DATE DUE

DEMCO 38-296

climate of
the unknown

Woodcut Engraving
by Herman Zaage

Against the Disappearance of Literature:

Essays, Interludes, Dialogues, Invocations on the Creating Word

by

Arlene Zekowski

The Whitston Publishing Company
Troy, New York
1999

Copyright 1999
Arlene Zekowski

Library of Congress Catalog Card Number 96-60696

ISBN 0-87875-470-9

Printed in the United States of America

Cover photo by Stanley Berne

Acknowledgements

"Manifesto 1962" appeared with *Concretions* by Arlene Zekowski, *The Dialogues* by Stanley Berne, republished in *Seasons of the Mind* by Arlene Zekowski, *The Unconscious Victorious* by Stanley Berne, 1969 (George Wittenborn, New York); *The Whole Cosmep Catalog* (Dustbooks, Paradise, California, 1973).

Assembling, Assembling Press, 1973
  "Sidelights" (feature excerpted as: "Notes on the Neo-Narrative" 2nd Series)

MARGINS/15, pp. 10, 11, 64: 1974.
  "An open letter to the Writer of *IT MUST BE SAID, I TOOK IT PERSONALLY*"

X—A Journal of the Arts, 1979, #6/7. "Mapping the Neo-Narrative and the Grammarless Language"

Bloomsbury Review, November 1985.
  "Cultural Suicide and the Decline of Literacy in America" (excerpted as: "The Cultural Crisis in America")

American Writing Today, Whitston Publishing Co., 1991.
  "Literature and Language for the Year 2000: Poetry-Prose Neo-Narrative Open Structure"

yefief: "A Narrative of Culture at the end of the Century," *Images For Media*, 1996.
  "The Managerial Technological Ritual Shakers and Makers of the World"

American Renaissance (Anthology, 1997).
  "The Treason of the Liberals: Their Renunciation of Literary Art"

Books by Arlene Zekowski

AGAINST THE DISAPPEARANCE OF LITERATURE
EVERY PERSON'S LITTLE BOOK OF P=L=U=T=O=N=I=U=M
HISTORIES AND DYNASTIES
IMAGE BREAKING IMAGES
SEASONS OF THE MIND
THE AGE OF IRON AND OTHER INTERLUDES
ABRAXAS
CONCRETIONS
CARDINALS & SAINTS
A FIRST BOOK OF THE NEO-NARRATIVE
THURSDAY'S SEASON
GIDIAN STANDARDS OF LITERARY VALUE

Anthology Inclusions

AMERICAN RENAISSANCE
THE LIVING UNDERGROUND
DICTIONARY OF THE AVANT-GARDES
AMERICAN WRITING TODAY
BREAKTHROUGH FICTIONEERS
ASSEMBLING
TRACE
NEW WORLD WRITING (No. 11)

Forthcoming

EVERY VERY PERSON'S FUTURE FORWARD JOURNEY OF
RETURN (A Trilogy)

I *Quickset*
II *En Route To Auron Winter Ski Station*
III *The Street Of The Bitter Well*

A C I R E M A (A Non-Fiction Fable)

Against the Disappearance of Literature

In America today, creativity is measured by super-market standards. Will it sell? Can it be advertised?

Because of this, we are more in danger, today, of losing our souls than of losing our lives. Challenge, idealism, faith, excitement from the unfamiliar, and the true and the new—all of this experience in being alive which art provides—is denied us by the dead centers of our society, which proclaim deafeningly into the ears of all—that the human being is an object of manipulation, to be bought and sold like the very objects it is told to buy and sell.

—Arlene Zekowski & Stanley Berne
MANIFESTO, 1962

Contents

THE PORTALES NOTEBOOKS

INTERLUDES

APPENDIX

Preface

In 1976, *IMAGE BREAKING IMAGES: A New Mythology of Language* and *FUTURE LANGUAGE* were published by Horizon Press. These were tandem volumes by myself, Arlene Zekowski, and Stanley Berne, each dealing in its own way with the problem of why our traditional language in its 18th and 19th century linear sentence grammatical structure, was obsolete corrupt strait-jacketed, impervious to innovation or change, was contributing to censorship of ideas, imagination and thought and bringing about the death of our culture and civilization.

Some of the issues we explored in these 2 volumes of criticism came into public focus soon afterward.

During the summer of 1977 the *Authors Guild Bulletin* of June-August noted with alarm:

> Conglomerate owned publishing firms and publishing
> complexes which have expanded by acquisition appear
> to be basing their publishing decisions more and more on
> 'the bottom line' rather than on the professional stan-
> dards that guided publishers when the industry con-
> tained many more independently owned firms. There
> are indications that books of merit are being rejected be-
> cause estimated sales, . . . are not high enough to pro-
> duce that return required by the bottom line.

About the same time the August 15th issue of *U.S. News & World Report*'s headline feature "Special Report": "America's Press-Too Much Power for Too Few?" described the accelerating swallowing up of independent publishers through the "Books: Boom and Take Over" of Corporate Publishing dominated by balance-sheet computerized psychology, which the 5000 member *Authors Guild* found threatening to obliterate altogether the already shrinking writers market. As John Hersey, chairman of the Authors Guild Book Contract Committee viewed the situation, "Publishers are now going for the big book; it is more and more a choice of whether a book will sell, not whether or not it will contribute to our culture."

A call for Government action through the auspices of both the Authors Guild and Representatives Morris Udall (Democrat, Arizona) and Robert Kastenmeier (Democrat, Wisconsin), urged the Department of Justice and the FTC to use the Clayton Antitrust Act's antimerger provision to overturn book publishing's ominous "trend to concentration: to order divestitures, prohibit mergers, and take other appropriate action."

In addition, Congressmen Udall and Kastenmeier called for an investigation of book publishing competition in their projected Competition Review Act. In an address to the Association of American Publishers, Representative Udall remarked:

> If any industry has a social responsibility, it is the publishers of books. We face the loss of communication and an acute absence of ideas in almost every other media, the principal culprit being concentration and lust for the dollar. . . . The people of this nation sense the corporate growth to bigness. They may soon tire of the trade publishers spoon feeding them best sellers and leaving the fresh and the bold to fend for themselves.

The fresh and the bold have been fending for themselves longer than Congressman Udall or the general public could possibly imagine. At least the 5000 presses and writers of the alternative small press scene (many who, like ourselves, emerged from the single and small cluster groups of the struggling and isolated fifties), know that this sudden public concern over corporate muzzling of the press with its concurrent *censorship of contemporary authors and their writing* is no isolated phenomenon but has been gathering momentum for the last 45 years or more.

The "merger psychology" of excluding contemporaneity and new ideas, respect for the independent dedicated editor, had already begun to surface about the time we had the good fortune to be included in the now historic original *New World Writing* series which in number eleven, May 1957, carried our "The End of Story in the Novel." We were vigorously attacked in the feature following ours in the same issue, by the editor of Noonday Press, Cecil Hemley, in his essay "The New and Experimental," that called for a moratorium on all new and further avant-garde or innovative contemporary creativity. This was his opening paragraph:

> What we need now in literature and in the arts is a re-
> volt against revolt. The immediate past is brilliant,
> the revolutionary innovators of the last fifty years did
> their work well, and revolt succeeded. But can their
> revolution be further extended? Ought we to march un-
> der the same banner they did? Can our slogan also be
> 'the new and experimental'?

This was how he continued:

> If one goes beyond Kandinsky, there is no picture; emo-
> tion becomes pure and inexpressible. If one goes beyond
> Mondrian, there is nothing to form; there is only the
> idea of form, and this too is incommunicable. These
> then are true limits. Along these lines no further exper-
> iments can be managed.

This was how he ended:

> It is time to say farewell to 'the new and experimental.'
> The way back is a way of rediscovery. But it is more
> than that. Since the realm of form is infinite, no one
> need worry that there will not be important things to
> do. All that is required is the genius to do them.[1]

Included in our eighteen page feature, "The End of Story
in the Novel," were excerpts from the frequently periodicaled
Phenomena (Berne) and *Decorations as for Prayers* (Zekowski),
as well as a preview selection from our forthcoming book of literary criticism: 29 essays "On the aims and purposes of the Arts
in our time," *Cardinals & Saints*, published the following year in
1958. Along with explaining the necessity for new contemporary
literary forms, a general condemnation of the already proliferating materialism and reduction of publishing to the business psychology of consumerism was elaborated upon in *Cardinals &
Saints* as in characteristic passages like the following:

> Nevertheless, with all this material nutrition about
> us, this push-button progress, . . . this general extension
> of literation has brought upon us, in the midst of the
> heaviest book business we've ever experienced . . . an
> underground of searching, a nostalgic and harried wa-
> vering and wondering as we backward glance at the
> time when entertainment was a searching to fulfill a
> hunger, and not a push of the television button to fill in
> time.   (p. 155)

> Modern literature must become revitalized. Otherwise
> it will die by killing off its readers; for once you have
> taken away spiritual hunger and extension, there will
> be no generation, and without generation there can be no

> life, and without life there can be no Art. It is time for
> Literature to be Literature, to be Art.[2]   (p. 156)

We were warning against mass-appeal schlock, in our plea
for excellence:

> Everything today is subject to this one yardstick
> only: *will it sell*! But the benefits of new forms may not
> always be apparent by this measure. Someone must
> bring a *new* yardstick to this problem so that Democ-
> racy may support the ideas it so inevitably inspires,
> and then fails to nourish.[3]   (p. 59)

> . . . culture cannot live by feeding on itself, by draw-
> ing life blood from its own neck;

> . . . a Democracy must have its elite, . . . Aristoc-
> racy must be encouraged once again—the Aristocracy of
> labor, the Aristocracy of knowledge, the Aristocracy of
> new forms. Democracy must have a minority of creative
> workers, creative consumers, creative thinkers; or else
> succumb.[4]   (p. 57)

Despite the fact that *Cardinals & Saints*[5] was surprisingly
well received, the deterioration on the American publishing
scene continued, amalgamations and mergers growing by leaps
and bounds with more and more featherbedding in the way of
"safe" publishing of the past and less and less of the present.

But the bottom line of schlock mass appeal did not con-
fine itself to publishing alone. It invaded the schools and spread
across the wasteland of television in one grand collusive narcosis of consumerism robbing thought from the mind as it mas-
turbated our sensations into a willing suspension of surrender to
majority mass collectivized taste. Big Brother televised consumerism soon became the surrogate for family, friends, lovers,
education and entertainment.

This great country of ours which had rescued shipwrecked
Europe and Western civilization from the tragic holocaust of
World War II and which had itself suffered through the violence of the political freedom struggles of the '50s and '60s was
losing its grip upon its own sense of national identity and character long before Watergate jogged us to attention over the thin
grey line between law and criminality.

When Stanley Berne and I evolved our twentieth-century
language for the year 2000 in our poetry-prose neo-narrative, little did we realize that our more than 40 year amplification of a

post-modern literary structure carried *political* as well as *cultural* implications.

Grammar as we know it and use it in the schools and in reading and writing and in its corruption into jargon in Government in the professions and in academe, is an obsolete gravitational drag upon our minds, riveting them into its 18th century structure, strait-jacketing thought imagination creativity from soaring into the 20th and 21st century now upon us, sterilizing literature and interest in books and ideas while science zooms into freedom and adventure into a renaissance age of Einsteinian space and time.

Is it not a culture shock to realize that books and reading and the language of the schools and of publishing is an 18th century one when what is needed is a 20th, 21st century structure of creativity and communication, a geodetic language from a geodetic society culture and civilization living in geodetic space?

The Corporate Publishers should, but won't acknowledge that the great writers of the past are their fossil fuels supplying their literary wells, through public domain. Should public domain continue to belong to the publishers as an ironic gift of the law, of literary noblesse oblige, when those very authors rarely, if ever, enjoyed any patronage themselves? Moreover, "public domain" publishing acts as a punitive legal instrument in defiance of the Bill of Rights denying publication to living authors while promoting exploitation of dead authors.

Should the royalties of public domain continue to enrich the literary scavengers who rape from the past or *should publishing reward those who add something new to creativity*? Should it moreover continue to overwhelm with gratuitous praise those who "steal" from other creators? "Best Sellers" are generally the products of short order cooks who can't originate their own recipes and so crib from the master chefs.

If the "bottom line" of mass-produced sludge is to ever slow down, if publishers are ever to be pressured into realizing their *social responsibility*, that neither government nor the public will continue to condone what Congressman Udall called in his time, "the loss of communication and acute absence of ideas . . . the principal culprit being concentration and lust for the dollar," then the law of conservation must be applied indiscriminately to publishing as it is to forestry: For every exploited dead author raped, bushwhacked, picked over clean, slicked into the publishing house organ "classic" providing the lumber of their house line of celebrated books and authors, for every dead author who enriches the publisher, like every dead tree the lumber industry, the forest of literature must be prevented from being further bulldozed or else there will be no forest at all.

Is it too late for the Corporate Publishers to obey and observe the law of literary conservation and ecology by encouraging, supporting—for every author of the past they pluck and process—a living contemporary author engendering *new literary forms and ideas?*

Against the Disappearance of Literature attempts to bring into focus the symbiotic relationship of language, literature, education, and publishing in their influence upon a nation's society and culture, why old ideas must change, what new more practical ones might take their place if the threat of cultural suicide and galloping entropy is to be circumvented and future horizons encouraged to emerge.

Arlene Zekowski
Skymount
Santa Fe

Notes

[1] Cecil Hemley, "The New and Experimental," *New World Writing* No. 11 (New York: New American Library, 1957), pp. 171-176.

[2] Arlene Zekowski and Stanley Berne, *"Cardinals & Saints": On the aims and purposes of the Arts in our time* (Croton-On-Hudson: Metier Editions, 1958). Available from American-Canadian Publishers, Inc., POB 4595, Santa Fe, New Mexico 87502.

[3] Ibid.

[4] Ibid.

[5] *The Times Literary Supplement, Etudes Anglaises* in Paris, *Amrita Bazar Patrika* in Calcutta, as well as establishment magazines newspapers and scholarly periodicals largely concurred with English poet, editor publisher James Boyer May in their assessment of *Cardinals & Saints*: "It shines with fresh flashing statements of neglected basic wisdoms. And rare humor, sword-sharp attacks and cool lucid reasonings. . . . The book is a jewel. . . . The book must be read" ("Some Items Received," *Trace* 35 [February 1959], 42-43). In addition, we began to receive encouragement and approbation from respected authors and critics (Marianne   Moore, Thornton Wilder, William Carlos Williams, Henry Miller, Virgil Thomson, Waldo Frank, Janet Flanner, John Lehman, Harvey Breit, W. G. Rogers, Donald Sutherland, Henri Peyre, Wallace Stevens) on this and other literary works of ours written in our own poetry-

prose "neo-narrative," characterized by John Martin Adams ("Fiction Chronicle," *Hudson Review* [Autumn 1962], p. 429) as "A device for responding directly to reality without the clumsy intervention of grammar."

Author's Foreword

Towards the Evolution of a New Literary Form

> Lo! thy dread Empire CHAOS! is restored,
> Light dies before thy uncreating word;
> Thy hand great ANARCH! lets the curtain fall,
> And Universal Darkness buries All.
> —Alexander Pope (*The Dunciad*)

For over 35 years, both myself and Stanley Berne have been engaged in a struggle against the "uncreating word," through a form of narrative that combines poetry and prose images freed from the limits of the sentence in order to more nearly approximate the language of the mind.

Dubbed by antagonists and academicians as the "grammarless language anarchists," attacked as the "Frankensteins," the "Bonnies and Clydes of the scholastic tradition" (London Daily Mail), we ourselves have characterized our evolutionary approach to a new literary form as *neo-narrative* .

In high-powered publishing and quasi literary circles, aridity and obsolescence have brought about the malaise and creative literary suffocation now proliferating for almost half a century in America; so that the average and above average book reader in this morass of confusion and illusion cannot distinguish between literary works that nourish the psyche, and commercial "bestsellerdumb" that cancerizes and lobotomizes the mind and soul.

Contemporary innovative literary art works are hard to find. You can rarely come upon them in the Shopping Mall Supermarket Book Chain mausoleums with their boomerang shout cover movie and TV celebrity titles and other "how-to" distractions of the mass publishing circus.

In fact, the mid forties and early fifties encompassed the last brief moment for truly innovative literature and art, at least in New York where the air was filled with anticipation, excitement, expectancy, and a fervor bordering almost on the religious, to welcome and proselytize all that was new, inventive, yes even outrageous. It was a generous time. It was almost as if hype had not yet been invented. The public, along with the artists (writers, painters, sculptors, composers, dance choreographers, etc.) sensed that they were participating in a "Revolutionary Pioneer Movement," the second wave of the "Frontier Emigration Westward," with its fountainhead not in America this time, but born of the great European cultural exodus-diaspora fleeing from the rubble, the chaos of the Nazi holocaust. Where the initial Westward Movement of Trappers, River and Mountain Men, Explorers, Adventurers, Gold and Silver Seekers, Ranchers, Railroad Barons, was Transcontinental-American, this second Westward Movement was European-Oceanic: the grafting of a revered sophisticated European Civilization upon a burgeoning youthful New World American Culture. Enthusiasm and excitement were often at fever pitch. Each art opening, each retrospective was treated like a happening, an operatic or theatrical event: Salvador Dali, Max Ernst, arch rivals, surrounded by their separate coteries of admirers at opposite reaches of Peggy Guggenheim's "Art of This Century" gallery-museum; Strip-Tease Artist Gypsy Rose Lee sheathed in decolleté black satin enveloping a stretch-pant tight-clinging derrière, mobbed more than the painters whose show she was supporting; Garbo black caped, in monumental black hat, black boots, frequenting the Madison Avenue Perls Gallery; Picasso's "Guernica" at the Museum of Modern Art packing in hordes of worshipful admirers as well as the curious, in queues that snaked around several city blocks. And the writers of significance and celebrity, crowding into Frances Steloff's Gotham Book Mart meet-the-author parties: Welsh poet Dylan Thomas bear hugging, womanizing a breathless circle of Wellesley, Barnard, Smith, Sarah Lawrence nymphets; the Broadway songwriters Comden and Green; literary critic Edmund Wilson in his perennial "watchman's" worn-to-threadbare brown coat; choreographer, modern dance pioneer Martha Graham, navy-blue suited, diminutive, unobtrusive, quiet, ascetic and non-theatrical, largely unrecognized offstage.

The Cedar Bar Village "loft" crowd, the Art Club on 8th Street, wine, beer and cheese hosting visitors and guests where Dutch-American painter Willem de Kooning, composer John Cage spoke as well as listened to Alsatian sculptor Hans Arp, French surrealist writer and theorist André Breton—whoever was in town. And most especially, there was poet and poetry anthologist literary gadfly Oscar Williams' Water Street terrace penthouse gatherings on weekend summer evenings, above the silent shuttered downtown Wall Street financial district.

It was then 20th century art history was being made: tall and thick-lipped Clement Greenberg, Oscar's celebrity guest art critic, surrounded by admirers and neophyte hopefuls eager for recognition and support in a fantasy dream of a possible "second coming" lightening strike wave of Abstract Expressionism following the Jackson Pollocks, Franz Klines, Willem de Koonings, Robert Motherwells, Mark Rothkos Adolph Gottliebs, etc., that finding themselves no longer bastards or orphans, realized they were a family with a lineage and respectable niche in contemporary art history.

* * * * *

And yet, despite all this cultural and aesthetic revolutionary ferment, no such event *then to now*, has ever taken place in American literary art. There has never been a "guru" for example, as literary critic—gathering the scattered, isolated, disparate idiosyncratic but related parallel complementary inventions, developments and directions of *writers as literary artists*, into any overall aesthetic of form, idea, meaning or purpose—no attempt at probing the *whole* picture, the *whole* perspective, of the language of poetry, prose, serious fiction or verbal invention in the 20th century, in contrast to what was accomplished by Clement Greenberg for the abstract expressionist painters.

Thus you have the phenomenon in the Fine Arts, of Cubism, Surrealism, Futurism, the Blue Rider School, Impressionism, Expressionism—all significant purposeful art movements of the Twentieth Century—whereas Literary Art of the 20th century has been either buried or suffocated under antediluvian Archeozoic Australopithecus Realism—with *Realism* exclusively a vehicle for the dying Novel, the commerce of television and the movies.

With the result that the writer as Literary Artist, Creative Intellectual has been denied visibility to the society at large, and its circle of quality book readers—swept under the carpet or locked in the closet, stuffed in the attic like some ancient fossil or relic of prehistory or poor relation never invited to the family gathering, ancestral feast, Thanksgiving, Anniversary, Christmas or New Year's Celebration, *The Serious Writer in America is consequently a pariah, a member of the forgotten or disappeared.*

One of the idiosyncrasies of being American, is the curious tendency of sweeping aside our own history, our own tradition, as so much Augean refuse, cleaning house so that nothing remains with which we can identify, so that we appear to have sprung from nowhere, a phenomenon of spontaneous evolution or accident of hybridization or the like. We re-write, we re-create our own history as we please, both good and bad: in politics, the extreme right, the religious fundamentalists and their kind, zealous to revise the Constitution and the Bill of Rights in their own fixated image and delusion of America as a religious nation, strait-jacketing our 18th century intellectually enlightened Founding Fathers—Washington, Jefferson, Franklin and their contemporaries—into "Christians" whereas in fact they were Deists fiercely determined to forge a secular republic free of bigotry and religious persecution through the revolutionary concept of separation of Church and State.

So that as Pericles wisely pointed out ages ago, Democracy, a free and open society, is always perilously on the brink of annihilation, open to attack to repression and to any fascist leaning revisionism.

This, however, is not any way the case in *Literature,* which in America, is *never* threatened, *never* in danger of attack, but on the contrary, suffers from intellectual apathy and neglect, remaining largely abandoned, moribund, maintaining the status quo of its history and traditions of the past.

When literary tradition is confined to the past, it loses its instinct and vitality for *evolution.* For what are history and tradition if we cannot build upon them, create a lineage of culture of thought that becomes a legacy of creative accomplishment for a nation? This has not been the case in America, because, unlike American Technology and Science, both innovative and the envy of the world, *innovative* Literature has not been granted recognition or encouragement. And that is why our American legacy of overall creative accomplishment in the 20th century is skewed and distorted, veering off in one extreme direction—Science, Rationalism, Pragmatism—with no balance, no tilting in the direction of creative Literary Art, which involves *the research of the soul through language*.

A considerable number of the essays, dialogues, interludes, critical and incidental pieces in this volume[1] highlight the importance necessity inevitability of *creative evolution in literary forms*, comparable to Darwin's biologic discovery in the previous century, of the inevitability necessity of *organic evolution in animal and plant forms*. Because philosophically, intellectually, our awareness of life today as in Darwin's day, and historically, going back to recorded time, all of our life forms (the biosphere itself), have always been in Heraclitean flux, never fixed, always evolving.

Language is no exception. This means, of course, pointing to the *future*, as we conceive and respond to *language*, involving our minds and sensibilities in an exploration of the self through exposure to a new kind of writing which I've referred to earlier in this selection as *neo-narrative*.[2] The genres, the pigeon-holed categories of the past (what formerly constituted traditional poetry, prose, fiction, essay, criticism—our inherited linear grammatical framework originating from the 18th century) are restructured in *neo-narrative* into 20th century *spatial* and *kinetic* images. The New Narrative moves as *interplay*, nuancing, exploring, merging, poetry with prose, fiction with poetry and essay, essay with poetry and criticism, and so on. What evolves is a new *texture* in keeping with a new approach to language and our perception of ourselves and the world.[3]

Throughout the literary history of Western culture, through Homer, the Beowulf author, Dante, Chaucer, Rabelais, Cervantes, Edmund Spenser, Shakespeare, Laurence Sterne, Góngora, Milton, Wordsworth, Whitman, Rimbaud, Proust, James Joyce, Virginia Woolf, Dos Passos, Gertrude Stein, Faulkner, William Burroughs, Michel Butor—the artist of language constantly seeks to fashion, enlarge and expand the possibilities, the horizons of verbal forms.

In America, for most of this century, however, there has not been any encouragement of the literary artist in his or her endeavors towards the *future*. Without the *future* the *present* is meaningless, stale, arid, corrupting, non-nutritive, even dangerous. Creativity, in language, as in all art, constitutes the essence of all life forms and must flourish for any society's well-being. It is time to alert and avert us from the continuing proliferation and consumption in mega publishing and the media of "Trash Tease Glitz and Sleaze." Language must be encouraged to nourish and revitalize the mind and sense for a culture to survive. Otherwise, good books and authentic literature will have no future for those of us who care.

Arlene Zekowski
Skymount
Santa Fe

Notes

[1] In this volume, note particularly "Essays In Dialogue" as examples of "neo-narrative," combining poetry, fiction and criticism.

[2] For critical discussion by authors Arlene Zekowski and Stanley Berne on the origin and evolution of "neo-narrative," see their joint critical volume of 29 essays: *Cardinals & Saints*: "On the aims and purposes of the Arts in our time" (New York: George Wittenborn, Inc., 1958). See also Arlene Zekowski: "Notes on the Neo-Narrative," in her volume, *Abraxas* (New York: George Wittenborn, Inc., 1964); also 10 Related Essays in *Seasons of the Mind* (New York: George Wittenborn, Inc., 1969) and her last book of criticism, *Image Breaking Images: A New Mythology of Language* (New York: Horizon Press, 1976). See also Stanley Berne: 6 Related Essays in *The Unconscious Victorious* (New York: George Wittenborn, Inc., 1969), as well as his last book of criticism: *Future Language* (New York: Horizon Press, 1976).

[3] Commentary by others on the Zekowski/Berne neo-narrative, is provided by scholar-playwright Gertrude Stein, biographer Donald Sutherland, and poet William Carlos Williams in *A First Book of the Neo-Narrative* by Arlene Zekowski and Stanley Berne (Stonington, Connecticut: Metier Editions, 1954). In Arlene Zekowski's *Abraxas* and Stanley Berne's *The Multiple Modern Gods*, see scholar, critic, poet Sir Herbert Read's Preface: "The Resurrection of the Word." By way of prefatory commentary in Arlene Zekowski's *Histories And Dynasties* (New York: Horizon Press, 1982), see "Language and Questioning" by critic and fiction writer Welch D. Everman, also "The Ego, the Id and the Word" by scholar, poet, critic Walter James Miller; in Stanley Berne's *The Great American Empire* (New York: Horizon Press, 1982), see the introductions: "A New American Epic" by Welch D. Everman, and "The Great American Empire: A Prose" by Walter James Miller. (All works cited are available from American-Canadian Publishers, Inc., P.O. Box 4595, Santa Fe, New Mexico, 87502.) In addition, see Richard Kostelanetz: *Twenties in the Sixties* (1979), as well as his *Dictionary of the Avant-Gardes* (1993); *X-A Journal of the Arts* (Winter 1979, #6/7): "Mapping the Neo-Narrative and the Grammarless Language," an interview conducted by Welch D. Everman; *Review of Contemporary Fiction* (Fall 1984): criticism by Welch D. Everman, of *Future Language* (Berne)

and *Image Breaking Images* (Zekowski); *New Frontiers: ZYX 5*: reviews by Arnold Skemer, Editor of *Future Language* (Berne) and *Image Breaking Images* (Zekowski); *ZYX 6* "Berne-Zekowski: Neo-Narrative and Its Paradigmatic Uses In Speculative Fictive Historicity," critique by Arnold Skemer of *The Unconscious Victorious* (Berne) and *Seasons of the Mind* (Zekowski).

Against the Disappearance of Literature

In the year 2000 a backward glance over the Seventies, Eighties and Nineties, might be regarded as some peculiar cultural phenomenon when consumers in supermarkets stashed canned and frozen foods, household goods, meat, fish, eggs, cheese, videocassettes, magazines and paperback books—into their food-baskets. But in reality is *book consumption* today any different from any other form of *consumerism*, whose aims and purposes are as immediate as ephemeral as ice-cream? Whereas ice-cream will always be magical and tempting, *literary* works today are disappearing without leaving any pleasurable lingering trace or taste behind. And nobody seems to care.

The target I wish to pinpoint here is not "reading matter" per se but the "book," the "good book" as the lifeblood of the literary creative artist, and its role in cultural history.

The *Book* as literary art must now be considered as much *endangered* as any wilderness, rain forest, sea, river, ocean life form—but not for the same reasons. Because no one today is in hot pursuit of literary art. No one finds it profitable to support nor does anyone feel called upon to voice any moral philosophical aesthetic commitment to "save" literature now and for the future.

A superficial but striking example of literature's lack of impact, in fact of books themselves, would be a "time capsule" for the year 2000 featuring junk foods, sport and running gear, sloganized T-shirts, videos, cassettes, camcorders, stereos, computers—but no *books*.

You may say for argument's sake that it is unfair to revert to a pop culture yardstick when more people are visiting art museums, supporting concerts, symphonies, opera, theatre, dance and performance art than ever before. Which simply proves that the hunger for the arts is being fulfilled and that the public know a good thing once they are exposed to it.

But who is exposing the art of the book, the work of literary art to these potential culture consumers? What publisher in the publishing world has remembered the unspoken hippocratic oath of *literature publishing* which is to provide what is best what should be known what enriches the mind and the spirit now and in the future: above all the *new* and *unknown*?

In an article written back in the '70s by way of rejoinder to a *New York Times* condemnatory review of *Breakthrough Fictioneers*, one of the few anthologies of genuine innovative literature to appear at that time, I underscored the publishing establishment's role in the disappearance of literature:

> The Publishing Establishment is perpetuating emotional, spiritual and creative impoverishment . . . in America, through the wasteland of garbage and boobtuboisie yardsticks they generate along their conveyor belt-mass-producteaze-pulp-pap Hollywood to consumer-junkey . . . best-sellerdumb. . . .
>
> Junkyards can be cleared. Air and water can be improved. But the conduits of creativity publishers have almost irrevocably destroyed in our time, by refusing to open their doors to new writers with new ideas and new approaches to the new realities of human experience in our time.
>
> What could be more ecologically disastrous, by way of a human energy crisis, in a world forever and always short on thought, reason and intelligence, where the sources, the outlets for encouraging more thought and intelligence and communication of the grace of the human spirit, have been deliberately cut off in one grand collusive machiavellian design, and are indeed second by second being reduced by every company decision of the board in every publishing conglomerate daily, as the group-think of corporations employing an army of thousands of editorial clerks and readers all vote as a majority of *one*?
>
> As if it were divinely possible for all of them to pronounce in pontifical agreement what is or is not a good book a great book a book for the present for the future or for vast eternity.
>
> What the 20th century philosophy of publishing in America has unilaterally decreed by its censorship of intelligence and creativity through the unwritten but no less operative protective tariff system of glutting the market exclusively with the expendable the meretricious the vulgar and the dead, is the promotion and

perpetuation of Illiteracy in America through the
closed-door policy of turning their back upon originality and all forms of creative research.[1]

("The American Samizdat")

"Creative research" is a term now generally replacing the
more traditional "avant-garde" or "experimental" which in the
last several decades has taken on prejudicial coloration born of
ignorance about any writing that is new and unfamiliar.

If we were to examine public attitudes in the last two centuries towards pioneers in Science versus pioneers in Literature,
we come up with some striking contrasts that we have difficulty
accounting for.

Creativity, original innovative research in Science, has
always been encouraged. No one has dared to sneer or pro-
nounce judgment upon any scientist's right or freedom to pursue knowledge or practice experimentation. And government
has always been generally lavish in its support.

But when it comes to private or public support of original
innovative creativity in language, in writing, the acceptance of
the new and the unfamiliar in Literature, then judgments and
pronouncements opinions misconceptions and general round-
house condemnations descend like doomsday upon the writer-
victim. So much so that this behaviour has perpetuated itself
into the form of a public myth that should be destroyed if we are
ever to effect any change.

The myth may be described as follows: Since the writer-
victim is made to suffer for nonconformity or nonacceptance of
the literary status quo, the writer's quid pro quo is stoic or self-
flagellating acceptance of "frustration, discrimination and
pariah-like neglect." What is more surprising, the public not
only accepts this myth of the long-suffering persecuted artist, but
perpetuates its necessity and incontrovertibility: i.e. the artist's
work would "suffer" if encouraged rather than maligned and
neglected. This would contradict Milton's celebrated line: That
suffering, not fame is the spur.

The literary artist who is a pioneer innovator then, would
seem to occupy an extremely neurotic and extremely unhealthy
position in society in contradistinction to the pioneer in science.
Why are the scientist's privacy and rights to creative originality
respected, while the literary artist's are invaded, exposed and denied? Is it because the scientist's language is a largely unfamiliar
private one and has been all through history? And because the

public has always instinctively recognized this, they take upon faith the scientist's right to plunge as much and as far as the scientist wishes into this arcane world of scientific language.

Unfortunately the language of the literary artist has always been a vehicle used by and familiar to all of us whether in its *literary* or *popular* everyday journalistic form.   Or, as I have commented in a previous piece:

> *Change* in language has always been a guarded and jealous and misunderstood affair, possibly because the tools are in everybody's hands whereas this is not the case in any other art or science.   And where the many not the few consider themselves the guardians of usage there is no way the single solitary creative visionary can be heard.   He or She or They are lost, muffled in the crowd of naysayers who insist that they know all there is to know about the obvious and familiar.
>
> But the language of the *unfamiliar* is what new literature is all about. . . .
>
> The symbols of communication of the scientist, the painter, the composer, are specialized private scripts or 'languages' if you will, whereas in an age aimed at total literacy everyone is taught the alphabet, taught to read, to write, to speak. . . . Which results in the lines of distinction between language as everyday as mundane communication and language as *art* as literature, becoming obfuscated, blurred.
>
> Writing, literature, as a métier, as an art, as a craft, as a vision of truth, of poetry, of intelligence, of spirit, of reason and of the feelings, has had to go underground, has had to become hermetic, hieratic, arcane, in order to realize its mission which is *cultural*, not *journalistic* or *mundane*.[2]

* * * * *

Perhaps never before as now in our 20th-21st century, have we felt as human beings, at a loss to embrace the mystery, the strangeness, the baffling ineluctable Faustian-like dimensions and temptations of existence and its everyday science-fiction-like nature where penetrating into the galaxy of other worlds is becoming a mere space station away where reproduction or simulation of our flesh and blood and muscle and heartbeat can be either cloned, making us all expendable or, on the other hand, where we can buy our way into the future beyond any Faustian dream, through body freeze preservation.   Never before in human history has humanity transformed so much in so short a time. And yet in our most precious endowment, the gift of speech, of language, we are frozen, riveted to the verbal signs, symbols and grammatical structures of the past, and not to present or future history.

To do with *language* what is already being accomplished and has been accomplished in other creative fields: in science, in music, painting, sculpture, dance, etc., is of the greatest urgency, the greatest challenge because *language* is unlike all these other media in being both a *private* and *public* medium of communication.

* * * * *

Leadership in language has always reflected not just global socio-economic political dominance but also a *spiritual and cultural mystique*. Assuredly one does not go through the trouble of learning a language and mastering it just for exclusively pragmatic reasons. Sooner or later there must follow the intimate communion of cohabitation generation or generation of its life and spirit. That is how all past global languages branched into living cultures and civilizations. And American English is certainly no exception.

But where is American English today and where will it be tomorrow? Is American English spreading humanistic as well as global power, worldwide? One hardly thinks so.

The technological bulldozing of the last quarter century has leveled principalities states nations empires as well as neighborhoods everywhere into spheres of influence that have conglomerated into supranational emperies and international power structures, impinging upon our individual struggle for human identity, privacy, idiosyncrasy, and that shared human community of language and culture that has always marked high civilization in its reach towards excellence, beauty, truth.

Vast industrial complexes now reach out across the planet excluding poverty-level regions while agribusinesses proliferate exploiting cheap peasant labor worldwide as the GIP (Gross International Product) reaches into the factory food chain supermarket adding necrophagous preservation via chemicals, pesticides, bio-genetically altered, and now even radiated spices, fruits, vegetables, poultry—with ground wood pulp, meat and fish scraps for added fibre.

In our national and multinational oligarchies proliferating biochemical and pesticidal adulterations of non-diary cream-
ers cokes boxed cereals calcium propionated pastries breads
monosodium glutamated nitrated reconstituted ersatz food
tailings of every kind category and form, last but not last in this
grim drama of our lives today is the technological malnutrition
of mind which the publishing industrial complex ("that Polit-
buro of electronic, cinema and advertising-super-sell and agentry
sensationaleze")[3] perpetuates and perpetrates through the
"wasteland of garbage and boobtuboisie yardsticks they generate
along their conveyor belt-mass-producteaze-pulp-pap Hollywood to consumer-junkey . . . best-sellerdumb."[4]

* * * * *

The *disappearance of fresh and natural food* and the *disappearance of literature* form the *body* and *soul* of the twin
monstrosities of technological change operating the gigantic
maw and profit hungry belly of corporate conglomeromania.

Malnutrition of soul of intellectual thought contributes to
"censorship of creativity; galloping entropy; cultural suicide; the
death of language and nations."[5]

Book publishing today has joined the ranks of all the
other corporate empires of food chains, oil and gas, television
and electronics. What was once humanistic idiosyncratic glam-
orous even if low-paying editorialdom, is now part of the bureaucracy of collective decision making associated with government and the other mammoth consumer industries.

In a volume of 29 essays written with Stanley Berne, *Cardinals & Saints*, published in 1958, we tried to voice what was already apparently happening—a tidal wave of consumerism that
would bury the distinction between literature and publishing—
when we said: "Literature was never a business. Publishing is."[6]

There was a time when fantasy belonged to its own world
of *Alice In Wonderland, Peter Pan, Midsummer's Nights
Dream*. Today this is not the case at all. Over the last several
decades the electronic media of movies and television have ri-
fled through literary classics, adapting and transforming the
book to their visual technology. A curious instance of television's show biz mass appeal taking precedence over professional
competence occurred on a PBS Dick Cavett two part symposium
on "What's Wrong With Our Language?" The guest speakers

were Harvard Economist John Kenneth Galbraith; Movie Critic John Simon; T.V./Radio Journalist Edwin Newman; and Choreographer of Movie and Broadway Shows Agnes De Mille. The scenario went as follows:

> —Insulting the minority and third world cultures in a presumptuous display of anglophile snobbery and patronizing superiority (John Simon).
> —An exclusive pedantic attack on the jargon of academe (Edwin Newman), circumventing its consumptive pervasive effects in government, law, journalism, and other professions.
> —Reminiscing over her adolescent romance with a dead language: Latin (Agnes De Mille).
> —The only participant apparently aware of being in alien territory who had the good sense to remain silent through much of the discussion (John Kenneth Galbraith).

Such a symposium should have included at least one literary authority or language historian. Frivolity based on incompetence is out of place, in bad taste, and insulting to *any* audience.

Ninety-nine percent of the versions of books adapted for television are adapted from novels and the "novel" is a favorite term as the media devours literary history in fiction that is now ground out and into the computerized mill for television's mass consumption:

> . . . the 'electronic book' the 'electronic newspaper'— television— . . . is now annihilating the visual representation of the *story* and the *novel* in its Gutenberg print form of the *book, magazine* and *newspaper*— through its greater economy and efficiency of recreating the visual of literature. . . . It takes far less time to see *War and Peace* on television than it did to read it.[7]
> —*Image Breaking Images*
> ("The Emperor's New Clothes")

It used to be "read the book then see the movie." But now fantasy has entered our everyday world so that we "see" the movie and then "read" the book.

* * * * *

In 1962, with the publication of *Concretions* (Zekowski) and *The Dialogues* (Berne) from George Wittenborn, we issued a manifesto with the following title: "*When Will You Understand That in So Far as Present Use Is Concerned the Novel as We*

Now Know It Is Dead." The gist of the manifesto called for support and encouragement of new and innovative forms of fiction to replace the dead and dying novel of 18th century narrative. It warned publishers and others of the impasse now upon us in sterility of ideas in books and thought if the perpetuation of *sameness* and *contemptuous familiarity* continued to be implemented at the expense of *innovation* and *encouragement of new forms.*[8]

What ensued was a curious defensive posture of attack often bordering on the hysterical and paranoiac, on these "enemies" of the classic two centuries old novel which publishing houses continued to grind out seemingly in defiance of our prognosis that the traditional novel was dead.[9] Meanwhile, as fewer and fewer novels sold, the "big" publishers decided to retool, blaming of course, sales, public apathy and ignorance in its surrender to a "pop" culture; instead of catering to the varied types of readerships the publishers found it more profitable to amalgamate into interlocking directorates that swallowed up the struggling independents. Thus was born the "movie book" package resurrected from the detritus of remaindered novels and potential works of literature that just didn't "sell."

So powerful and pervasive was the electronic takeover of fiction and the novel that some who shall be nameless went so far as to proclaim that books were at an end instead of naming the real culprit of this gruesome melodrama: *the almost three centuries old subject verb predicate lineal latinate grammar structure of the English language itself.*

* * * * *

> In every aspect of American life Americans have accepted innovators and innovation any and every form of efficiency and have promulgated innovation and efficiency and contemporaneity world-wide. In everything except *literature.* . . . When it comes to language and literature, Americans are the most fanatic traditionalists the world has ever known. . . . We are thus far a frontier people who yet reject *Literary Frontiers.*[10]
> —*Image Breaking Images*
> ("Why Johnny Can't Read," pp. 94-95, 102)

> Why is it difficult to teach the sentence in grammar? Because in reality the thought continues. The unit of 'thought' of perception, if you will, is not a 'sentence' but a cluster of clauses or images. When does it end?

Certainly not mechanically or arbitrarily with a period. The period is merely a mechanical device invented by the grammarian's fanatic sense of logic and
warped sense of truth.[11]   ("Because He Won't Read")

The sentence in literature, then, must go, because
like Newtonian physics which 'fits only into the
framework of classical mechanics where time and space
are absolute and where an inertial system is assumed to
exist,' the *sentence* too is part of an *inertial system*
which no longer can comprehend the contemporary universe of time and space, *neither of which is absolute.*[12]
                                —*Image Breaking Images*
                                ("Selected Criticism," p. 160)

Is it not a curious and sick anomaly that in a country
which prides itself rightfully on being a pioneer of innovative
expression in the sciences; in technology of every kind from
laser, solar engineering, multiplex fiber optic cable, phone, mi-
crocomputers and printers, interactive painting, sculpture,
dance, music, art and communication media, only *Language* has
remained in its 18th century "command grammar" mold, in-
hibiting thought and expression and bringing on cultural stagnation?[13]

In politics, sports, entertainment, advertising, education—
our whole society—is embalmed, drugged, doped, mesmerized
packaged by the philosophy and propaganda of "consumerism,"
and language is no exception: the grammar of old structures
(from Greek through Latin into English) replayed over and over
again into conformity and rigidity whose most dramatic, most
flagrant expression is now being waged as two enclaves draw up
their forces over the 20th-21st century version of the 18th century Battle of the Books: the elitist superstar "token" professors
and traditionalists—old line manipulative Prussians of logical
positivism, mandarin scholasticism, scholarly academicism—
pitted against the modernist, contemporary future-oriented innovators. So the battle wages (in the schools) between the disci-
plinarian analytic *fanatics* and the more youthful contemporary
enthusiasts while the ship of fools in schools of liberal arts desperately gasps for breath, clutching to retain courses and curricula that do not "make," that do not "sell" while administrators
"fire" the professors or institute RIF (Reduction In Force) policy
guidelines or simply faze out the senile liberal arts altogether as
professors and their courses retire and fade away through natural attrition. Symptomatic of the cynicism and malaise long

permeating academe is the following anonymous dispatch I once received:

> Office of the Persistent
> Re: New Program to Facilitate Termination of Surplus
>   Personnel
>
> New Directive for which I take full responsibility
>
> 1. In accordance with the present policy of phasing out all surplus personnel the RAPE (Retire All Personnel Early) program will go into effect immediately.
> 2. Employees who are RAPE'd will be given an opportunity to seek other employment, provided that while they are being RAPE'd they request a review of their record before the discharge takes place. This phase of the operation is called SCREW (Survey of Capabilities of Retired Early Workers).
> 3. All employees who have been RAPE'd and SCREW'd may also appeal for final review. This is called SHAFT (Study of Higher Authority Following Termination).
> 4. Present School Policy dictates that employees may be RAPE'd once and SCREW'd twice, but that they may get the SHAFT as many times as the Administration decides.

Where professors are consumed by their courses and universities by their bread and butter foundation and federal subsidies, no one asks the beleaguered student why he/she no longer is attracted to literature, and turns to business or fine arts or electronic journalism, political or social sciences instead. There still exist students who refuse to be passive, conformist, teem-oriented, unwilling to spectate instead of speculate—against collective consensus making and me-too-ism—individuals searching out *innovative* not *derivative* ideas.

The absence of contemporary relevancy in curricula designed to enrich young people with a cultural continuity from past to present, underscores the problem today of liberal arts, its emphasis upon a *dead* rather than a *living* literary heritage. Such academic mandarinism projects the concept of literature as either elitist or fossilized and drives away potential lovers of the humanities and of books and of creative ideas, which they subsequently regard as ivory towerish unrelated, and of little value to the development of their own individual lives.

* * * * *

> The regularization of both grammar and spelling
> was the likely result of seeking to apply Law and
> Order to the human spirit.
> The enforcers of the Sentence are the enforcers of
> thought control: teachers, and the police. Both are no-
> ticeably little thought of.
> The Sentence has become, unhappily, an industry or
> factory wherein youth are manufactured, if they allow
> it, into exact replicas of the demonstrated failure that
> the humanities have become.
> The Sentence is the argument of Dictators to read
> arbitrary law to the impenitent political prisoner
> about to be sent to the camps.
> The airplane defied walking, as the imagination
> defies the earth-bound Sentence.
> They do not speak or write Sentences on Mars.
> Messages sent into space by radio are written in
> anti-linear symbology, so they can be read.[14]
> —Stanley Berne, *Future Language*

Perhaps far worse than ignorance of authentic literature on the part of both publishers and teachers whom they serve, is what educators themselves have perpetrated in the cause of grammar bordering on fanaticism.

It is a peculiar and strange anomaly that every one of the last three or four generations of public school, private, college and university students respond identically to the proverbial *intellectual and creative servitude* that characterizes their race memory of the English "grammar class" or "college freshman composition."

Invariably it is *grammar* that turns off students from reading, from literature, from the uses of the creative imagination which shapes everyone's emotional and intellectual life.

Why the idea of *discipline* inflicts inquisitorial terror upon the searching and fervid imagination of young people, and in its most generally recognized form: grammatical fluency, which snuffs out originality and individuality with a thoroughness a finality that the directors of any prison or concentration camp would rightfully envy and want to emulate, would be regarded most assuredly as strange and curious by a visitor from beyond this planet. Most certainly the study of grammar, grammatical analysis, sentence diagramming and the like, is as successful a form of brainwashing if not the very essence of verbal sodium pentathol, totally guaranteeing docility and subservience as well as fear and anathema of the very program that stamps its boots on their victims' consciousness.

The heated opposition will expose its aversion to freedom-license and the pleasure principle by insisting that *discipline* is good for body and soul. And so it probably is. However, it is not discipline that is being questioned as the innovative enthusiasts contend, but the uses and sources of that discipline: *the language itself.*

* * * * *

> But words will never do what the grammarians insist upon, for words belong not to those who have imprisoned them *but only to those who set them free. . . .*
>
> As sounds are for music, as colors are for painting, as form is for sculpture, words, in the end, after all is said and done, are the bone and marrow and structure of all literature, past, present, and future. . . .
>
> Thus, in art, the sentence must be destroyed because it never existed.
>
> Only words exist. And words engender thought.
> —Arlene Zekowski, *Abraxas*
> ("Notes on the Neo-Narrative")[15]

When Samuel Johnson carved out the principle of sensitivity to language through creative examples of usage and good taste, he was not using grammarians but writers as the authorities. Unfortunately in that very same 18th century a species of verbal parasite emerged from the woodwork of the scientific laboratory and proceeded to codify language into an analytical framework of formulaic definitions, propositions, and applications. Thus was latter-day grammar born. But for it to become entrenched, it had to sweep the schools in an epidemic that ended in a plague, killing all opposition including *literature* itself. *Verbal communication*, ever since, has been suffering the *cancer of language separated from literature* and has become the humpty-dumpty of our time.

As a result, the battle of communication has run riot in an Alice in Wonderland fantasy of verbal chaos: placing the cart before the horse, the skeleton before the living body, matter before spirit. Is it no wonder that we drive potential burgeoning intelligence and creative minds away from literature and from reading through the bureaucracy—autocracy of the English curriculum?[16]

When we need servicing on our car or repair on our body we turn to the professionals, the mechanic and the physician. But who enlightens us with the mysteries of language, the world of ideas, the creative imagination? Surely the area of mind and soul also require professional enlightenment. But instead of turning at once to the fount of language, the professional writers themselves, we are exposed to the ritual of verbal hazing, a traumatic rape of beauty and the dream world of poetry and the literary imagination by being subjected to the boot camp of grammatical march and drill, diagramming sentences, memorizing rules, analyzing structures of word particles and etymological fragments, as if we were students of anatomy slicing or shredding or dissecting a corpse. Is it any wonder that the subject of English turns young people off and away to other more alive and relevant areas of commitment and that there is a remoteness surrounding the neglected author wrongfully blamed for the bad taste and insensitivity of the Napoleonic ego-swollen jargon-bound pedestrian grammarian.

Today, Dullness, such as Pope never dreamed of but sardonically prophesied, has finally filtered down into the sewage of rote, bonehead English, along with "advanced composition." Self-study programs in Junior College and Freshman College English classes geared to grammatical proficiency instituted by our entrenched fanatics of rule and rote, only prove that some students are more docile more politic than others in succumbing to the discipline of rule and example—demonstrating deductive and inductive reasoning can be indoctrinated into any system, including grammar. Moreover, in countless studies where the rebellious imagination or a rash of individuality breaks through, student scores plummet, further ensuring traumatic discouragement while in no way reflecting verbal creative aptitude. In point of fact those who score well are curiously adept at composing illiterate paragraphs while those who fail, more often soar or at least show competency in composition thus proving no correlation between arbitrary scientific test devices and freedom of expression.

Grammar then, from its very inception, has been and always will be a failure.

It is ersatz, artificial and inorganic, a product of the linguistic laboratory, soulless, fleshless and dead.

* * * * *

Unknown to the public at large and unfortunately to students already lost to English literature from early disillusionment with a sterile and arid curriculum, a "grammarless" language of authors has evolved, snowballing into rapid intensity in the last 75 years of our own time into what I should like to call a veritable renaissance of non-linear innovative fiction initiating with James Joyce, Virginia Woolf, Gertrude Stein, William Faulkner and reaching as far back as Shakespeare and Laurence Sterne.[17]

But because publishers have succumbed to the bureaucratic conglomerate consumerism of "best sellerdumb" and university professors to their feather-bedding of the classics of the past, no one knows what is going on except the writers themselves, in what is called the "alternative scene."

It is only the latter working in innovative forms, the majority of whom should be enriching literature who for the most part have shunned the dead or moribund "museum" of higher education for alternative life styles as independent bookstore owners and managers, small press editors and publishers, printers, distributors, desktop computer specialists, art gallery and museum curators, video artists, solar energy new-age environmental architects, agriculturalists and the like.

This is the alternative underground Samizdat world of multi cross-cultural media where innovative music, painting, sculpture, dance and literature have converged and combined since the late '50s to produce the "grammarless" texts and forms largely unknown or ignored by the larger culture whose consciousness the alternative scene has been trying to change. But literature still has the hardest struggle because it has yet to be given a proper hearing to show a twenty-first century language of creative forms and ideas beyond the earlier Surrealism, stream-of-consciousness, linguistic and other literary inventions of James Joyce, Gertrude Stein and Virginia Woolf.[18]

Support of the new ultimately lies with the book publishers who, unfortunately, will not change or adapt. But surely they are no worse and no better than the multinational oil and other conglomerates they have chosen to emulate: Mobil, Gulf and Western, Texaco and the like.[19] And if oil in the guise of Mobil and Exon, beds down with public arts programs to improve their own public image, it is surely time for the mammoth publishing network to remember that once they actually published literature, and that they must do so again and in perpetuity, if freedom of expression, the encouragement of new ideas are not left to die.   Otherwise Fascism's preview and promise of the forties will indeed be fulfilled in the nineties.   It is simply a matter of shifting gears and changing one's point of view: Literature is not the business that publishers think it is.   It is an art.   And art involves research.   And as research is supported and has always been, so must literary art.   Because like any other form of research, the language of literature, even if it is a new non-linear 20th century language, is a language that we will all be using and be affected by, sooner than later.

* * * * *

> —The Prostitution and Corruption of the literature
> of Commerce has nothing to do with literature. But in
> America, in a county so morally righteous, it is not the
> 'literary' prostitute: the pulp porno-sensation ghost non-
> book movie script hack writer who is an outcast a non-
> person. He or she is commensurately rewarded and en-
> couraged to pollute and corrupt. Their books are mea-
> sured like slabs of meat on meat hooks awaiting packag-
> ing and distribution. The only yardstick is Mammon.
> Will it sell. No different than selling heroin, sex or
> cheese. This is the 'Mafia' world of publishing which
> the literary artist and innovator cannot accept.[20]
> —Arlene Zekowski, *Image Breaking Images*

A distinction that once existed must be reiterated loud and clear: there is the *literature of commerce* (akin to applied science) and the *literature of research* (paralleling theoretical or pure science).   The one is best-sellerdumb, consumerism, the other is craftsmanship, art.   Best sellerdumb's yardsticks are in universal quantitative sales, literature's are in specialized qualitative readership.   This has been and always will be so that literature at first attracts a different but nevertheless powerful articulate audience, a minority of the best and most sympathetic imaginative informed and sophisticated who will eventually spearhead the vanguard of new ideas they are exposed to.   But first they must be exposed to the generally *unfamiliar* so that it can become *familiar* and then, of course, accepted.

* * * * *

Following the example of the small press scene which exploded into print through the multilith revolution of the sixties, demonstrating the feasibility and success of small yet attractive economic editions and which has been disseminating its methodology ever since, through workshops, symposia, exhibitions, communal printing centers, city, sate, national and international book fairs, the big establishment publishers can no longer afford to bury their heads in the sand of "in-house" publishing, whining eternally and repeatedly over the profitless futility of encouraging innovative authors, or continue to perpetuate our chronic national infirmity since America's inception, of *literature by default*, treating its authors like it still does minority cultures: *as exploited slaves, white niggers or second class citizens.*

The philosophy of consumerism based upon mass appeal and the gross profit yardstick does not work and never has worked for literary art. It never worked for Poe, Hawthorne, Melville, Whitman, Gertrude Stein or Sherwood Anderson, to name just a few out of our vast array of neglect, extending now beyond the first 75 years of this century where resistance to change in recognizing the exciting forms and innovations of a 20th-21st century language has amounted to a literary muzzling of free speech/censorship of all that is alive, vibrant, meaningful and contemporary.

* * * * *

Unless literature becomes innovative and adventurous like science, willing to accept the new and the unfamiliar it will continue to recede into oblivion and totally disappear. When language is no longer functional, like any other technology, it finally dies and others take its place. Cultural history is strewn with the detritus of at least a hundred languages that died and disappeared: Babylonian, Egyptian, Cuneiform, Hittite, Phoenician, Mycenean, Etruscan, Rongo Rongo and innumerable others including scores of Amer-Indian ones, as well as classical Greek and Latin.

We owe to Dante the first technological leap into the modern era of Western civilization when he decided that Latin as a universal language was no longer serviceable or functional, when he created a literary structure from the contemporary speech of a country dialect—Tuscan. He thus established the precedent which all great writers and all great languages and literatures have followed since: to be alive and meaningful is to be contemporary in both matter and manner, literature and language.

America has neglected far too long being contemporary in language and literary art while forging ahead in almost every other contemporary direction. But a culture leaves its imprint on history in both its spiritual psychic roots as well as its inventions. We can not substitute matter for spirit. No culture ever has and we constitute no exception.

All bureaucracies in the end accomplish the same thing: *they preserve what is already dead.* That is how cultures die and literature and language disappear: *by opposing change.*

* * * * *

Literary prizes and awards are a supreme example of our warped philosophy of relying on what I've called "the mediocrity of collective decision making" which angers and frustrates the many more than it satisfies the lucky few.

In America we tend to admire aggressive competition using collective and communal yardsticks at the expense of unique invaluable idiosyncrasy and creative originality. *Imagination and thought are sacrificed to patronizing conformity of a majority consensus.* The team spirit of board decisions is perpetuated throughout the fabric of our multiple and tentacled bureaucracies from executive and legislative consortia in government, to college and university postgraduate schools, publishing editorial boards, to literature bodies of the National Endowment for the Arts. If worth can not be measured by consensus yardsticks what criteria should we, can we use?

In *A Room of One's Own* Virginia Woolf demonstrates the futility of literary judgments:

> At any rate, where books are concerned, it is notoriously difficult to fix labels of merit in such a way that they do not come off. Are not reviews of current literature a perpetual illustration of the difficulty of judgment? 'This great book,' 'this worthless book,' the same book is called by both names. Praise and blame alike mean nothing. No, delightful as the pastime of measuring may be, it is the most futile of all occupations and to submit to the decrees of the measurers the most servile of attitudes. So long as you write what you wish to write that is all that matters; and whether it matters for ages or only for hours, nobody can say. But to sacrifice a hair of the head of your vision, a shade of

its color, in deference to some Headmaster with a silver
pot in his hand or to some professor with a measuring-
rod up his sleeve, is the most abject treachery, and the
sacrifice of wealth and chastity which used to be said
to be the greatest of human disasters, a mere flea-bite
in comparison.[21]

Literary judgments fail in their time as do many other aesthetic judgments in painting, music, dance, because any judgment must rely not only on a special familiarity with, an expertise in a body of creativity, but more often on the magical power
of the divining rod with regard to its impact: will it last, will it
affect or play a role in the future? Unfortunately this power of
vision instinct or insight very few mortals possess, and even if
they did, you won't find such shamans, prophets or magicians
on literary prize boards and most assuredly not on the literary
board of the National Endowment for the Arts.

And yet knowing the impossibility of casting the right
prediction, decisions are made and prizes awarded generally to
the wrong people or to writers who will disappear into the oblivion of their time without leaving a shred or trace even for ob-
scurantist scholars or imaginatively sterile English PhDs to re-
suscitate on a "long lost writer jag" for the latest publish or perish project.

* * * * *

One of the most flagrant forms of fascistic censorial behaviour, is hidden in the recesses of postgraduate liberal arts
higher education. Nowhere else is the American disease of conformity so well, so solidly entrenched as in doctoral programs
purporting to train young impressionable converts in "literary
scholarship and research" while in reality weaning and expung-
ing their souls from all imaginative incentive creative potential
or endeavor.

Where in reality intellectual creative life should begin,
the postgraduate priesthood insures its demise, so that the emer-
gent body of doctoral acolytes are ready in their turn to inculcate
in others the aridity and sterility of preserved scholarship and
conformity to a dead tradition.

William James in his time called this phenomenon of the
postgraduate doctoral ritual "intellectual servitude." But where
and how did it all begin?

Education cannot be separated from dissemination and dissemination from what education insists upon promulgating. What better way and what greater power for the education business or church than its own elite house organ university press along with the more mundane textbook publishers, to perpetuate the mandarin philosophy of its Byzantine world: to instill awe, fear and respect by virtue of the vast horde of dead immortals sung and eulogized in snug anthologies who ironically sadly in their time were sacrificed and scorned to neglect, starvation anathema or oblivion: Blake, Shelley, Keats, Poe, Whitman, Hawthorne, Melville, to name but a few.

Is it not an irony of ironies that creativity must suffocate under the weight of ponderous endless scholarly research instead of inspiring or perpetuating further contemporary creativity? Why must each generation of creative writers suffer anew the slings and arrows of its family of illustrious suffering forbears? And why must heavy-handed jargonized constipated scholarly research regurgitate its tomes of aridity in a soporific sea of post-doctoral pollution?

* * * * *

To be creative is to question or criticize things as they are, to insist on being free, to take risks, to be unafraid of making mistakes, to grope toward change, to try the unfamiliar, to experiment in order to discover and expose a new idea, to occasionally unearth a diamond in the rough, a new star to steer by, to be reborn and to give new life to others, and above all, to inspire.

How many doctoral programs in English literature accept a work of seminal literary criticism or a creative work itself (poetry, novel, drama, story) in lieu of the proverbial dismal tedious scholarly thesis? Even after several decades following my own departure from five long grinding doctoral years in one of the more prestigious of these institutions of higher learning, having been denied, at the end, the doctoral on this very basis (despite the many publications they were offered from this writer's already growing number of books of literary criticism, essay, drama, poetry, short story)—precious few.

Intellectual and creative discrimination, the strange neurosis-psychosis *conformity* syndrome is bureaucratizing American life from the government to the private sector, from education to the publishing media.

What good is any kind of power, intellectual, political, economic without ideas to feed it? Otherwise *conformity* will bury us in the hoist of our own petard and fascism will surely come.

Reform is needed but will it be heeded?

* * * * *

Cultural stagnation extends into all segments of society and is another way of referring to cultural malnutrition. Freshman college students, for example, experience a "Time-Lapse" and "Jet-Lag" that is biologically as well as psychologically unnerving when their imagination and sensibilities are not engaged because of being strait-jacketed into writing, reading, according to structures which are *sterile, analytical* or *abstract*, rather than *esthetic, dynamic* or *literary. Beauty* and *form* which are a part of nature as well as literature are thus denied them. They do not know for example that language soars from the printed page in its metamorphosis into sound, rhythm, tone, accent emphasis—elements of voice, speech, music, etc. As a result they are tone deaf as well as tactually inert to what words say and mean and feel and their sensory power is lost, buried in the jargon of grammar and composition surgery performed upon, what is for them, already lifeless matter.

* * * * *

> But words will never do what the grammarians insist upon, for words belong not to those who have imprisoned them *but only to those who set them free.* The word serves the artist, the poet, the creator above all who allows the word its head, much as a good rider does his horse. Only then can accomplishments be made, *when movement takes place.*[22]
> —Arlene Zekowski, *Abraxas*

If I were Emperor or Empress as the fairy tale goes, I would eliminate all rhetoric and memorizing of grammatical rules from the classroom and consign to the rubbish heap grammarial pundits posing as writers. The only "professors of writing" I would include would be those who do not profess but who are genuine writers. Taste begins with exposure and so instead of the proverbially American "sugar pill" bureaucratic majority-consensus of feeding everybody the "ordinary" I would begin with the extraordinary and the unique which is what literature is all about and what great writers write.

Since language is the creation of those who make language we would dispense with those who have been freeloading for over 250 years upon those very creators—the grammarians and linguists (let them do their philological psycho-linguistic thing in postgraduate schools where language science today has become a scholar's toy for doctoral acolytes to play with).[23]

It is time we confronted the possibility that language was not created by writers to intimidate readers but to embrace and liberate them and where better to demonstrate this to the intellectually and creatively starved than in the freshman English class?

But how will they learn to write? To think? Certainly not by memorizing or applying the 300 rules of English grammar.[24]

You never hear a writer write or talk about those 300 rules of grammar. He probably does not even know them or much less care, as long as he knows how to write. A writer writes because of the need to transmit sensory experience, beauty, philosophy, or knowledge, to others. Form and substance to a writer are as instinctive, organically interwoven with each other as the root of a tree to its trunk, leaves and blossoms.

* * * * *

Literacy, after all, is what we are after: learning how to think, learning how to read means learning *what* to read. You cannot discriminate without choice, and choice means taste. Beginning at the bottom the mediocre the ordinary and eventually proceeding upward will alienate and discourage those whose quickened sensibilities are being vulgarized insulted or frankly not aroused. Beginning with the best literature will at least engage the *quick* and perhaps teach the *slow* something worthwhile to grasp for and rise up to.

No one reads unless reading becomes compelling, an act of love, of need, of engagement, not a duty, a chore. *Enthusiasm* has and always will be the key to bridge the literature of the past into that of the present. There should be no segregation of that past from the present. Unfortunately it is the *present* which is being denied access today and which largely accounts for the indifference to reading and for the impinging threat of literature's disappearance.

Librarians and teachers, for example, should be engaged in a joint effort to make more available, the contemporary renaissance of the alternative small press scene of books and periodicals (germinating since the multilith revolution of the sixties, from a handful of presses to over 5000 today). Ironically the reverse seems to be taking place today in many college and university libraries.

Not only personnel but cultural resources have fallen victim to the budgetary knife of economic efficiency so that periodicals in particular (not subsidized as book purchases are by local bond issues) are being redlined and riffed out of existence. Since important writing first appears in periodicals and not in books, the censorship of creativity and access to a free press are threatening the healthy functioning of a democratic society.

* * * * *

Books are not at an end as some would fashionably theorize. It is *language* and *language attitudes* that need to be changed. And it is *language* that has been and is being changed in the renaissance of writers denied publication in the corporate publishing establishment controlled by electronics and combined multinationals of every kind and species (see especially footnote 19). Centralization may be more efficient and economic for many types of industries and services but when it comes to language and literature magnum control must necessarily exclude polylithic idiosyncrasy and contemporaneity upon which freedom of speech and expression in Western society depend.

That is why the alternative small press scene is our vital link to what is contemporary and meaningful in our present civilization. Moreover, as general statistics prove, the most important writing of this century—over 75 per cent of most authors' works—was launched in the contemporary small press magazine scene and only 20 per cent through books of the establishment presses.

With most fiction publishing being "packaged" by Hollywood, T.V., blockbuster book/movie mergers, the small press scene has become virtually the only outlet for contemporary exploratory expression in literary fiction today.

If, as Virginia Woolf penetratingly observed, you cannot legislate taste, why does so much opinion and prejudice underlie who gets what part of the public bankroll in the issuing of the yearly NEA prizes and cash awards?

* * * * *

At a working session of the Literature Panel of the National Endowment in Santa Fe and at the subsequent bash the evening following, sponsored by a member of our own Rio Grande Writers Association, a very prestigiously placed NEA board member urged me to consider becoming part of a "power block" in order to swing the opinions and votes in a more sympathetic direction for innovative literature.

Like any other government bureaucracy, members of the Literature Board of the NEA represent power blocks the way congressmen respond to the lobbies and pressure groups of their own constituencies.

But the NEA derives its power from public taxes and where the public is involved, criticism and reform are also public, not private issues.

It would perhaps take a Solomon to reconstitute the voting procedures of the National Endowment for the Arts to balance out a more participatory, more democratic procedure. But voting stems from philosophy or policy and this we should change so that the *new*, the *innovative*, the *experimental*, the *investigative*, the *exploratory*, the *truly contemporary* are not perpetually denied a hearing, as has proverbially been the case.[25]

Clearly rationality and common sense are against the present procedures where authors who derive their forms from the inventions, discoveries and sacrifices of others—who in their time never enjoyed encouragement and support, but more often suffered neglect—should be lavishly rewarded for popularizing old ideas while those practicing original and momentous literary breakthroughs are discriminated against.

The two general areas of literature: the *traditional* along with the *innovative* should receive *equal* representation and support. Otherwise the future of literature is compromised and will disappear.

* * * * *

> Of accepting and supporting *the unfamiliar the un-*
> *known the new* whether it is understood or not. Of al-
> lowing challenge, novelty, strangeness, exotic and un-
> known forms of liberation in literary directions to take
> place, of *tolerating* what is foreign and unfamiliar and
> what is more of *encouraging* what is inventive and cre-
> ative, not sneering and suppressing it. . . . We are thus
> far a frontierpeople who yet reject *literary frontiers.*[26]
> —Arlene Zekowski, *Image Breaking Images*

Opinion cannot enter into the area of the new and the
unknown either in literature or in science. That pioneering instinct so characteristically American, so full of vitality and exciting energy has been warped until now in being withheld, denied
to literature all through our cultural history. We are, we shall be
no farther along today than we were in Henry Adams' day if we
allow this attitude to continue. Richard Chase in "The Fate of
the Avant-Garde" describes it as follows:

> As we have been told at length, the serious writer
> of the nineteenth century was painfully on his own. We
> are not surprised to find two of the most isolated of
> these writers pleading for what we should call an
> avant-garde movement. Thus Melville begs his con-
> temporaries to 'confess' immediately the greatness of
> Hawthorne without waiting for the slow judgment of
> posterity, which, whatever it may be, will do neither
> Hawthorne nor his generation any good, at least not
> while they still have the power of further accom-
> plishment. 'By confessing him,' in Melville's well-
> known words, 'you thereby confess others; you brace the
> whole brotherhood. For genius, all over the world,
> stands hand in hand, and one shock of recognition runs
> the whole circle round.' Yet Melville's plea had no
> more effect than the similar plea in Henry Adams' let-
> ter of 1862 to his brother Charles Francis: 'What we
> want is a *school.* We want a national set of young men
> like ourselves or better, to start new influences not only
> in politics, but in literature, in law, in society and
> throughout the whole social organism of the country—a
> national school of our own generation.' As it turned out,
> Adams' broadly based insurgent intelligentsia was even
> less possible than Melville's more purely literary
> 'brotherhood.'[27]

* * * * *

If we could reform the system of literary awards for innovative literature by avoiding prejudice or a priori opinion, what then is to take its place? A policy or philosophy at least more in keeping with our American sense of fair play finally proffered to those who have experienced the most neglect longest: one that leaves out opinions, prejudices, demonstrates respect for those who have accomplished most: in essence a *seniority* system for authentic creativity that avoids subjective judgments, that applies as in a court of law, the *evidence*, the works produced (both published and unpublished) upon which to propose awards. That much of the publication will be in presses and periodicals of the independent small press alternative scene goes without saying since those largely published by the conglomerated mega publishers—Random, Viking, Doubleday, etc., are hardly "neglected" authors.

For the last 30-40 years, denying zero new forms of literary art, is enough to elicit the endemic despair that we who are part of that coterie of pariah-like neglect, are experiencing to the point where we can almost touch, feel and smell doomsday's breath upon a dying and disappearing literary culture in America.

If Culture and Civilization do not feed on the life of the *new* and the *contemporary* then they feed on no life at all. And no life means decay and death for individuals as well as societies.

If the contemporary and the new are given at long last their due, in America, then there is hope that creators in literature like creators in science, will reap their legitimate and long overdue respect and recognition. Perhaps we will then, as a nation, begin to enjoy proper cultural recognition in the world to offset the exclusive political soul-less superpower dominance that still turns others more humanistically inclined, away from us.

* * * * *

Looking over the Nobel Prize laureateships, it is shocking to see that the greatest artistic accomplishments of the twentieth century were left outside the magic circle of winners. Proust, Joyce, Stein, Apollinaire, Valery, Kafka, D. H. Lawrence, Virginia Woolf, Chekhov, Conrad, Henry James—the greatest sources of contemporary artistic consciousness were passed over by

the critics, and the laurel was given instead to their adapters. This oversight must clearly indict twentieth century criticism, large as it is in output, with the monumental failure to recognize 'truth' in terms of lasting literary merit.[28]   —Stanley Berne
The Unconscious Victorious

No one is ahead of his time, it is only that the particular variety of creating his time is the one that his contemporaries who also are creating their own time refuse to accept. . . . Those who are creating the modern composition authentically are naturally only of importance when they are dead because by that time the modern composition having become past is classified and the description of it is classical. That is the reason why the creator of the new composition in the arts is an outlaw . . . and it is really too bad very much too bad naturally for the creator but also very much too bad for the enjoyer, they all really would enjoy the created so much better just after it has been made than when it is already a classic. . . .

. . . Now, of course, it is perfectly true that a more or less first rate work of art is beautiful. . . . Of course it is wonderfully beautiful, only when it is still a thing irritating, annoying, stimulating then all quality of beauty is denied to it.

Of course it is beautiful but first all beauty in it is denied and then all the beauty of it is accepted. If every one were not so indolent they would realize that beauty is beauty even when it is irritating and stimulating not only when it is accepted and classic.[29]

—Gertrude Stein, *Selected Essays*

* * * * *

Is not the system of bestowing awards on the basis of *productivity* and *seniority* just as much a gamble? No more than the present policy of coals to Newcastle by exalting the known, the established, the familiar, of even proclaiming this or that best seller the great novel of the future, moreover, of politically caballing for the author to receive the coveted Nobel prize. *No great novel of the last 75 years of this century was ever a best seller and certainly no best seller was ever a great novel.* Ultimately the risks of glorifying the popular writers of the moment are far greater than lavishing honor upon unknown authors creating new forms. Any scientist will defend *risk* as the very life blood of pioneering discovery. Without the courage of exploring the new, of accepting risk, how can a great country hope to maintain its leadership over others?

In addition to pioneering new policies of awards and subsidies for creatively innovative authors, the National Endowment for the Arts could also make accessible continuously emerging presses of the small press alternative scene, to public and private libraries, colleges, and universities.

This can be accomplished on a revolving basis via NEA subsidy (outright purchase) of a selected number distributed gratis or through philanthropic foundations and trusts. Only then can the public become aware of the dynamic vitality and diversity of the contemporary writing scene.

Some 20 years ago I characterized this scene as follows:

> Thus, for the very first time in our cultural history we are realizing at long last (and hopefully not too late), a fellowship, a brotherhood and sisterhood, a loose pluralistic, diversified cosmopolis of floating and flowing communities continent-wide from California to New York, from Montana to New Mexico, Westerly North to Westerly South, Mississippi East, Mississippi West, from Maine to Key West, from Peoria to Kalamazoo to San Antonio and Austin to Kansas City, all across the geometric checkerboard of farms and prairies and high and low deserts and Sangre de Cristo . . . Rockies and rivers of the Rio Grande and Pecos and Susquehanna and Great Lakes and Louisiana Cajun canalways and sleepy lagoons of the Mississippi.
>
> All united and determined never again to suffer in silence or neglect, the Hawthornes, Melvilles, Whitmans, Poes, in their time, to promulgate a new way and a new wave of the avant-garde of the written and spoken word in all its diversifications and philosophies and eccentricities, idiosyncrasies and coteries, both democratic and aristocratic with multiple sensibilities and voices of every form and feeling: feminist, black, Chicano, native american indian, gays, . . . transvestites, joycean, steinian, woolfian, anaïs ninian, haikuian, concrete sound poem, long-poem, collage, wall-poem, experimental prose-poem and poem-prose, avant-garde comic pop satirics . . . multilinguals and numbersystems, skywritings, happenings, science fictions and antifictions, spoken and unspoken words, verbi-voco-visuals, pop and cubistic cinémathèques and dial-an-author, esoterica . . . from: 'Pot-Hooks and Hangars,' to 'The Second Coming of St. John,' to 'Schmuck'![30]   —*Margins*, 1975

* * * * *

But the most powerful, the most irresponsible, the most blameworthy sector insidiously contributing to the proliferation of idiocy, dullness, cultural suicide is the press of the publishing establishment itself in denying access to all creative innovation for the last 45 years and more—an unprecedented censorship of literary ideas and expression festering in a country priding itself on technological freedom in all   other areas of human invention.

Certainly the impotent weary argument that experimental literature is not "profitable" will not do. It is like saying it is not "profitable" to be honest, dedicated, idealistic, or that writing that inspires, encourages curiosity, generosity of thought, elevation of spirit, stimulation of imagination, ideas, a sense of beauty and form—is not worthwhile.

Support of the arts and participation in every form of cultural activity and performance—museums, theatres, concerts, operas, etc.—testifies otherwise to the public's hunger for self-enrichment.

The publishing establishment can not continue to ignore all this arts activity when the facts are staring at them accusatively that they have become culturally repressive almost fascistic in their consistent denial of access to new writers and new writing.

They are no better, perhaps even worse, than the American Medical Association in obstructing a humane national health insurance, worse than the lethargic and muscle-bound auto industrial giants in not encouraging more enthusiastically, solar-electric generation, worse than the Energy Administration itself in not closing down nuclear-powered plutonium polluting plants, in favor of United Solar Systems 1995 online abundant pollution-free *silicon alloy* solar panels at 12 cents per kwh surpassing photo-voltaics at 50-75 cents per kwh.

Certainly Literature is a *human resource* as much as any and all of these others for how can we even conceive of culture or the creative imagination without Literature?

Then why bother with the establishment presses at all? Why not let them go their sterile vulgar bureaucratic obsolescent way?

Not only are we subsidizing the waste the featherbedding pollution via yesterday's remaindered dead texts but encouraging an exclusivity policy of raping public domain, which is tantamount to exploitation of the "dead," but what is worse, denying less and less publishing access to more and more contemporary authors: the more you publish and republish the past and the dead the less room there is for the present and the living. It is like building a house or an apartment complex and setting aside for each individual occupant, one whole room as a mausoleum or funeral chapel for ancestor worship. Can we afford to go on this way "censoring" denying the present through greedy rape of the past?

If the gargantuan publishers themselves will not publish economically feasible editions of *innovative* works let them at least show their good will in righting the wrongs they have perpetrated through their half-century closed door policy of avoiding the contemporary scene by at least taking on original works of independent small press publishers for recommendation in college and university bookstores, libraries, and literature courses.

Active support of the contemporary and the new would demonstrate that social, intellectual, cultural *responsibility* most American publishers have denied their readership for far too long. Certainly freedom of the press and healthy encouragement of that freedom is as much a hippocratic oath of literary publishing in a free society as its ethical counterpart in medicine. It is time the publishers repaired the moral cancer they themselves have created through their Mafia Hollywood-T.V. blockbuster-movie buck-success psychosis.

* * * * *

American culture is dying, hovering over its own precipice and burial ground which it itself has dug and already filled with the detritus of dead forms and dead ideas of books of the past from its gargantuan corporate press mill threatening total dumbed-down conformity of the society it is pledged to serve. At least before we gasp our last breath let our two century-old nation attempt a surgical miracle—for only a miracle can save us from the suicidal course corporate bigness and profit paranoia have brought about: let *literature*, a truly *living literature*, a *literature* of the *present* and the *future* breathe not its final, but is first breath on this continent of ours and maybe, who knows, along with the great European and Asiatic Oriental cultures of the past a Western Hemisphere culture, a distinctive culture of the Americas will leave its heritage of spirit and mind for present and future generations to remember, cherish and be inspired by.

Notes

[1] Arlene Zekowski, "The American Samizdat: Why There is an Active Literary Underground Renaissance in American Today," *Margins: A Review of Little Mags and Small Press Books*, 12 (June-July 1974), 50.

[2] Arlene Zekowski, "A Preface to the American Samizdat & Post-Modern Anthology," *Margins: A Review of Little Mags and Small Press Books*, 24, 25, 26 (September, October, November 1975), 12.

[3] "A Preface to the American Samizdat and Post-Modern Anthology," *Margins*, 24, 25, 26 (September, October, November 1975), 13.

[4] "The American Samizdat," *Margins*, 12 (June-July 1974), 50.

[5] For a book-length exploration of these and other related topics, see Arlene Zekowski, *Image Breaking Images: A New Mythology of Language* (New York: Horizon Press, 1976).

[6] Arlene Zekowski and Stanley Berne, *Cardinals & Saints: On the aims and purposes of the Arts in our time* (Croton-On-Hudson: Metier Editions, 1958). Distributed by American-Canadian Publishers, Inc., P.O. Box 4595, Santa Fe, New Mexico 87502. See Chapter 25, p. 155.

[7] Arlene Zekowski, "The Emperor's New Clothes: Beyond the Visual," *Image Breaking Images*, Chapter 7, p. 67.

[8] The 1962 Manifesto was reissued in Arlene Zekowski, *Seasons of the Mind*, and Stanley Berne, *The Unconscious   Victorious* and *Other Stories* (New York: George Wittenborn, 1969), pp. 303-304, 307-308.

[9] In *New World Writing*, No. 11 (New York: New American Library, 1957), publisher, editor of Noonday Press, Cecil Hemley in his essay, "The New and Experimental," viciously attacked all innovative experimental avant-garde writing, as well as our feature, "The End of Story in the Novel." (See "Preface" *Against the Disappearance of Literature*, p. x.)

[10] *Image Breaking Images*.

[11] Ibid., pp. 115-116.

[12] Ibid. See especially: "Relativity and the Neo-Narrative," *Seasons of the Mind* (New York: George Wittenborn, 1969 and Horizon Press reissue, 1973), pp. 161-173.

[13] Journalists like Edwin Newman think that by exposing jargon we can "purify" language, prune it back to its grammatical source, not knowing that we're pruning an already diseased corpse. Jargon is the product of the corruption of language and the corruption of language the product of its obsolete structured *grammar*, derived from an already dead language, *Latin*.

[14] Stanley Berne, *Future Language* (New York: Horizon Press, 1976), pp. 25-29.

[15] "Selected Criticism," *Image Breaking Images*, p. 155. See also "Notes on the Neo-Narrative," *Abraxas* (New York: George Wittenborn, 1964), pp. 23-29.

[16] For a further treatment of this topic, see "Why Johnny Can't Read," "Because He Won't Read," *Image Breaking Images*, Chapters 10 and 11.

[17] For a lively witty illuminating mini anthology of "the grammarless language" in both literature and advertising, see Stanley Berne, "A Little Appendix of the Grammarless Language," *Future Language*, pp. 131-143.

[18] See "Free Association: The Liberation from Logic," *Image*, pp. 46-56.

[19] Some typical examples of conglomeration: according to *Publishers Weekly*, Gulf and Western Industries, which owns Paramount Pictures, has swallowed Simon & Schuster and Pocket Books. RCA owns Pantheon Books, Alfred A. Knopf, Random House, and Ballantine Books. Litton Industries owns Van Nostrand, Reinhold Company, American Book Company, and Delmar Publishers. ITT owns Bobbs-Merrill Company. Bantam Books now belongs to the Italian industrial group I.F.I. International, which makes Cinzano and Fiat. Filmways, Inc., purchased Grosset and Dunlap, Inc. Xerox owns R. R. Bowker Company and Unipub. CBS Inc. owns Holt, Rinehart, & Winston, Inc. Raytheon owns Atheneum Publishers. See also *U.S. News & World Report*. "America's Press—Too Much Power for Too Few?" (August 15, 1977); *Booklegger Press*, "Publishers Acquired By Publishers: Publishers Owned By Conglomerates" (September 1980, as first published in *San Francisco Review of Books*, June 1980). More recent developments include the German media/entertainment conglomerate, Bertelsmann AG, owner of RCA, Arista Records, Bantam, Doubleday, Dell, publishing companies—now landlord of a one million square foot 46-story Broadway Tower on New York's Times Square (*New York Times*, April 25, 1994).

[20] "Why Johnny Can't Read," *Image Breaking Images*, p. 98.

[21] Virginia Woolf, *A Room of One's Own* (New York and Burlingame: Harcourt Brace & World, Inc., 1957), p. 110.

[22] "Notes on the Neo-Narrative," *Abraxas*, p. 28.

[23] A case in point is the transformational grammar crowd who loudly reject the structural anthropologists, structural linguistic and behaviouristic psychology people in favor of their own modern linguistics and the abstract generalizations of philosophical grammar. While professing concern for the "creative aspect of language," they themselves largely derive from 17th century rationalist scientific views projecting into their own contemporary idea of grammar. Protesting against the criticism leveled against them that theirs is not "prescriptive" but "generative" and a "natural science," what is so mystifying in such professed terms of theirs as "deep" and "surface structure"? Are these not simply a pretentious verbal shuffling for "semantic-figurative" (deep?) as against "literal" (surface?). Whom are they obfuscating with such academic cosmological skullduggery? Admitting that creative intelligence is the highest form (above animal and "normal" human intelligence) their whole theory or science of language and mind upon which their generative grammar rests, fails of its own weight through lack of logic, since creative intelligence in language cannot be demonstrated by grammarians, linguisticians or even computers but only by a particular species of human being: the literary artist/craftsman. Their intellectual evasiveness in providing no allusions, ref-

erences or specific illustrations of the creative language of the writer is a dramatic but monumental omission that only proves the ineptitude of any language, science or scientific language theory to account for the "mysteries" of creativity in language. So eminent a psychiatrist and psychologist as Jung acknowledges this simple yet profound point. Underscoring the transformationalists' ignorance of 20th century verbal art forms, is their total lack of reference to Freudian free association, its role in shaping the stream-of-consciousness in 20th century literature, and the art movements of Dada and Surrealism. (For an exploration of these relationships see *Image Breaking Images*, Chapter 6, "Free Association: The Liberation from Logic," Chapter 7, "The Emperor's New Clothes: Beyond the Visual," and Chapter 8, "Spatial Language, Open Structure, Words as Composition in Movement.") How can any language theory like transformational grammar, based on 17th century rationalist 18th-19th century positivist concepts consider itself in harmony with 20th-21st century alineal spatial-temporal philosophies of mind, language and creativity? I consider this another example of the sterility and archaism and reactionary scholarship of academe.

[24] In Stanley Berne's *Future Language*, the 300 rules have been revolutionized and reduced to two: the period and the comma. For explorations and examples of the *kommatic* and *periodic* styles, see in particular Chapter 9, pp. 56-65 and Chapter 11, pp. 74-82. In *Image Breaking Images*, see Chapter 14, "A Neo-Narrative Sampler," pp. 138-147.

[25] In a characteristic NEA announcement of 165 literature fellowships to fiction writers, playwrights, poets and essayists in 38 states, only 2 were awarded to writers of innovative forms. Significantly, not one of the Advisory Panel responsible for the awards represented innovative writing or writers.

[26] "Why Johnny Can't Read," *Image Breaking Images*, pp. 101-102.

27 Irving Howe, ed., *The Idea of the Modern* (New York: Horizon Press, 1967), p. 149.

[28] Stanley Berne, "Related Essays," *The Unconscious Victorious and Other Stories* (New York: George Wittenborn, Inc., 1969 and Horizon Press reissue, 1973), p. 164.

[29] Gertrude Stein, *Selected Writings*, ed. Carl Van Vechten (New York: Vintage Books, 1972), pp. 514-515.

[30] "A Preface to the American Samizdat & Post-Modern Anthology," *Margins: A Review of Little Mags and Small Press Books*, 24, 25, 26 (September, October, November 1975), 11.

Works Cited

"America's Press—Too Much Power for Too Few?" *U.S. News & World Report*, 15 August 1977, pp. 27-33. Note representative issues of *Publishers Weekly*, also *Literary Market Place*, 1961-1978 for annual listings of book mergers.

Berne, Stanley. *Future Language*. New York: Horizon Press, 1976-1977. Declining literacy, reading ability, and interest in literature: "Open Structure" as the cure. Word Language vs. linear grammatical sentence structure. Its universal application to all modern languages. Features author's bibliography and "A Little Appendix of the Grammarless Language" from Shakespeare through Sterne, Joyce, Stein, Woolf, *The Wall Street Journal*, etc., to the present.

—. The Unconscious Victorious and Other Stories. New York: George Wittenborn, 1969 and Horizon Press reissue, 1973. The new story/short novel. Poetry-prose, notes, essays, interviews, Sir Herbert Read corres.

Chase, Richard. "The Fate of the Avant-Garde." In *The Idea of the Modern*. Ed. Irving Howe. New York: Horizon Press, 1967. A wide-ranging anthology of distinguished authors characterizing the avant-garde artist and society.

Harris, Frank. *My Life and Loves*. New York: Grove Press, 1963. Penetrating literary portraits of the most celebrated authors of his time.

Hemley, Cecil. "The New and Experimental." In *New World Writing* , No. 11. New York: New American Library, 1957.

Kostelanetz, Richard, ed. *Breakthrough Fictioneers*. West Glover, Vermont: Something Else Press, 1973. The most representative, comprehensive and courageous anthology on the post-modern writing scene. A veritable "Who's Who" of the groundbreakers in contemporary innovative new literature at that time. For a contemporary update, see Richard Kostelanetz, ed., *American Writing Today*. Whitston Publishing Company (Troy, New York), 1991.

Stein, Gertrude. "Composition as Explanation." *Selected Writings*. Ed. Carl Van Vechten. New York: Vintage Books, 1972.

Woolf, Virginia. *A Room of One's Own*. New York and Burlingame: Harcourt Brace & World, 1957.

Zekowski, Arlene. *Abraxas*. New York: George Wittenborn, 1964. Distrib.: American-Canadian Publishers, Inc., P.O. Box 4594, Sante Fe, New Mexico 87502 (poetry-prose neo-narrative). Preface by Sir Herbert Read; Authors' Exposition; Forward; "Notes on the Neo-Narrative"; Selections from *Cardinals & Saints*.

—. "The American Samizdat." *Margins: A Review of Little Magazines and Small Press Books*, 12 (June-July 1974), 50, 80.

—. "A Preface to the American Samizdat and Post-Modern Anthology." *Margins: A Review of Little Magazines and Small Press Books*, 24, 25, 26 (September, October, November 1975), 8-13, 201.

—. *Image Breaking Images: A New Mythology of Language*. New York: Horizon Press, 1976-1977. Zekowski's "open structure" and the grammarless language. Language and its relation to elitism, racism, science, literature, the arts, feminism, third world. "Command grammar's" censorship of contemporary thought and writing. Galloping entropy. Cultural suicide: the death of language and nations. Rigor-mortis, education and publishing. Projects a new mythology of language: curvilinear organic and universal. Author's bibliography and 20 years of "Selected Criticism" by and about Zekowski and Berne.

—. *Seasons of the Mind*. New York: George Wittenborn, 1969, and Horizon Press, 1973. The new novel/neo-narrative "open structure." Poetry-prose. Radio interviews. Sir Herbert Read corres. Legends. Manifesto. Major essays on innovative literature.

Zekowski, Arlene and Stanley Berne. *Cardinals & Saints: On the aims and purposes of the Arts in our time.* Croton-on-Hudson: Metier Editions, 1958. Distrib.: American-Canadian Publishers, Inc.: P.O. Box 4595, Santa Fe, New Mexico 87502. 29 essays: "comic, bawdy, ironic, authoritative, elegant and urbane," on literature, painting, science, television, dance, theatre, publishing, education, aesthetics, literary criticism, American customs and culture. A classic in its field.

—. "When Will You Understand That in So Far as Present Use Is Concerned the Novel as We Now Know It Is Dead." Manifesto. Issued September 1, 1962, upon publication of *Concretions* (Arlene Zekowski) and *The Dialogues* (Stanley Berne). New York: George Wittenborn. Published in: *Trace*, 47 (Fall-Winter 1962-1973), 262-263. Excerpts: in *Third Assembling*. Eds. Richard Kostelanetz, Henry Korn, Mike Metz. New York: Assembling Press, 1962. In *Whole Cosmep Catalog*. Special one-time supplement to *International Directory of Little Magazines & Small Presses*. Paradise, California: Dustbooks, 1973. Reissued: in *Seasons of the Mind* (Arlene Zekowski). New York: George Wittenborn, 1969, and Horizon Press, 1973, pp. 303-304. In *The Unconscious Victorious and Other Stories* (Stanley Berne). New York: George Wittenborn, 1969, and Horizon Press 1973, pp. 307-308.

—. "The End of Story in the Novel." In *New World Writing*, No. 11. New York: New American Library, 1957. Excerpts from *Cardinals & Saints*. *Phenomena* (Stanley Berne). *Decorations as for Prayers* (Arlene Zekowski).

Essay

Tradition and Its Limitations

I should like to talk with you and to you, to all of you and some of you and any down to a few, in fact to anyone who wants to participate, howsoever and whatsoever about *tradition*, different kinds of traditions, and eventually literary tradition.

Perhaps you might say this is presumptuous on my part, a literary person, a writer, to talk about so general and so sweeping a subject which appears to belong more to the realm of say social history or philosophy, etc.

Well, in the Preface to the *Literary Ballads* I believe Wordsworth ventured to be what was then perhaps considered bold by suggesting that the poet was like other human beings only more so, that is, more human. What Wordsworth was suggesting to the reader then, in a nice and polite pre-Victorian-like way, was: the artist, the creator is an intensification—exaggeration—magnification of some part or whole of each and all of us. Moreover the creative artist—writer—poet can bring the beyond the *mystery* that repulses and attracts, that puzzles or frightens but that also charms us into focus.

Call the creative artist shaman-wizard prophet sibyl medicine man or woman, what is important is that the creative person transforms the ordinary into the extraordinary or unusual. Since most of us recognize the truth of these remarks as partaking of rather common knowledge in our dictionary of commonplace ideas, we must also accept the premise that the artist has just as much a right as any specialist-scholar to show us in some perspective of the artist's own—what tradition is all about.

One characteristic of any tradition, whether ethnic or literary or cultural, is that it creates comfort and security and self-assurance and literally charms us *out of thought*. And *out of being*.

When you accept any kind of tradition it means that you have accepted what were once other people's creations for your own. By accepting this legacy of other people's properties and inventions and possessions you have had to accept the conditions upon which they have been passed on to you. And whether you realize it or not, these "conditions" are as serious as those that Faust accepted when he sold his soul to the Devil. Everyone pays, societies and nations, all of us, in full acceptance of any and all gifts we receive. And the gifts of tradition are no exception to this rule.

All inheritors of any and all traditions, for example, are buying *death* as against *life*. Does this shock you? It shouldn't. When we accept the creations of other people we are really substituting their lives, their adventures, their struggles, their ideas, their imaginative and intellectual and sensory existences, for our own.

When we accept tradition, the whole body of other people's accomplishments, their languages, their customs, their morals, their laws, their ethics, their sex, their music, their architecture their art, their literature, their prejudices, loves, hates, education, scholarship, myths, religions, inventions, we are in effect refusing the gift of our own creation, the possibility of becoming and being, of being and becoming, an *unique* instead of an *eunuch*, a servant instead of a master.

Tradition has always involved enslavement. Look at the Middle Ages. Look at the enslavement to ignorance and disease and death in the history of the plagues of Europe. Look at the *Empire* syndrome all throughout human history: Egyptian, Babylonian, Persian, Greek, Roman, Holy Roman, French-English-Indian-Asian, English-American Colonial, European-African, Russian-East European, Japanese-Pacific-Asian, American-Southeast Asian.

Not too long ago when I earned my bread in academia, I actually believed that culture, art, civilization, literature, music were in essence life-giving and so preached and so sustained myself and so occasionally inspired young people to carry the torch of what I and they considered to be the enlightenment of the good, the true, the beautiful and the wise—that heritage of all that has survived, all that has been preserved, all, in a word, that has been capable of being embalmed!

* * * * *

And so as a novice to the religion of culture I had adopted, like so many other Americans without a faith in America and what it could offer or deny an American who grew up feeling more like a displaced European, I made my pilgrimage.

But the pilgrimage unfortunately was largely more often to broken shrines, to those "bare ruined choirs where late the sweet birds sang," to Avranches and St. Malo and Dignes and Calais and Etrétat and Quiberon and Fécamp and a dozen other Norman and Breton towns and villages where the ghosts of the Middle Ages of the fanned vaulting and the charred buttresses, the ribs of their skeletal pillars, altars, sacristies thrust to heaven stood out, every part and particle shattered forever—lost stained glass, and brick and masonry and stone, shimmering in sunlight or shadowing in grey rain but always eventually against a blue sky. And you wouldn't believe it. Or you didn't want to. That the engines of the 20th century could, and did, like it had done 2 decades previous, seek and find the destruction of beauty in time and place.

And then you could understand why a writer like Proust was trying so hard to hope and to prove that he could suspend the ugliness of time's waste by soaring into memory and grasping the significance of the stones of architecture and of art and their possessiveness and love-embrace upon the human spirit.

And so I half closed my eyes to the terrible, the utter destruction but I knew it was there all the time. I knew, for example, that it lurked like an ominous invisible translucent shadow against the shimmering minaret-like spires of *La Sainte Chapelle* in Paris housed in the grey eminence of the Law Courts, even though it weathered the ravages with every millionth stained glass removed and returned intact, a marvel, a miracle of preservation.

Yes that was culture. Every particle of flesh and brain and heart and soul of my being immolated itself and received and drank like a sponge and sopped in the wine of ages and millenia and centuries of European darkness and light. And though I could not *be* everywhere I *was* everywhere. Like a modern Caesar: "I came, I saw, I conquered." And there came a time after I had possessed it all, that there was nothing more to possess. My hunger had at last been satiated.

I gathered together the leaves, the scraps and shreds of anger and fear and passion and defiance accumulated over the years and they were published by a small Paris printing house,

Parnasse Presse, that was then just issuing the now renowned classic series on avant-garde French film: *Cahiers du Cinema*. My book of 73 pages of 40 poems called *Thursday's Season*, I hid behind the pseudonym of "Zephyr Jans," which later I took pains to discard along with the shyness that called forth that *nom de plume*.

Shortly after publication, literary critic and long time Paris resident George Slocombe whose studio apartment atelier fronted celebrated Père Lachaise cemetery, reviewed *Thursday's Season* and excerpted "Lines on the Death of Three Jewish Youths," in the Paris edition of the *New York Herald Tribune*.

Reactions in Anglo-American and French-European circles were mixed. French playwright and friend Audiberti for whom I often served as translator at the Montparnasse Cinema's American film showings, liked it. English journalist Cecily Mackworth said it was the poems only a prose writer could write. A Spanish Count-expatriate from Franco Spain on the staff of *Cahiers d'Art* loved it, especially the format. Welsh novelist friend Richard Jones rejected it as doing violence to the English idiom. He heatedly insisted you could not cancel out the heritage of the past along with the tradition of language structure.

There were other reactions but then it was I knew I would write no more poems. Or almost no more. One or two but especially one I later wrote at Cagnes in April of the year of my return to America, "The Sweet Soft Light" was published in *Southwest Review* shortly afterwards.

Then it was I knew, with the book's publication, that Tradition and Culture had served their purpose, that what I would now engage in as a writer would be unfamiliar both to me and to the reader. Yet not entirely. The fragments of that "silver cord" of richness that was Europe that was and could be almost every American's hemisphere race-memory, would not be entirely erased in the memory of the living.

I remember how they looked with shock on the whole episode of my departure, that crowd of American English Europe-watchers, suspending themselves mournfully and haphazardly like a lost flock of homeless pigeons along the established flyways of Europe's delectable cities of delight.

They asked what it was I was going back to.

And frankly then I didn't really know. All that I did know was that I had to go back.

But what I learned soon afterwards was that I didn't go back to anything. I rejected all tradition, all death, in every form, but especially in the form and structure and sensibility and "idées reçues" (received ideas) of language, of the language of both prose and poetry.

I wanted to write in what seemed like the dimensions of the sensibilities of the poet. But for a long time this new structure as it emerged was so arcane, so hermetic, so hidden even to ourselves (author Stanley Berne and myself)—that it didn't occur to us until the publication of our first joint volume that we were groping into the creation of an entirely new genre of writing that had no precedent in any of the more or less established genres and categories of prose and poetry and that this new genre which we called *neo-narrative* was so fluid, so spontaneous, so unpredictable and so unrecognizable and yet so inevitable—as utterly demanding in its new structure as any and all previous established genres. Moreover, what was at once delightful and yet painful in our neo-narrative was that it allowed for every kind of structuring of sensibility and idea, that it was or could be *all inclusive* as the other traditional genres were each of them *exclusive*, that it could and did include: epic, poem, novel, essay, short story, play. That its subject matter roamed everywhere and was more often not of a literary nature: geology, myth, science, physiology, architecture, art, music, philosophy, history, religion, anthropology, archeology, etc., were all structured in our neo-narrative. But what became most important to both of us, each in our own separate ways and distinct styles, was our disgust over the stranglehold of grammar on the multiple literary structures of all the possible and potential multiple literary languages and idioms that were waiting to be explored.

After all, the *convention* of language was just another horrid example of the stranglehold of the past, of the death throes that all forms of culture and tradition carry like a plague, a succession of diseases within their embalming preserving riches of infection.

What does any infection do? It spreads. It takes hold like a virus upon the race. And like a virus the pattern of grammar acts like an iron vise upon the literature. So that we have reached in the last decades of the 20th century the second stage and age of Byzantium and we await the 2nd "Turkish" invasion to flush out the language embalmers of the culture and tradition of the past, as they came and did in the 14th.

The Portales Notebooks

Anaïs Nin

Wednesday, September 27, 1967

Reading Anaïs Nin's *Diary* (Vol. II, p. 172), one finds a passage which explains a great deal about her rather strange attitude to the work of art. She finds fiction to be an "alchemy," a transmutation of reality which smacks of artifice in the denigrative sense, and extends this attitude to all works of art which she feels comes "out of the factory." Painting, rugs, sculpture, poetry, architecture, the creations of art in all forms she finds artificial.

This attitude towards creativity is indeed a curious one, for as she admits, it is intermingled with fear. Is it because of this fear that she rewrites her books: *Winter of Artifice* 1939 and *Winter of Artifice* revised 1945, etc., etc.—the same action of revision which sets up a confusion in the reader's mind as to how many books she's written and which version to accept?

Her concept then of the art work is that it is artificial, that it is contrived, and by her implication (in view of her fear of it, in view of her curious idea that it smells of the factory) that it is *false*.

In addition to this as being a curious assumption on her part, it is also a *dangerous* assumption. For by extension of this kind of attitude about the work of art, Anaïs is implying that the creative accomplishments of Western Civilization, the works of the Chaucers, the Dantes, the Blakes, the Wordsworths, the Shakespeares, the Whitmans, the Hawthornes, etc., are falsifications of reality because of the *form* in which they are written, because of that conscious-unconscious, cerebral-intuitive, intellectual-sensuous, rude and polished, symbolic-direct, literal, figurative, polarities, idiosyncrasies, contradictions, monotonies and varieties one finds in much of what we appreciate in belles-lettres.

Great art after all is like the systole and diastole of our very breathing, and contains within it both the vulgar and the sublime, the ordinary and the extraordinary of what it is to be human. Wordsworth reminds us that the poet, after all, is a man like other men, just more greatly *human*.

I think Nin is afraid of fallibility in her books of making the wrong stroke.

Her attitude might be compared to a piano or violin virtuoso who must not make a mistake, who craves acclaim, applause, who is never a person, but *always* the performer, the actor and sometimes the ham! The desire for approbation (which after all is human in us all) is dangerous if it interferes with the truths, the authenticities which the work of art must convey to a greater or lesser degree and which stamp its originality.

That is why I cannot agree that it smacks of the factory. Things of the factory partake of the assembly line. The work of art is an *original* of which all the imitations are *copies*.

It is perhaps for this reason, this difference of attitude on the part of Anaïs, that I find she has put her art, her vision of life, not in her books, her creations, but rather in this amazing and frank *Diary* which contains the rough surfaces, the crudities, the breathtaking insights sparkling like a many-faceted diamond, the fresh air of life itself that her books do not have.

When I read her books I admire the performance without lingering over the meaning. I also feel closed-in, in a kind of hothouse atmosphere whereas I feel the clear light of day shining on these *Diary* pages, and the truths, the insights into human beings are here in the *Diary*. Her frankness constitutes its art.

It is also a limited view to suspect art or creation as a *male* activity and the kind of flow she achieves in the *Diary* with the breath and sinews bone marrow and blood of life itself as particularly *female*.

An artist, whether male or female, is defined through the authenticity of the work itself, not in categorizing whether this or that is male or female but whether it partakes of the human in all of us. Likewise when she concludes men are abstract and women concrete, is no conclusion but a prejudice and a distortion of the truth. Abstraction and concretion partake of the thinking processes of all human beings. Such sweeping generalizations are distortions of the truth no less than of logic itself. If one pampers ones prejudices too much, the organic totality of one's perspective results in myopia.

Thursday, October 5, 1967

When Joyce and George Wittenborn presented us with Volume Two of the Nin *Diary*, Joyce remarked how irritable Anaïs made her feel, that in fact she was on the verge of penning an angry note to Anaïs Nin vis-à-vis the whole affair.

Now that we have become reoriented to our own dearly beloved Southwestern milieu, I've had an opportunity to surmise what Joyce meant. At least I think I know now the source of irritation that does overwhelm one, sometimes to a greater, sometimes to a lesser degree.

In the *Diary* Anaïs leaves out the yin-yang relationships, the usual, biologic casual relationships and insights we expect of a woman writing about the world of men and women.

Stanley is struck by her almost Victorian reticence. In commenting upon Henry Miller's relationship with women, Anaïs comments on the fact that Miller sees women only and exclusively as beings "with a biological aperture." There is a certain precocity an over-nicety in this and other remarks through the *Diary* which creates an artifice, a pose, in the dimension or portrait or persona of herself Nin is deliberately trying to create. The point is when the artist is dealing with observations of life which reveal certain hidden truths, those truths cannot be distorted into niceties or manipulated (as one feels Nin is doing) so that one (the artist) is all things to all human beings. The artist can never be a diplomat in his creations, only in his person as another human being. In his uniqueness he must not falsify or create the impression that he is doing so, as Anaïs does. I believe part of the root of her problem is not distinguishing between Anaïs the writer and Anaïs the person amongst other human beings. She is constantly projecting illusions in life, about life, about art.

For example, in commenting, towards the end of the volume, (Vol. II) about the effect of the reality of World War II, she presents a false ego as if she were trying to convince herself that what she was saying was true. She comments over the difference between herself and all her acquaintances, their poignant realization about the transitory quality of life, their suddenly living and loving desperately (pp. 341 bottom and 342 top), their regrets. For any writer to state by way of contrast: "I was never careless, inattentive, thoughtless, indifferent, absent, or asleep," is the kind of sweeping generalization that constitutes both a falsification in logic and human psychology. Either Anaïs is trying to create the perfect and therefore false persona that she is not, or she is living a life of illusion and really believing that she is not human but superhuman.

Another disturbing aspect of the *Diaries*, one that I touched upon in an earlier paragraph to today's entry, is her unnatural preoccupation with the female. The entries on the male (Waldo Frank, Henry Miller, Durrell, etc.) are all of an intellectual nature, as if they existed only as ideas and not human beings.

In her discussion of the female, on the other hand, there seems to be a latent or secretive lesbianism which furtively, and rather awkwardly rises to the surface.

Her jaunts into Harlem with Rank, describe her attraction to the beauty of Negro women. Are not Negro males handsome? I have always found them so. What could be a handsomer sight than the Negro male on Saturday nights, decked out in all his peacock colors?

Her trip to Morocco is another instance of the same character. Where did Anaïs spend most of her time? Peculiarly, visiting harems, talking girl talk about how to paint eyelids, overcoming her revulsion over the dirtiness and squalor of the Arabic women's public baths, describing instead her fascination with the bodies of Arabic women in all their nakedness. Nowhere does she record an encounter with the male of Arabia and yet it was he who surrounded and protected her in her visitation to Morocco.

There are countless other instances over this sexual imbalance of interest in the Nin diaries. She teases the reader into the belief that she is a full-blown woman, enjoying fully the ecstasies of sexual orgasm and gives no proof of substantiation.

She appears or presents herself to be some immaculate medieval idealized Virgin of mercy and misericord in male-female encounters. While there is a strange excitement she cannot sublimate or suppress vis-à-vis her female friends and acquaintances.

Is Anaïs Nin a reformed lesbian? She doesn't say nor would she want to reveal this to the reader. That is why, despite some scattered and worthwhile insights, I find the *Diary* not a true diary, not a human document revealing an integrated personality. It is too much of a caprice, a divertissement, a work of artifice to be taken whole. One reads it with both amused and bemused reservations.

October 6, 1967

I am still smarting over Anaïs Nin's uneducated generalizations about men and women. There is a certain segment of the previous generation of writers Faulkner, Miller, Hemingway, Anaïs Nin that maintain a romantic overly neurotic attitude and one that is completely false, that the intellect, or intellectual activity is antipathetic, in fact harmful to a writer's organic and psychic development. Valery intimated as such, or at least underlined this half-latent fear in comment on the fact that he dare not read too much for fear of endangering his creative powers. Balzac did not feel this way, in fact claimed that the writer, the important writer, must know everything.

Between Balzac's deliberate exaggeration and the previous generation's anti-intellectual pose, the truth lies somewhere in between.

One cannot prescribe rules, regulations for everybody. A writer is a human animal with all the idiosyncrasies that make human beings the individuals that some of them are. But to subscribe to Anaïs Nin's view that men are intellectual and lovers of art, that women are not is carrying a particular writer's idiosyncrasies too far!

I perceive myself as I am, not as Nin perceives herself and all women to be. I speak for myself as a writer and as a woman, but not as a woman writer. A writer belongs to a genus not a gender, the genus being the human race in all of its yin and yang manifestations. You cannot exclude one sex from another, neither in nature nor in human life.

These attitudes which Nin nourishes and cultivates like a mother hen over her brood may be all right for Nin. But her doubts and rationalizations of them come forth in her insistence that she speaks for all women. Isn't it enough for a writer to speak for himself or herself? I think it would be.

I first became acquainted with the name, personality and "legend" of Anaïs Nin in Henry Miller's essay-portrait: "Une Etoile Etoilique," or was it "Un Etre Etoilique," from his volume: *Max and the White Phagocytes*, which I read in Paris. Upon my return to New York in 1951 and marriage a year later to author Stanley Berne, we both met Anaïs Nin for the first time, on two occasions, first in Greenwich Village when she did a radio interview at "Circle in the Square," followed by her invitation to us to come along with her to Luis and Bebe Barron's place afterwards. Correspondence and exchange of books[1] (an autographed copy of *Cities of the Interior*), then some years later, her invitation to visit her and Ian Hugo in their Washington Square apartment.

Note

[1] George Wittenborn, the New York art and literary publisher, who published *Concretions*, with illustrations by artist Milton Avery (1962); *Abraxas* (1964) with Preface by Sir Herbert Read; *Seasons of the Mind*, with essays on the new (neo-narrative) novel, interviews, plus Read correspondence (1969) by Arlene Zekowski, . . . *The Dialogues*, with illustrations by Matta (1962), *The Multiple Modern Gods* (Read Preface) (1964,) *The Unconscious Victorious* (1969) with essays on the New Story, author interviews, and Sir Herbert Read correspondence, by Stanley Berne. George Wittenborn committed suicide in late 1969.

The Portales Notebooks

Paris to New York, New Jersey, Brooklyn,
South to Southwest,
to New Mexico

Thursday, September 28, 1967

Richard's comment about Americans being inhuman to Americans is an interesting observation, based upon his experiences in visiting the Eastern coast and the Virginia tidewater land of our fathers.[1] He chose the cradle of the past to visit rather than the heartland of this country and its future—the West.

The East is finished for the present. It literally drove us out almost 20 years ago. Struggling in our poverty, the poverty which I was familiar with from my three years in Europe, living mostly in Paris in first the Rue Monsieur le Prince in the very hotel where Gertrude Stein's brother had resided (so I was subsequently told by the son of the manager) then later moving to the Hotel du Panthéon, finally being driven out by the rats of Paris, denizens of its old sewers who would work their way up through ancient patched-together scaffoldings of buildings that aged and decayed and were used over and over again with a cover-up of paint now and then. I loved the view from the French windows of my room which abutted onto a balcony onto the Square where the great expanse took in the old law buildings of the Sorbonne with the pigeons and their excrement of centuries mottling their façades to dull greys. Below me was the Bibliothèque Communale - Ste Geneviève where I poured over books and took out cartloads every week, and the Commissariat du Police where every night the police smuggled in those poor Algerian "vagrants" who were the city's fruit and rug vendors (I never passed one without buying fruit), on the pretext that they either had no license or were violating some secret regulation of the city. Paris's second-class citizens were its Algerians. This act was emphasized in a daily and nightly round of arrests right under my window. Then finally the rats drove me out because at 3 AM like clockwork they invaded the paper basket and rustled, scratched, scraped, for hours, here, there, everywhere, so I sacrificed the view of the vast square with Rue Ste. Catherine in the distance and the Pantheon itself and the wild orgiastic celebrations of the Beaux Arts students below in the square once a year and moved to the student tenement in the Rue des Fossés St. Jacques which I understand has since been condemned and razed. My rent there was $10 a month without heat. It was an egalitarian decision. No heat since most of the students couldn't afford it. And much of the time neither could I if the classes I taught at Berlitz were few in a slow season. Some nights I slept with every sweater I owned over my pajamas and some days I sat in bed when I did my writing, to keep warm. But much of the time after a breakfast of coffee and chicory (the coffee was still rationed and so they sent me coffee from home from time to time) made on the alcohol lamp, and half a baguette with demi-sel cheese, off I headed for a warm café and did my writing there.

Stanley Berne and I met, about the 16th of May, just a few days after my return from Europe in 1951. It was my cousin, the artist Charles Seliger, who introduced us. Charles had the quaint idea that since I was a writer and Stanley was a writer and both of us smoked "Between the Acts" cigars, and since Stanley was his best friend, we might be attracted to each other. The rendezvous was arranged in the Empire State Building a way up somewhere in the office of Charles' friend, an English painter working on some industrial projects.

This was how Stanley and I met. In about a week all my worldly belongings were moved into his dingy flat of three rooms in Union City, New Jersey. My parents were chagrined and embarrassed because of their Victorian views but did not interfere. I was determined.

Miracles can not be talked about. They just happen. It was this way with both of us. We never questioned. We never wondered. We were often awed and afraid over how such an accident happened. It was deliberate on the part of Charles, my cousin. But Charles was only the means, not the why. Stanley's divorce came through a year later and we were married at City Hall, Brooklyn. The clerk who officiated wore dirty underwear. But this memory was effaced in the splendid seafood lunch we all had (my mother hosting) at Gage and Tollner's afterwards, with Charles and his wife Ruth, who was also an artist, Herman Zaage, artist-engraver, later, Fellow at the New School, illustrator of 5 of our books, and his wife Sylvia, German refugee, Phi Beta Kappa Hunter College graduate and laboratory chemist. Then the "bourgeois" party followed the Sunday following with friends and family.

In the East everything happened with the speed and animal energy of a country on the move, a country which swallowed technology whole, exported it to the world, and now is regurgitating from the mistakes, the human mistakes it made because it buried the human in the world of profits and machines. And the symbols of these mistakes are the slums, the race riots, the urbanization, the smog from the traffic.

So Stanley and I, struggling on odd jobs, preparing for teaching licenses, writing our books feverishly in the moments snatched from the world's work, storing our manuscripts in cartons, in the oven of the apartment kitchen, then taking them out when we had to roast a meat loaf, cook a lamb chop, moved slowly Westward, first to Connecticut, then to Texas, back to upstate New York (Highland Falls, Croton-on-Hudson), then to Louisiana and finally out West here to New Mexico.

It was while we were in Louisiana at L.S.U. studying for the doctorate, that we took off one summer in the old cadillac, hoping to make California. We broke down in New Mexico (the car was always getting vapor-lock from the changes in altitude which we repaired by placing a grapefruit-half over the fuel pump), fell in love with the mountains, the history, the traditions, and its idiosyncratic people—Anglo, Spanish, Indian. We dreamed of returning. And our dream materialized.

Note

[1] Richard Jones, Welsh writer and friend from the London and Paris days, lives in London and works for the BBC.

The Portales Notebook

Underground Cinema

Thursday, October 19, 1967

On Saturday night last, we went again to the Underground Cinema at Don Pancho's in Albuquerque. The "George Dumpston's Place" by Ed Emshwiller was a visual poem in color, tracing found objects, discards of metal, wood, papier-mâché, old dolls, photographs, broken statues, rubber tires, machinery parts, crockery, garden pieces, hardware, all massed in a leafy shadowy forest retreat reminding one of a modern Walden surrounding and invading the ramshackle one room discard hovel of its owner, an elderly negro looking like some wizened Oriental Buddha, quietly, calmly, placidly smoking his pipe in this nondescript wilderness he chose to live in and by. Good, really excellent photography with only one shortcoming: Emshwiller did not know where to end the repeats. His camera lingered too long and too frequently over his bizarre still lifes. But aside from this factor, the technique was excellent, almost painterly.

In "Allen for Allen: London 1965," by Barbara Rubin, the attempt was to *create* a collage in black and white with the hand-held camera. It seems the hand-held camera has in itself an obvious drawback and this is its relationship to the onlooker's eye. If a technique such as this, is meant to introduce new directions in cinéma nouveau, it is not contending with its obvious limitations which are physiological. The onlooker becomes or feels dizzy and struggles to maintain his interest, his objectivity if you will, against the more fundamental physiological impulse to withdraw his view from what disturbs the eye itself. As Ginsberg read his poem "Kaddish" (very well articulated), the viewer was exposed to various scenes superimposed one upon the other which were meant to symbolize the feelings, the ideas, the experiences conveyed in the words and images of the poem. The idea was excellent but the execution was deplorable (actually one of the worst expressions in experimental film). First of all, the images were accidentally and carelessly contrived so that their deliberate impact was lost. The photography was poor or shall we say "dirty" (in the sense that a painter cannot handle his colors) as against the "clean" perfection of the Dumpson piece. I had the feeling that the photographer was attempting to palm off her photographic "errors" as unusual inventions. An improvement or a correction might have been realized in fixing the images, deaccelerating them so that the onlooker would not have found them so blurringly dizzifying. In sum, though the concept of collage in moving picture was excellent, the execution was disastrous.

The other films dealing with the life of a prostitute (J-24), a study in paranoia (Shoot the Actor) were uninteresting because they were telling conventional stories in a conventional way. They lacked inventive subject matter.

"Report" by Bruce Conner was a tasteless collage of news events and advertisements treating just about the most dreadful, painful event of our times—the assassination of John F. Kennedy—as burlesque. The idea was to render incongruity as it exists so often in life itself. But the treatment of it in this film was a tasteless vile disaster, violating every sincere human fabric of emotion.

Stan Brakhage's "Wedlock House: An Intercourse," was dishonest. Every attempt was made at conveying an authentic adult biologic and physiologic experience as a coy unnatural titillating self-conscious embarrassment. The picture was shot with a flashlight and the scenes were repeated over and over again monotonously—a long corridor, a kitchen, a bedroom, all of which you couldn't see because the filmmaker was shying away from his subject matter rather than confronting it head on. Why select a subject if you're afraid to treat it. How Victorian Mr. Brakhage!

What Underground Cinema needs in sum are new gods, new subjects, new dimensions. It is bored with visual literature and it says so. It is, however, unacquainted with the literature of the unconscious, of the contemporary psyche. And that is what it needs to use its camera techniques upon. When I say this I am thinking in terms of the magnificent possibilities, among several other contemporary examples, as well as in our own work in the neo-narrative, which combines images of the poetic and fictive imagination where image and narrative are treated in non-linear space-time simultaneities of multitudinous human perceptions and sensibilities.

The Portales Notebook

Paris Reminiscences—Picasso, Mme. Lipchitz

Monday, November 6, 1967

The recent reports in the *N. Y. Times* involving critics Kramer and Canaday in a re-evaluation of Picasso's work based on the present exhibition at the Museum of Modern Art, reveal just how far Picasso's exhibitionism masks him, his real nature, even from the critical public.

The underlying confusion or mystification about Picasso in both articles was expressed in defensive attitudes on the part of each critic.

Both are clearly overwhelmed by the "quantity" of the Picasso sculptures (almost 300 pieces in all) and the reputation of Picasso. Clearly, Picasso must be "great"!

Picasso's many modes, poses, improvisations, his various "periods," so to speak, create the dramatic effect of the sensational persona Picasso constantly affects in all of his moods and attitudes and stances. Picasso has striven hard to be the artist engaged, not with his art, but with himself as artist-personality, and with the public, aiding and abetting and whetting his appetite for public acclaim.

What makes Picasso suspect is that one cannot detect any organic spiral or direction of search leading to further investigation, development, amplification, etc. In other words, you cannot read his pieces into the book of an oeuvre such as you can with a Cézanne, a Léger, a Tobey, a Pollock, a Kandinsky, a Klee, etc. His pieces stand as pieces, like the improvisations of any virtuoso, without leading the spectator or art lover into a series of experiences or revelations about the artist and his attitude towards life. Important art—if it is to influence the culture of its time in a profound and not a superficial way—must stem from a direct confrontation with life, and not be, as Picasso's art is, of the museum, or produced from other art or other art influences exclusively and inclusively. Not that artists are not influenced by other art. Cézanne studied classicism by copying from museums. But the study, the skill, is only a point of departure for the artist, only provides the means for an organic statement about life. If the skill, the prestidigitation, the emphasis upon improvisation and academic form constitute the end-product as is true in Picasso's work, then we are not dealing with a first-rate creative intelligence.

Thus, in Picasso, as in all other academicians, you have inbreeding, which is, of course, unhealthy, producing seeds from other art instead of seeds of its own from a life of its own based upon organic living, breathing, vital life experience. Consequently, Picasso is all pastiche, all virtuosity, to convince or try to, in order to satisfy his Ego—his vulgar, if dazzling witty often mischievous but all-consuming ego—even at 85, which cheapens whatever Art there is in his consummate virtuosity and flair, which exercises the hubris and destroys whatever necessary humility he ever had as an artist.

When I was 13 or 14 or 15, I saw Picaasso's "Guernica" at the Museum of Modern Art, and though I found it unlovely and on the level of superb caricature, but nevertheless caricature, I defended it as a prognostication of things to come, which, unfortunately, later never came. Picasso, I feel, was a disappointment to our generation, whereas his one-time best friend Lipchitz, the sculptor, was not.

Mme. Lipchitz (who in early years had entertained Gertrude Stein, Picasso, Hemingway and others at the magnificent town house-residence, reminiscent of the multiple decks of an ocean-going luxury-liner, built in the then revolutionary poured concrete by their friend, architect Le Corbusier) often revealed to me, and alluded again and again, to the rift between Picasso and Lipchitz that later developed, following Picasso's sudden and heady rise to fame. His friends apparently sensed the difference, the change in his personality, and did not enjoy being in the company of Picasso the celebrity, rather than Picasso their former friend. It was while I was in Paris in the late '40s, early '50s, that these and other revelations by Mme. Lipchitz were confided to me.

I recall meeting her quite by accident at the restaurant Orestias in the Rue du Bac off the Blvd. St.-Germain (owned and operated by a three generation family of Greek émigrés) which I invariably frequented for dinner, and which she usually frequented for lunch. One day I came for lunch (usually I could not afford lunch, being perennially low on funds until the monthly check from Berlitz arrived), so I usually skipped lunch, except for a quarter of a kilo of lentils or other cooked vegetables (*haricots verts, choux-fleurs*, etc.) or fresh herring from a neighborhood delicatessen-kitchen (*characuterie-chaud*).

Mme. Lipchitz, if she did possess a head of hair, never revealed it, for she was always coifed with a black and white chapeau-like band which emphasized her Slavic, eastern, almost oriental appearance and predilections. She was born in Russia and spoke both English and French with a Russian accent.

A lover of literature, she always insisted on my reciting parts or selections from the book of 40 poems just recently published in Paris. Although she possessed a complimentary copy she preferred hearing me stumble over my own words (I have always experienced difficulty trying to remember anything I've written) from *Thursday's Season* (Parnasse Press, 1949). Often she would have me translate particular lines or phrases back into French.

She was quite argumentative and picturesquely emotional, a kind of Slavic *grande dame*, always striking in appearance, large and bulky in size but impressively so, her appearance dramatically accentuated by her proverbial black dress and coat, or cloak.

We must have met in winter time and I believe we were introduced to one another by Minna Harkovy, an American sculptor whom I met aboard the Marine Marlin tanker that took us both to Europe in the summer of '48. We both occupied the same stateroom, sharing it with four very frightened Scotch-Irish ladies who prayed each morning at 5 am chapel, that the old unsteady merchant ship now on her final voyage to a Frankfurt, Germany dry-dock, would make it safely to Cobh, Ireland. The ship was crowded with innocents abroad, like myself, and those not so innocent, but all of us happy in our pilgrimage to an old but now ravaged Europe clinging to the last and final shreds of a romantic past of culture and civilization that would endure by the force of the momentum of its past. We lived on excitement, celebrations, romance, intoxicated, or sleepless with intoxication and hemisphere change, napping on deck under the stars, using the stateroom only to shower and change clothes for

another round of the day or night fantasy of it all.   The Scotch-
Irish ladies were silent in their rather grim vigil of fright, but
direly critical of our frivolity, paying for a stateroom that was
barely used for sleeping.

* * * * *

Mme. Lipchitz was constantly complaining of the cold
museum piece that passed for a home.   The plumbing or the
heating or sometimes both, that Le Corbusier permitted to be in-
stalled, was not sufficient for the damp, dank, foggy Paris win-
ters. So Mme. was always walking or running from one café to
another to keep warm, or to telephone Le Corbusier frantically
about her unending complaints over his budding architectural
creation-feat in modernity.   His rejoinder to her criticism was
always a proud: "Madame, I'm an architect, not a plumber or
heating expert."

At any rate, towards a less cold spring, I finally acquiesced,
accepting her frequent requests to spend a weekend at her Le
Corbusier house on the edges of the Bois de Boulogne. I remarked on the lonely isolation of her bosky locale. And she
agreed she was always a bit fearful when alone, since she was located at least half a mile from the nearest bus or metro stop.

The weekend I spent there was idyllic, with the moon
playing fantastic effects between the leafy shadows of the woods
outside, silhouetting the vast window-paned volumes of the ascetic ship-like hallway-corridor—rooms and passageways dis-
playing excellent museum-piece, authentic originals of African
sculpture. (The late '40s was a period when African sculpture in
Paris, was collected by the true afficionados before Africa was
"discovered" and corrupted into producing the ersatz mass
products it perpetuates today.)

Mme. was somewhat impatient of my desire to always
linger in the garden filled with massive Lipchitz sculptures left
behind to her care when Lipchitz emigrated to the United States
(I believe today she is divorced or separated from her sculptor-
husband.) She would allow me only a quick look at the pieces,
as if looks could steal. At any rate I never knew why she did not
let me linger. But then, she was quixotic, unpredictable, but always interesting if sometimes exasperating in her willful deter-
mination to do thus and so and force another, regardless of the
other's feelings or inclinations, into doing likewise.

In describing the old Bohemian days of Picasso, Lipchitz, Gertrude Stein, Kandinsky, Hemingway, etc., she said that they had wonderful parties, wonderful feasts, because artists made the best cooks. In this I *would* concur.

I shared her tremendous energetic enthusiasm for exploring many haunts of old Paris, including the Levantine quarter with its casbah-like atmosphere in the Rue des Rosiers, which Balzac, in his time, frequented in his avid gourmet search for those blends of coffee that finally contributed to his early death.

Mme. Lipchitz and I searched out cheap but unknown excellent restaurants, in addition to visiting the environs of Paris (walks in the grand royal forest of Saint-Cloud, eating mussels with beer), and the haunts of the demi-monde. Always deluged with complimentary theatre tickets, I would occasionally accompany her to the opening of an existential play (Anouilh, "Antigone") or to a private opening at some art gallery and usually at the Musée de l'Art Moderne where she was invariably treated as an honored and distinguished guest. Always her conversation was sparkling with intellect and emotion. She was earthy and inquisitive, sensitive like the poet she thought she was. At least she was a great *amateur*. And at that time, for the yet partially inchoate, searching, creative explorer that I was, her great sympathy for the intellectual and the artist, her fundamental humanity and the generosity of this humanity, sufficed in considerable measure, my communicative needs for, and towards others.

The Managerial Technological Ritual
Shakers and Makers of the World

—The tabula rasa is the clue to each and every one of us.

—How so?

—Americans are carpet sweepers. Not carpet makers. Except the Navajos. Whose weave is just as tight and strong and beautiful as the Persian.

—But not baroque.

—No. Abstract. The lines. All mostly angular. As sharp sure to their mark and accent as the purpose of the arrowhead to sever life from game. As the metate to grind out grain from bean of corn. The angles and the waves of airy space. The rods and thunderbolts. And 4 winds. Prayers of season into harvest. Into rain and wind. The water of the dry and arid plains. The dry steppe waving bayonets of green grass rush. The purple smoke of tamarisk. In puffs of mist and cluster. The purple sage. A million and a million more of tufts of tumbled heads of hair upon the prairie. In the rock as shoulder to the wind. In arroyos brushing on the mesquite. And the palo verde. And the seeds as snow of cottonwood in spring. But mostly boulders. And the layers of the purpled clay and red adobe dust and silver into white as quartz. And fine as talcum. All striated in the gash of hillside slashed on each side for the roadbed of the highway. That will link the lonely fright of space across the blue horizon. Never-ending to the sight it makes with seas of grass. As high as flood tide breakers of ocean crashing down upon the nothing behind the engine of the car that's you. A dot of slanted shadow cast by sun. That rages and that paints the dust in day. The sunset that is heartbreak for its colors dazzling. No way that is contained by word or picture. Impossible to photograph or paint. To say that it is arrogant of all the color casts and shades and hues of every spectrum of the rainbow. After rain. And then again in actual shower. To say that it is blood red. Not like blood. But azure turquoise. Speckled like stone malachite. Pomegranate in a stunning way. Too bright to look upon. Or blinding like some bronzing into gold. Would be a way to say the way the sun dives under. And leaves its wound of color glowing. Refusing to give way to purple darkness. Which blinds bewildered eyes in night. As sun glow does in day. In every way the human creature. On horizons of the West. Feels helpless if not hopeless and alone. The magnitude of space and thorns of cactus. Of goatheads scarifying tissue. Of briar thorns of Russian olive trees. The dry metallic wind. A hot mistral of spring. That corrugates and wrinkles up the skin. The tumbleweed of skeletal balls of briars. That cousin up to their sister-brother barbs of wire fence. And hold their own as ballast on the wind. That scrape against you as the interfering figure. The bastard stranger. Complaining in his wail of things that be. That oh the West would be so beautiful. If only no more wind. If only all arroyos weren't dry. The sound of water trickling like a waterfall. Instead of rustling paper shuffling sounds of leaves of aspen. Or the sough of branches of the mesquite. Or the cloud of cotton tufts of balls of seed and flower and fruit of cottonwood trees. If only all of this and more were not so harsh in grandeur and in size. And beauty that surpasses every human challenge to touch embrace describe.

—I did not know you felt so strongly of the beauty. Of the land so often you complain of.

—It wants taming. And never will be tamed. It fights back where it hurts. The wind the dust that flays the skin. And leatherizes every bark of tree and human flesh.

—What did you mean before a moment ago when you said Americans were carpet sweepers? Except the Navajo.

—Oh yes. We are not fatalists you know. We don't accept things as they are. And yet. And yet. We are medieval in other ways without the fatalism.

—How?

—Well we are rude and crude and hierarchical. From the corporate structure pyramidal. We are the new Pharaohs. The new Egyptians. Tending towards the stasis. The solidity of monopoly. The oneness undivided. Of power absolute. The managerial technological ritual shakers and makers of the world. Multi-kinged. And multi-nationed. Babylons of conglomerates. Industrializing sky water earth. Worshippers of death and putrefaction. Which we convert to fossil fuels. And nylon stockings. And plastic ladies corsets and brassieres. And rubberless garden hoses. And childrens toys. And artificial additives to foods that are mass-produced no differently than cars. Or sewing or washing machines. Or lawn mowers. We are medieval. But instead of heaven as our afterlife. Our world of future adoration is in the here and now. And no it is not of universal man. But of universal machine. Of overcoming flesh and blood and heart and soul and spirit. With machines and networks of wires of command and artificial body parts and laser beams that kill and heal according to command. And computerized pleasures of canned emotion and sound and image and huckstering hard and soft sells tuned in to supermarket and drugstore and auto factory sales. Mesmerized to purchase and consumption. And we go to the boob tube for satisfaction. As man medieval. Went to mass. And we pray for our securities and stocks and bonds. The way medieval man prayed. Against the scourges of the devil and the plague. At least he could recognize a spirit—saint or devil. But all we see is the machine. And we know that every labor-saving device. In the end. Is what we serve.

—Worshippers of the machines we serve.

—Exactly. The ultimate carpet sweepers. Hiding the dust. Sweeping everything under the rug. A conscience sloth-like. And upside down. But our closets are full of discarded machines. Not family skeletons. We take the land. An acre of trees a scape of forest of rock a cowpath a route of the Western cattle drive a valley between mountains. A swamp. An island bought with a bauble of beads from the aborigines we found squatting. Worshipping the bison. And bartering shell beads. And contemplating nature. Through the smoke rings of clay pipes. We seize the island. The valley. The cabbage patch. The ditch. The meadow. The dust bowl. And buy and sell. And plunder. And skin it dry. The earth the land of blue mountains. And copper red sky. Becomes our land of smoke. Of factories of fire. Better than the ones aboriginal. Of Vulcan of Pluto the father. The smoke the haze the noise the macadam blasted and refilled the whirring machines that bury our own invisible whine. Smothered by the whine of the machines. We are the remakers of nature. The engineers of death. We thought first to out-perfect Nature. When we found we could not. We thought we could outrun the wily Goddess. And we are succeeding. Nature is al-

most nowhere to be seen where She was once pliable and yield-
ing. But where She is harsh. In the wind and the dust and the
dryness. And the vast emptiness that frightens. She refuses the
tabula rasa. The plundering. The bushwhacker. She is her own
engineer in the West. Her own tabula rasa.

Patterns. Or. The Gap.
(The Great American Package)

—Exits and entrances. As the ways for sure. Of nothing overlooked. In crowds. Assemblies. And the like.

—You speak in riddles. Riddles of words.

—I always almost always speak in riddles. As the words. The words are new. That is the patterns are. And words are nothing but the patterns they assume.

—Than words themselves are not irrevocable?

—Nothing is. Not even patterns. All dissolves. Sooner or later like ourselves.

—Then where's the fun in flux?

—Exactly where it's at. In flux.

—Why then be earnest?

—Why then indeed!

—I'm asking.

—And I'm telling. It's all in the gesture. Don't you see. The pattern and the wave. The star. The sunset. And the cloud. The whispering branches in a breeze. The desert plains. In choke and muzzle swallow. Of the wind and water cells at 50,000 feet. Hovering to smother. In glacial hail balls. As the break of itself. In the soughing and the clap of thunder. Predetermines what will muster after. In the retrospect. When damages pay homage to its passing. A broken barn. A mud slough of a road. The axles and the wheels of tractors spinning. And overturned. The shattered window glass strewn on broken wires. Naked and bleeding and alive-live. To electrocute whoever and what-ever is unwary. The tensions of the wires in the city. Shorted. Like the wires in the body of your nerves. All blown. And bursting from the pressures. Airless. To the brain and atmo-sphere of life and death around us. Haunting. And on the brink

of the threat that didn't come. The tornado passed above us.
And beyond. And lost its anger. In the wind and rain.

—These then are patterns? Patterns of what?

—Of what didn't happen. The threat of what might be.
That never was. It's all a joke. A jest of all that's visible. Invisible.

—Such miracles I could do without.

—It's better not to think. Or even plan. Just go along
with it as I am.

—Your rhyme is full of no sense.

—Nonsense. The human in us all. Is all our weakness.
Of the male and female. Of our own bêtes noirs.

—And what are these?

—Surely you must know. Their power is in never giving
up. So long as we give up in fighting them. Or vomiting or
voiding them as best we can.

—Do we always have to face our fears?

—Sooner or later. They will drown us otherwise. We
shall overcome.

—I grow weary in the groove of what it is to be American.

—I know what you mean. It is the struggle of facing what
you are to yourself. And what they (all others as Americans) are
to you. And what you are to them. I know what you mean. Indeed in deed.

—To trace the pattern from where it is. To its beginnings. . . .

—Exactly. There you see. It always comes back to patterns.
What are patterns you say to others and to yourself.

—Indeed. What are they?

—I know the patterns of club fungi (basidiomycetes).
Mushrooms, toadstools, puffballs, smuts and rusts. Club shape
structures (basidia). Twenty-five thousand species of them. The
most advanced of the fungi. Or sac fungi (Ascomycetes) about
30,000 species. Or the saprophytics. Penicillin, yeasts cup fungi,
truffles and morels. Or the blue mold ripener of Roquefort or
Camembert or the yeasts of baking and brewing. The carbon
dioxide rise of baked goodies. The alcohol of beer and other fer-
mentors. The antibiotics of medicine. The *Aspergillus* of citric
acid. The *grisiofulvin* that cures fungal skins. Single or many
celled. The patterns are multiform and faceted. Of endless use
and destruction. I could go on.

—Stop with your tangents. I am no student of botany nor care.

—You should care. You should watch and wait on the passion of the rude green olive tree. That pares its barbs to attack the unwary. Nothing can stop its beauty or its strength. Not wind or rain or sand or caleche or aridity or vetch weed or tumbleweed barbs in the spring winds or caterpillars invading in July. Its yellow flowers of violet size perfume like body talc or baby's breath. Its olives feed the birds. Its branches hide and house them from the cats. In every rude ditch or line of property. They outline ageless peace and color. Their blue green quicksilver paper leaves. Confetiing the air and line of sight. On highways ditches gardens and windbreaks. Green and silver and blue. In 3 seasons out of 4. In spring. In summer. And in fall. They will and do prevail. They are there. And here. Because they last. They insist that suffering will not overcome them.

—Do we suffer too? Of course we do.

—Yes we suffer. But do we overcome our pain? Or do we carry it like a cancer which will target to its mark.

—You sound ominous. You don't think Americans as people. As persons. Have guts?

—Well we are gutsy. We have *hutzpah* I think they call it. But our ambitions our purposes are new.

—New to whom?

—New to ourselves. To strangers. To all. We are a melting pot you know.

—And what does that cliché symbolize?

—It means that we prefer *stews* to *soups*.

—You're being silly. What's the difference?

—A stew is potluck. A soup is a dish. A creation of the pot. A potage.

—You mean we're not deliberate but accidental.

—Brilliant. Exactly. A people of hindsight. Not foresight.

—Our knowledge comes after the fact. That's pragmatic. What's wrong with that?

—Nothing. Except that our experience is based on accident or catastrophe. We're full of synapses. Short circuits. Frantic. Hectic. Abrupt. Schizoid. Hysteric. Paranoid. Impatient. With low thresholds of tolerance. We'll always be on the edge of the frontier. On the edge of racism. And gangsterism. Violence. Hatred. Frustration. We want to reason with the world.

To lead the world. When we have not learned to reason with each other. With ourselves. You can't grind everything into a package. A stew. Some things will not do. To be ground into a stew. We fear what is different in ourselves and others. Will we ever stand side by side different? Or must we always assembly-line all of us and everything into the GAP?

—What is the GAP?

—A variation of the G.N.P. The "Great American Package."

—How does it work? Like the GNP?

—Well not exactly. Though the world has embraced the principle of the GNP the pattern of the GAP is as yet invisible. It is the part that makes the whole. Once the world understands the miracle of its pattern the pattern of the GNP in the exposure of its sine qua non, the GAP, then it will be like all other idols of the crowd, an eventual disappointment. Unknown and aloof as it is now, it is exotic and exciting. But we who have lived with the GAP all our lives know it as dry stale dust in the mouth, not gold. It has substance but no spirit. And yet we go on and on. Making more and more of its kind. A world of packaging without end. We shall go down not as the modern Romans. But as the modern Egyptians.

—How so?

—We'll produce dynasty after dynasty. Of living death. A death in life without end. Not a life without end. Eternal. As the Egyptians wanted. As we the Americans. Their modern descendants want. But a death without end. In the packages that consume and surround us and smother us and embalm us. In their glitter and gadgetry and convenience. Making us all. Rich and poor. Pharaohs of all that possess us. Encaged imprisoned. Entombed in all our possessions. Our gadgetry of surrogate flesh and soul and feelings and mind and thought and affections and food and hunger and yearnings and energy and will, surrendering in a vast sleep of wake to the wake of our deaths in full and prone and mute subservience to the service of the GAP. We are ourselves the Great American Package. Just as the ancient Egyptians were themselves. In their living eons of lives and lives of eons. The very essence of death. In their pyramid upon pyramid of embalmed embodiment of the body's embrace of death without end. As the answer to the search for life and soul. In the *body*. And *not* the *soul*. And that was their mistake. As it is ours. Our pyramid is the GAP. Our body and our soul. As the pyramid was theirs.

Essay

Cultural Suicide and the
Decline of Literacy in America

Of all the constituencies that make up life in these United States, the *writer-creative artist* is the one most threatened with *cultural suicide*—and the product of his art—with *cultural extinction*.

Since the mid-twentieth century, the differentiation between the *literary* as against the *commercial* or popular writer, has become increasingly more obfuscated, as America adopted the forms, attitudes colorations of *empire*, with political economic concerns taking precedence over moral aesthetic ones.

In space science rocketry because of Sputnik, it became expedient to surge forward, not because of any intellectual commitment to knowledge for knowledge's sake. Whatever human value accrued for the benefit of humanity was merely the result of pure chance, a spin-off from more deliberate pragmatic objectives.

Likewise, in the era of Johnson's Great Society and its ensuing civil rights affirmative action policies, the objectives were more *political* than they were *humanitarian*. For if they had been *humanitarian*, we would not be today, a society with its educational system in intellectual and creative disarray.

Instead of developing a program to benefit the whole of our society, the powers that be decided that all of education would become egalitarian and populist, serving society in the mass, rather than the human beings that make up that mass.

Egalitarian thus became vulgarian, a *caste* society separating the masses from the corporate bureaucracy that manipulated government and education. Discriminatory practices against excellence and intellectual and creative goals, were suddenly introduced in the guise of discouraging individual differences and capabilities (interpreted as *elitism*) versus affirmative action procedures. The formerly racially deprived were now leading the pack and determining the standards, so that education would become the same for all, and hence, *democratic*. As a result, public education became more and more, an adjunct of government tyranny over a political democracy in a growing corporate state where populist, pragmatic attitudes captured the former free-flowing emphasis on knowledge for enlightenment and psychological enrichment.

So that from a society we could heretofore characterize as the deprived versus the advantaged, what has now emerged is *a society of the totally deprived*—eroded more and more by a government of the privileged in a corporate empery, and not a democracy at all.

As education in the United States deteriorates further and further from the Western intellectual tradition and disciplines of knowledge and enlightenment, a junk society of pop-ism street-smart subculture rock-jazz-drugs fast-foods television-exploited sports and celebrity-hollywood-oriented masses—buys, sells, proselytizes, arrogates and dictates what American life and "culture" is all about and where it's at.

It is a *passive* society sybaritic in its values, viewing its aims and purposes as a never-ending pursuit of the pot-of-gold rainbow of making it "success-syndrome," preferably without the effort of struggle or the necessity or responsibility of earning what it thinks it has a democratic right to possess, by virtue of membership in a free society.

But Education was not the only chaos that resulted from corruption into political ends.

Mega Publishing, heretofore concerned with free and open dialogue of ideas, preoccupation with the intellectual and creative responsibility in encouraging quality books and literature, became dominated exclusively by the identical empiric criteria that affected Education.

Catapulted into vulgarian egalitarian populist political bureaucratic interests, Big Publishing became shamelessly committed to the profit motive, "bottom line," without its former tempering self-regulatory checks-and-balances dedication to the publication of contemporary new ideas and forms.

So that today the large conglomerate publishers in their glut commercial pursuit of mass *bestsellerdumb* show biz bottom line schlock—promote *illiteracy* and *cultural suicide* as callously, as blatantly in their way as public education has in its way.

Where then is the literary artist-innovative writer in all this morass of junk in what appears to be a dying American literary culture?

* * * * *

The *literary artist* is alive, struggling to perpetuate the *tradition* of literature from being garbaged into the sewer of trash, Conglomerate Publishing has brought about in the last three decades.

From the very onset of the first wave of the war against literacy through the Conglomerate's initial attack-strategy in the 1950s of the mass paperback—the literary author, in order to stay alive, was forced to go "underground," through the movement known as Alternative Publishing.

In effect, this action on the part of the serious writer in America, placed him or her in the company of his surrogate peers in the Soviet Union since both samizdat movements derived their raison d'être from denial of publication through *literary censorship*: The Russian writer *for political reasons dictated by the State*; The American writer *for economic reasons dictated by the publishing giants' corporate politics*.

In a free society there are basically no precedents other than libel, as to what publishers can and cannot publish. And publishers can and have always published trash along with quality, but never approaching the monumental dimensions of today. It is only the *tradition of literature* that prevails all through civilization's cultural history—an unwritten law akin to the Roman example underlying our present civil law—that in a civilized society the reading public must have access to imaginative literature to reinforce their sense of literacy and of being civilized.

But this is no longer the case in the America of today. The literary artist operates in a limbo we can only characterize as a *diaspora*—a state of suspended exile without a country or visible audience he/she can identify with.

Rising from the very barricades of establishment publishing's *conspiracy* against the new and contemporary, the movement of the "literary refused" emerged from their samizdat underground beginnings, from the Fifties and Sixties on, to create what is known today as the Small Press Scene of over 3000 U.S. and some 10,000 independent presses worldwide where writers themselves became their own editors, graphic artists-designers, distributors and publishers. (*International Directory of Little Magazines & Small Presses,* lists 6000 markets in the 1019 pages of its 1994-1995 30th Edition.)

* * * * *

Television (though still in the medieval state of its technology), and for all the criticism leveled against it by mandarin academics in particular, has succeeded in transcribing into electronic form, the Novel of our Ur Television past: the technology of the 18th, 19th to mid-20th century fiction being primarily *visual*, it is not surprising that Dickens, Tolstoy, Flaubert, Balzac, Fielding, Twain, Melville, Hawthorne, Hemingway, Faulkner— could be successfully foreshortened from the *linear* printed page into the *spatial* immediacy of movies and television, effectively ringing the death-knell of the Novel of the last 250 years (with the notable exception of Joyce, Stein and Virginia Woolf whose works are still struggling to reach a more general audience).

As a result, sophisticated readers have turned away from the Novel. Its only audience is a semi-literate one, devouring the more corrupt commercial degenerate forms of today's fiction: *popular romances*, along with its commercial television equivalents: soap opera, sit-com, detective who-done-its and the like.

* * * * *

Just as U.S. Steel deserted its commitments to labor by diversification into areas of financial self-enrichment instead of industrial innovation—attempting to pressure the Federal Government into a globally threatening economic dead-end protective tariff system—Publishing Conglomerates have acted correspondingly.

Closing their corporate minds and doors to *innovative technologies* of *new fiction* beyond the 250 year old *story* and artificially contrived *plot*, they have opted instead to abandon contemporary literature altogether.

(See the Booklegger Press exposé in the June 1980 *San Francisco Review of Books* of "Publishers Owned by Conglomerates" and "Publishers Acquired by Publishers," for a behind the scenes revelation of Mega Publishing's monopoly-control adventurism into major Television, Radio and Cable Networks, Film Companies, Movie Theaters, Newspaper and Bookstore Chains, Popular Magazines and Book Clubs, Restaurants, Hotel, Fast Food Chains, Electronics, Computers, Data Processing, Mines, Pesticides, Missiles, Aerospace and Military Defense.)

* * * * *

With Education likewise neglecting contemporary innovative writers, particularly in college literature programs, accelerating the demise of literacy, imaginary thought, creative ideas, we are now paying for this vacuum of cultural aridity through the rise of evangelical anti-intellectual fanatic tyrannical back to religious basics, parochial schools proselytizing to capture, circumscribe and program the minds of the young, fomenting an atmosphere of fear and prejudice against our constitutional heritage of freedom of thought and expression. This erosion of American secular education is reflected in a recent Administration's political right wing staffing of the Department of Education with former members of the New Right conservative think tank Heritage Foundation's special projects director, Charles Heatherly, along with the executive director of the fundamentalist Moral Majority, Dr. Robert Billings (whose doctorate was awarded by an illegal state-dismantled now defunct Tennessee "diploma mill"), and their kind. (See Julie Kosterlitz. "The Department of Re-Education." *Mother Jones*, January 1984, p. 8.)

* * * * *

Bit by bit the conviction was forced upon me that if the American democracy does much to level up the lowest class, it is still more successful in leveling down the highest and best. No land on earth is so friendly to the poor illiterate toilers, no land so contemptuous-cold to the thinkers and artists, the guides of humanity. What help is there here for men of letters and artists, for the seers and prophets? Such guides are not wanted by the idle rich and are ignored by the masses, and after all, the welfare of the head is more important even than that of the body and feet.

> What will become of those who stone the prophets
> and persecute the teachers? The doom is written in
> flaming letters on every page of history.
> Frank Harris: *My Life and Loves*[1]

In an earlier time author Herman Melville was faced with a similar problem of awakening an indifferent public and an indifferent intelligentsia. At that time the American intellectual elite and, by extension, the book buying public, were more attracted to the cultural life of Europe than they were to that of America because they sincerely believed that America had no cultural intellectual life or tradition of its own. We recall Melville's words largely overlooked in his time, pleading with his contemporaries to recognize Hawthorne "without waiting for the slow judgment of posterity, which, whatever it may be, will do neither Hawthorne nor his generation any good, at least not while they still have the power of further accomplishment."

Now a century later, the same attitudes stubbornly persist in America, of elitism and prejudice vis-à-vis America's new contemporary writers who are experiencing more than ever intellectual cultural economic censorship and neglect on the part of scholars critics as well as editors and publishers who fashionably tout European avant-garde writers instead.

Is there some peculiar masochism indigenous to the American psyche that takes pleasure in breast-beating itself into a corner, of believing that world intellectual opinion is right in assuming that "the business of America is business" and nothing more, that we have no contemporary intellectual, cultural aesthetic ideals, when in fact we do, in the most vital contemporary writing scene in the world, but which is largely ignored by American literary critics tilting to Europe instead, whose elitism moreover, as reflected in the January 7 and 28, 1983 letters of *The Times Literary Supplement*, draws upon critical theory rather than an interest in primary literature?

A 20th century cabal against contemporaneity and new ideas had already begun to surface back in 1957 when we ourselves appeared in *New World Writing* #11 with the 18 page feature "The End of Story in the Novel."[2] We were vigorously attacked in the same issue by the late Cecil Hemley, then editor of Noonday Press, who called for a "revolt against revolt," an end to any further experimentation beyond the forms of Joyce, Stein, Mondrian and Kandinsky. Declaring that no further forms exist while admitting "the realm of form is infinite" but insisting "no further experiments can be managed" he called for a "farewell to 'the new and experimental.'"

In a similar vein, *The Kenyon Review*, in a 1980 promotional flyer self-righteously proclaims that it is neither avant-garde nor a "little magazine" (to which we certainly would agree, but for *our* not for *their* reasons), while acknowledging "these magazines have been invaluable to the promotion of fresh art and ideas, yet often have not outlived the ideologies they were born to promote," concludes that "the avant-garde has grown old . . . and fossilized."

Any writer, editor, critic, reader, exposed to the little magazines remembers them with deep abiding appreciation for publishing over 80 per cent of the works of authors of the past including those who reached celebrity, who were eventually taken up by book publishers. Which was, of course, their function: to make available what was new and contemporary and needed to be known. To state categorically and unequivocally that today the avant-garde is "fossilized" is tantamount to believing that no new authors or new ideas existed after the 20s, 30s and 40s, as if no new discoveries in science were developed after Newton or Darwin.

It would appear to us that the taste makers and taste breakers—to whom, alas, Melville was long ago pleading to largely deaf ears and closed minds—do have an intellectual, aesthetic cultural responsibility to inform the reading public about what is new and contemporary, whether or not they agree, disagree, like, dislike, those new ideas and new forms of writing. If we writers, critics, editors and publishers don't exert our influence upon the reading public, who will? Nobody.

Do not think there is not a danger in apathy or inaction. There is.

The fabric of America's cultural intellectual life has been threatened since the 1950s with FBI and CIA probings and penetrations both at home and abroad into people's private and public lives. Now in the 1980s and 90s this has accelerated through the fundamentalist ethic of immoral and illegal censorship of ideas, libel suits, book bannings and burnings, dictating through fear and ignorance what fear and ignorance demand and dictate to the public at large what it should or should not think, write or read.[3] We are truly courting cultural disaster along with illiteracy if literary critics, editors and publishers do not encourage, support and make known literary writers, instead of perpetuating the perennial adversarial aggressive dominatingly antagonistic attitude that is already America's image in the world towards others and its own. If we care about this country's present and future, we must change American consciousness so that America and not just Europe expresses the intellectual creative cultural aesthetic discourse of our time.

In an immature, success-oriented society such as ours, living on illusions of elitism, fame and wealth, what really exists, what really counts, are Ideas—if they can be heard! Nobody listens unless the party speaking or recommending is known to some public imaged in the public mind as a "name." Whether you like or don't like innovative new writing is not the issue. What is at stake is nothing less than cultural suicide, illiteracy and the disappearance of literature in America, if we don't exert our utmost to make innovative books and ideas known precisely because they are unknown, to that segment of discriminating readers responsive to the new and contemporary.

Notes

[1] New York: Grove Press, 1963. Penetrating literary portraits of the most celebrated authors of his time.

[2] New American Library, 1957. Excerpts from *Phenomena* (Stanley Berne). *Decorations as for Prayers* (Arlene Zekowski). *Cardinals & Saints* (Arlene Zekowski and Stanley Berne).

[3] See the 1984 re-publication of the 1953-1972 "Freedom to Read" joint statement of the American Library Association & Association of American Publishers endorsed by over 21 national organizations including the American Civil Liberties Union; National Council of Teachers of English; P.E.N.-American Center; American Booksellers Association; Anti-Defamation League of B'nai B'rith; Association of American University Presses.

The Treason of the Liberals:
Their Renunciation of Literary Art

In a social structure such as ours today in America, is there not some ironic gross-reverberating imbalance in the fact that every group or sector which feels exploited persecuted or in some way put upon has the opportunity to speak out to air all real and sometimes even imagined grievances with the total glaring exception of the serious artist-writer in this country? Is it not curious indeed quite strange that the universally recognized Platonic ladder of sensibility of excellence, of creative accomplishment has been reversed in America so that what all through human cultural history has been conceded as *first*—the Sublime—has in our time been reduced to *last*?

I have used Julien Benda's term "Trahison" in the title of this article to call attention to the consequences of intellectual political and cultural extremism in America today and to expose some of the motivating forces in our society which are possibly responsible for our present cultural-intellectual imbalance and psychic malaise.

That the most educated the most urbane, the most civilized, the most cultivated class in American society has turned its back upon the philosophy of humanism, cultural enlightenment, enrichment, allowing itself to be politicized in the most blatantly reactionary material sense, is indeed a "Treason" such as I fear thus far the history of human civilization has rarely known or witnessed.

Never have so many worked for so few and so paltry little.

Never have so many worked to emphatically destroy the multitudinous efforts of cultural struggle, the voices the ghosts of dedication and accomplishment in our time in Letters—the

Keats and Shelleys Arnolds Hawthornes Melvilles the Condorcets the Jeffersons and Mallarmés.

Never have so many worked to destroy the concept of an advancing culture, of self-leadership in America and later the world.

For as Gertrude Stein stated: "we are the first to enter the 20th century." She also said that she despised liberals. It is also quite apparent America can take credit for having been first in developing the philosophy of the new meliorism: dedication to the effective functioning of a mass society based upon the greatest good for the greatest number.

However, let us all be reminded that the greatest good for the greatest number, regardless of some nebulous Marxist idealism upon which its original impetus was based, has come to be: *the greatest numbers of material goods for the greatest numbers of people.*

What then has happened? The original leaders of the masses (those famed liberals of ours whom we all can recognize) are themselves now the captive of those whom they formerly harangued patronized and cajoled into rising up against their "oppressors," the privileged few, the educated, the eggheads, the eccentric iconoclasts of aesthetic "obscurantism," the cultural snobs, ladies and gentlemen, like ourselves.

So that those, who with the help of the liberals, threw off their political and economic chains, now exult in the power to enslave those whose philosophical and cultural idealism might have further realized the humanism of our forefathers who were as proud of their aristocratic cultural idealism as their democratic political pragmatism.

Indeed, the two ideals were not exclusive but complementary, a corollary of each other. A great people should strive for those aristocratic ideals of excellence and public service in every realm of human taste and sensibility. Was not Thomas Jefferson, humanist of letters and culture, as much teacher, linguist, author, academic, architect, inventor, bibliophile, antiquarian, agriculturist, as he was progenitor of our legal and political democratic tradition?

But the liberals, in the first three decades of our 20th century, whether out of a sense of frustration of embarrassment over their own selfishness of being self-serving, self-oriented, discovered ironically how to be even more self-serving, more opportunistic, while pretending to be the leaders of the exploited the repressed and despised masses.

They stooped oh how they stooped! They were not going to be accused of repeating the mistakes of their European avatars who had spat upon the crowd as did Flaubert who spat upon the bourgeoisie as did Baudelaire who went down into the darkness of death, scorn, despair, disillusionment and oblivion as did Matthew Arnold when he exposed the philistinism of the intellectual and barbarism of the uneducated in the already downward disintegration of culture through the rising technological industrial materialism of the Victorian Age.

No they would turn their back upon all that was "evil" in themselves: that intellectual and cultural snobbery (an excess of the over-zealousness of cultural idealism and aristocracy of excellence) would heretofore be irrevocably stifled, calumniated in those peers who refused to accept their reactionary "cultural" Marxism as a replacement for the uninhibited pursuit of creative research, that free and open advance guard in letters as has always existed in science.

In order not to commit the treason of political non-involvement these "humanistically" educated liberals turned their backs upon humanism and its fertile democratic possibilities, became instead tyrannical cultural reactionaries, politicizing, perpetuating our great American success myth up and down the country, (so tragically exemplified in Scott Fitzgerald and his generation) that "greatness" means production and consumption of what the many covet—goods as against what is good for them.

Thanks to our engagé-involved intellectual liberals, we indeed have finally succeeded in becoming the very grotesques that we feared our arch communist enemy was insinuating into the world—a plebeian society on the way to classlessness. Not the humane and elevated democracy that Jefferson or Whitman had envisaged. But instead a society where the value judgments the opinions, the self-serving goals, the prejudices, the overriding covetousness of material possession all contribute to the *triumph of mediocrity* and pragmatic efficiency, crowding out *aristocracy of excellence*.

There is no room for excellence in our present American social fabric, only for equality.

Equality as we practice it and promulgate it means,—thanks to our dedicated "liberals"—not educating people to rise, but lowering the standards so that all will be levelled and the "risers" the upstarts the idiosyncratic ones, the individualists, ostracized, neglected, forgotten, abandoned.

Who said that only the Soviets practice the condemnation of personality?

Who is more a "*Non-Person*" today in America than the dedicated creative writer as against the writers in commerce who get published by the big General Motors Publishing Syndicates whose wires of media influence spill over and out into Radio TV Hollywood and Madison Avenue as well as the Big Magazines of Mass Audience appeal?

Nor will we exclude from the accusation of treason (from the dedicated creative artist's point of view) the mammoth establishment of mandarin academe in the mummified realms of scholarly gangrene through their ritualistic perpetuity of intellectual conformity and servitude: their selective snob class support of scholarship to the exclusion of creative thought and originality.

I label academe treasonous because they successfully encourage a "hatred" of the vast parade of letters of original creative thought upon which goods of ideas and gems of precious beauty, of seminal truth, their whole degree factory their whole museum of higher learning and professional accreditation and acceptance depend for survival and perpetuity.

That which they truly abhor upon which their reputation depends they succeed in exploiting, in lowering to the degrading level of a collective research without the irritations of idiosyncrasy, ingenuity, obscurity, originality, insight, imagination or the unexpected.

Scholiasts they are. Not Humanists. Materialists, Conformists, Intellectual Reactionaries, enemies of an advancing culture, scholars of Keats whom they would have hated in his time, just as they hate us in our time who are of the same psychic temperament fabric and lineage. As we condemn academe moreover so we condemn academe's publishing.

How many University Presses (as many as there are Trade Presses) realize their obligation to perpetuate not just the *Tradition of the Scholarly* but equally (if they believe, as they claim to that they are educating the public to think) the antithesis as well as corollary of the Tradition of the Scholarly and the Classic: seminal original research into unknown realms of letters, both critical and literary. As a consequence, the Gargantuan Academic Establishment is by the mathematics of elimination and therefore of subjugation and reneging of its responsibilities vis-à-vis the realm of intellect and truth,—a corrupt and insulting travesty of itself. With its emphasis exclusively on the pedagogical and scholarly it too perpetuates our American philosophy of the greatest *goods* for the greatest number not the greatest *good* for the greatest number.

All big publishing then, University, Trade and Magazine is corrupt and parasitical in the most decadent sense of the term.

Just as our society is empire-oriented, so our publishing is. By this we mean, it disgorges its profits from the health and wealth of the precious organism of life upon which it feeds, like the colonial planter who became swollen with the riches of the wealth of the land, for which his slaves drew the blood upon which he sucked and battened his greed and his flesh.

What do the great backlists of the publishing houses symbolize if not the very blood and marrow of life they exploit and depend upon for their existence and their profit? Ladies and Gentlemen, Men and Women of Good Will: the ghosts of art, dedication, beauty, truth, all that is best in the history of culture form the ironic unwitting testimonial, the precious pearls, upon which the *colonial empire* of publishing externally feeds, which, if it had the courage to stand up and be counted, would have been in earlier times not the promoters but the very detractors of those who only in posterity taste the fruits of fame and immortality which their times irrevocably and cruelly denied them.

In these dreadful times for contemporary letters in America how then do letters in spite of such harrowing conditions, in spite of the deliberate anti-creative, anti-intellectual, anti-humanistic scorn heaped upon the tatterdemalion raggle-taggle stubborn dogged coterie of pure researchers in original and new forms of human sensibility, how do these indeed sustain themselves, since their brothers-sisters in education in class have abandoned them, have indeed denounced them and their open-ended philosophy, to the reactionary subculture of the masses that they lead and whom they now serve.

There is only one way to remain uncompromising in any doggedly dedicated art. And that is not to be tempted.

As we all know, recognizing the power of the Devil's Advocate in all of us, temptation means corruption, that which is capable of being eroded by matter, dying in the spirit, while the body delights itself in the orgy of ephemeral self-gratification of some sort.

Letters after all can only be perpetuated because Letters partakes of *spirit* not matter, even though matter may and does exploit and benefit from spirit. That is the conundrum. The *Pure* is of itself incapable of corruption.

But the pure you might say is created by those who are, like writers, only human. And indeed this is true. But the dedicated and therefore driven spirit in us recognizes how vulnerable the body is and instinctively like the mother protecting her young seeks cover, seeks support, seeks protection and encouragement.

The Arts in society because they partake of the spirit and not of matter cannot, therefore, be judged by society in terms of matter: material profit, efficiency utilitarian value, etc.

Art does not partake of commerce by its inception nature, and evolution, only perhaps centuries later in consumption through publication after it becomes intellectually and culturally accepted by the Establishment.

It, therefore, appears to me that the pure researcher in the arts must find some way to affirm the value, to the spiritual body of society—*the irrevocable value and importance of the artist* in his single-minded innocence, dedication to that which beckons to him or her as new frontiers of human consciousness and expression.

Furthermore, the concept of *letters* should properly be distinguished and recognized as quite distinct from the commerce of the best-seller the movie, book and television script in publishing, just as the realm of theoretical science has perennially been distinguished from applied science throughout its history.

Where, for example, would applied astrophysics be without Einstein's Relativity Theory which ignorant laymen respect and accept without at all understanding? By that token, analogically we should not allow our ignorance over the nature of aesthetics, of letters dictate opinion, prejudice and the vagaries of book trade economics, just because we can read.

Literate, after all, has as little to do with being knowledgeable in literature as the ability to read endows us with the gift of understanding or becoming a Gallileo, a Newton, a Planck or an Einstein.

It is time in America we place our priorities in all realms where they belong and where we begin to respect our individual and separate talents and potentialities whatever they may be. Then perhaps we as a fragmented pluralistic society will begin to value our diversity in multiplicity and the richness thereof rather than emphasizing the narrow bitter a priori opinionated, bigoted fanaticism of our present self-serving, intolerant adversarial behavior as a nation and society.

The Arts throughout the history of civilization have always suffered from supreme neglect because of their appeal only to the most privileged enlightened members of any society who find the highest forms of virtue spirit vision intelligence taste and beauty not a *luxury* but a *necessity*.

Whereas the vast majority of any society finds the high art of literature painting sculpture music etc., mysterious, obscure, frightening and above all without even as much use or practicality as a Rolls Royce or a Champagne vineyard, in a word the opposite of practical.

These are bigoted social attitudes and like all bigoted attitudes can and should be changed just as we have been driven into tolerance and respect for other races, religions, minorities, so we can be driven to respect, accept and not necessarily understand, that which is different, new, obscure, precious, rare, seemingly impractical but beautiful and a challenge to the spirit. In a word—Art. Encouragement must develop into an attitude and practice. *Support the artist.* Just as we encourage all other sectors of society to help themselves, why should the literary artist be ignored, persecuted through neglect?

Elevation of soul, of spirit in literary art as well as in many of the other arts, is far more "hallucinogenic," transfixing, more psychically fulfilling than the narrow circumscribed authoritarian ego-greedy fixations of religious fanatics and fundamentalists who prey upon the fears and prejudices of the unenlightened and uneducated, or the addictive despair, unlicensed decadence, self-indulgence of the drug-driven spoiled rich and the deprived poor.

What is at stake here is not so much numbers of individuals clamoring for attention and insistence upon their uniqueness (although there is certainly no dearth of these), but more importantly, what the most elevated Art encompasses, expresses, represents to the society at large: exhaltation of *Spirit*, creative liberation of thought.

In the end, a nation that does not exercise its potential of the human imagination—which the highest Art and Creativity provide—to enlarge its intellectual and humanistic horizons, will perish and leave no appreciable legacy in the record of great nations upon this planet, to emulate or be remembered by.

Essay

About Neo-Narrative

"*Language* evolution in Literature,
through exploration of the modern consciousness, is long overdue. That is essentially at the root of the contemporary problem of literary forms that
have long since ossified into obsolescence and why a crisis exists in modern
fiction and why the modern novel lacks
an appreciable audience of readers and
enthusiasts as against the audience it
carried in previous centuries."
        —"The Crisis in Modern Fiction"
                        Arlene Zekowski

My approach to writing has some analogies with abstract
jazz, poetry, music video, science-fiction (in its wide-ranging
subjects) and free-association in psychology.

What you see, what you experience on the page in "neo-
narrative," is, like all of these media, a way of overcoming the
jet-lag and time warp of our horizons of experience, which in
the case of *traditional prose*, pulls back and retreats into its
umbilical embryonic subject verb predicate *sentence structure*
without advancing or elevating itself from the *straight line* or
the *paragraph*.

As we move in our minds, bodies, feelings, sensations,
ideas and perceptions from the 20th to the 21st century, it is necessary to have a vehicle, a language in literature to carry us from
place to place in time and space so that we can react to the phenomena of existence with satisfaction, pleasure and fulfillment.

To accomplish this—during some 40 odd years of writing—I have had to rearrange the elements of what we call *the
sentence*, shorten, simplify its structure so that it could be han-

dled much like a sculptor molds and shapes clay into resilient objects and forms.

Thus you find fragments of rhythms, phrases, one or several word clusters, run-on patterns similar to poetry, or, as in the apocopation riffing and syncopation of jazz or music video, themes developing in a *narrative* that creates its own *plot* and *story* in its own *space* and *time*—on occasion slow and static, meditative, at other times fast and dynamic—but *contemporary* with what it wants to express.

The most significant difference in my word patterned "periodic" style of neo-narrative writing (which the *Hudson Review* described as "a device for responding directly to reality without the clumsy intervention of grammar"), from the familiar squared-off page line of prose is its *spatial* ability to travel in thought, to go anywhere it pleases, to do what it wants to do, not only in a totally unpredictable unforeseeable manner—especially from the reader's point of view—but to accomplish this efficiently, without wasted verbiage, padding, bombast, or "purple prose," to get at the *essence* of the *substance*, so to speak, so that, although the reader arguably objects to something visually and structurally new to adjust to (since we are all characteristically lazy as part of the human condition), the process of reading, of both speeding up and extending the thought simultaneously, of not wasting time, of cultivating our brain's synaptic potential, is, to my mind, exciting, to say the least.

Believe it or not, we already use, we have adjusted our mind-set to this process of speed and efficiency in the reading of newspaper headlines and in advertisements; these are not written in categorical grammatical subject verb predicate form but in "Shakespearean style" images with nouns as verbs; adverb as verb or substantive or adjective, thus destroying the canard even in Elizabethan times of regarding a word as a particular part of speech!

Words, in my writing, may function as *words*, but more importantly, they act as concretions of images for the thought. Or, as I have stated in "Notes on the Neo-Narrative," from my novel *Abraxas*: "Thus, in art, the sentence must be destroyed because it never existed./Only words exist. And words engender thought." Critic Walter James Miller, in his Preface to my last published book, *Histories And Dynasties* (Horizon Press, 1982), refers to my style as "word bursts" and "clusters of images" expressing "problems, urgings, goals of the larger psychological life," which the everyday language of traditional sentences cannot do.

How words were adapted from discarded Latin to Vulgar Latin to French, Spanish, Italian, Portuguese, Romansch, all of which were originally nothing but dialects, the so-called Romance Languages, how Dante rejected Classical Medieval Latin for the local Tuscan which became modern Italian, how Chaucer adopted the London dialect which evolved into standard British English, are just a few of the many examples of how word structures were adapted from traditional outmoded patterns, to create new approaches to language in both everyday communication and literary usage.

Need we add that the purpose of all these breakthroughs of the past was to prevent language from dying, as well as to provide creative evolution in literary forms, comparable to Darwin's discovery of animal and plant evolution in biologic forms?

That is my purpose, in developing "periodic" neo-narrative images, not only to enlarge the frontier of the patterns of the written word, but to suggest new approaches and concepts beyond the overworked familiar predictable *novel* and *story*; nonliterary areas of human engagement perception and pre-occupation: art, science, history, myth, religion, archeology, philosophy, geology, etc., many of which have appeared from time to time in my own writing. In this way (as I have stated in "Towards the Evolution of a New Literary Form"):

> The New Narrative moves as *interplay*, nuancing, exploring, merging, poetry with prose, fiction with poetry and essay, essay with poetry and criticism, and so on. What evolves is a new *texture* in keeping with a new approach to language and our perception of ourselves and the world.

Interlude

Life and Living in San Miguel: I

The aging divorcee of San Miguel.
Graduate of Smith.
Artists model.
Peripatetic tourist global world traveller.
Survivor of 30-40 lawsuits by way of a rich alimony settlement.
From an impotent rich alcoholic paranoid of a husband.
Who schemed and succeeded.
In 6 or 7 asylum commitment incarcerations of his victim
      spouse.
Now liberated and luxuriously alimonied.
She suns and gossips her broken bereaved spirit.
In dreams of authorship.
Where her only claim to the pen.
Is the liberal check she writes.
To the anonymous writer.
Who ghosted the record of her fantastic life.

Life and Living in San Miguel: II

You must rent a villa.
With a drab exterior.
On a cobblestoned street.
The stone and the plaster façade rain weary.
From heavy ponderous lethargic continuous rains.

But life is cheap in San Miguel.
The villa must be beautiful only with the door closed to the
    street.
Where the fountains of your pink-laced-stone-sculptured patio
    and the rainbow colors of the earth and pebbles and the
    bougainvillea and bird of paradise and the hummingbirds
    and parakeets
Where all this beauty is invisible to all other eyes but yours.
For the people, *la gente*, here in San Miguel are *mala mala mala*.
The tourists and expatriates bribe them to free breakfasts and
    hand-me-down clothing.
And buy their kitsch-camp trinkets and call them "native crafts."
And decay dilapidation and no plumbing.
And the bargain rents of 60, 70, 80, per mo.
Now inflate to more "picturesque" *precios*.
The patron of the *Vista Hermosa*.
Gives us a room with a view, plus a secret a joke we both share.
The door of the room has no actual lock.
A lock that doesn't lock!
No matter.
It is "drawn" on the door.
A thief only sees what he sees, not what's there.
He knows nothing of *trompe l'oeil*.
The rest is properly *pinturesca*.
Checquered black-white tile floors.
Metalcraft lamps.
Tile and brick fireplace.
Beamed ceilings.
Rush chairs of palm.
Oyster shell alcove with *santos*.
Señor Patron is his own *sereno*, his own nightwatchman.
All night long he locks and unlocks *la entrada* to the doorbell
    rings, sleepy, never getting his sleep.
Because the *serenos* are also *mala mala*, never to be trusted.
They fall asleep by 9 PM!

Sunday
April 21, 1974

Essay

The End of the Absolute
in Language and Literature

Language, like everything else that impinges upon the human consciousness, lies in a shambles of confusion, piled like the dust, the rubble, the leavings of waste and refuse crushed by the noise and din of the building cranes and the concrete mixers and the bulldozers—the vast monstrous grotesque erector toys—that house us enclose us in an atmosphere of leisure of work of shelter of escape of gregariousness—the social and private structures that try to program our loneliness our confusion our unnamed fears and dreads into an order of rationality and behavior that we know is both arbitrary and hopefully acceptable.

The reading of books is at an end and not because of other machines which have substituted themselves for the book. It is not the book which is obsolete. It is the language, grammar and structure, plus the tradition of ideas beliefs rituals which the mystery of words in their form enclose, that have brought on to reading and literature as they stand today, the threat of civilization and culture finally dying.

The problem within structures of *thought* (all forms and modes of knowledge) and structures of *form* (grammar, mathematical symbols, sound systems in music, symbols, scripts, codes in lingual structures, laws of physics, etc.) is in the nature not of what they *include*, but of what they *exclude*.

All language, for example, has hallucinogenic power. It has the power to induce deliberate states of consciousness: and through these states of consciousness, emotions can be released into visions actions or both.

Hitler's language brought on the death of the soul in those who became the instruments of the real death of others. Millions of others! Exterminated!

Lenin found the language of intellectuals artists writers humanists a threat to the structure of his tyrannical ordering of proletariat mass man because their language defied obedience to his program. And so the flower of the middle class was wiped out in the hope that the memory of their language and literature would be also.

But in spite of this, the reason that creativity will not die is because the *human imagination* is *arbitrary* and *Heraclitean*. It eludes every law, every tyranny of order, tradition, form, structure, conditioning, philosophy, logic, that seeks to impose itself upon it, enclose, crush, threaten, civilize, programmatize, brainwash, propagandize proselytize or kill. It eludes stasis, in *flux*.

To state, for example, that electronic media (the audio-visual) is the form the imagination (the proto-soul, spirit essence of our human biosphere) has arbitrarily opted for meaningful extension in place of the linear-verbal (the book) is ridiculous.

Here is the syllogism our "Medium-Message-Massagists" would have us believe: Pre-literate (oral mnemonic analphabetical) → Alphabet - Manuscript → Print (Gutenberg) → Electronic (verbi-voco-visual).

This syllogaic formula of the progression of human consciousness in the techniques of the parade of the history of its forms may intrigue and ingratiate us by its surface logic. But the *logical is not always true* despite its own implications of validity.

Homer in his original pre-alphabetic form is unknown to us. The Rememberers—Rhapsodists perpetuated him several centuries until the code of the alphabet effected his preservation and culturalized him into history. The process of recording did not alter Homer. It simply *guaranteed* his becoming known. It *multiplied* the original.

Though I as author live in the electronic age, I write in the "antediluvian" form of the pen, the manuscript-holograph. The manuscript to me is symbolic of the craft of the creator in words—which means I try to make or originate from imagination via pen to page.

Any technique that multiplies or makes copies does not originate. Thus Print, the press, the typewriter, the computer are assembly-line techniques of reproduction of an original form or idea into multiples of communication copies.

Thus the camera that photographs the painting of the artist multiplies makes known to the many its value but does not create or form its value which is always in the priceless original—the source.

Creativity, the imagination, the new, the *original* is *always* a source of the *copy* and *never* the copy. That is why any media of multiplication is not the same as the product it multiplies, but only a form, a means of transmission.

As far as the verbal imagination is concerned it does not exclude any of the previous forms of transmission and communication, but may and does include any and all of these: the auditory, the linear-visual, the print-visual, the audio-visual.

It seems to me each age of technology each technological invention enhances enriches multiplies the levels and approaches to the original in communicating the One to the Many. Thus, for Painting, the Museum can function as the Book—the Library, and the Book—the Library, as the Museum. Thus, for Music, the Recording can function as the Concert Hall or Theatre and these can function as the Recording, the private Concert, Audition, or Original Score.

However, whenever a process of transmission can replace and do better what the original art once did but no longer can do as well, it is time to reexamine that art. I am speaking here of the literature of the novel and why the novel of literature is no longer dying but already dead. The analyses and details of this subject have been explored in a book of essays: *Cardinals & Saints* (with Stanley Berne, 1958), and in essays included in my 1964 and 1969 fiction volumes: *Abraxas* ("Notes on the Neo-Narrative," along with Herbert Read's Preface: "The Resurrection of the Word"), *Seasons of the Mind* ("The Novel as Inscape"; "Rhythm Texture Communication"; "Poetry and Prose in the New Novel"; "Relativity and the Neo-Narrative," etc.), as well as in my latest book of criticism: *Image Breaking Images: A New Mythology of Language* (1976).[1]

The aim of the Novel in Literature throughout its history has always been potentially electronic or imagistic or visualistic, has always tried to grapple through its journalistic origins, with the pretense through fiction and story of recording time through images of events in recognizable moral patterns of society. The language of the novel has always been as arbitrary as the plots it invented for the sake of unraveling or bringing everything to an end, a denoument, much as in Classical, Traditional, Drama with the resolution of the plot.

But since the inventions were largely *lies* for the sake of conveying *moral truths* and since progression in Time was *not relative* but an *arbitrary absolute* of *beginning middle end*, the language *died* as the process for dramatizing the sense of Time developed into *spatial* and *kinesthetic* dimensions associated with cinema.

Since the arbitrary form of the sentence in the paragraph of the chapters of the novel could not be speeded up to convey the dramatic reality which imagination alone can enjoy, the cinema which could visualize for the many the multiple dimensions of levels of consciousness through the slowing or accelerating of images as symbols and symbols as images of ideas, the novel died in its former linear structure of language.

Today the novel is videotized, has come full circle, a subject for the imagination of mass consumption relayed through the cathode tube.

But the language of the literature of the Book from which the Novel projected has hardly been contaminated by any shock waves of new ideas.

Not only the Novel but all the Literature of Prose will die if there is not permitted a revolution in the structure of verbal communication in Prose. Each word, each part of speech must free itself or be freed from the arbitrary logic of the syllogism of the thought, of any thought as grammatical entity.

Note

[1] All books cited have been published by George Wittenborn or Horizon Press, New York, and are available from American-Canadian Publishers.

Essay-in-Dialogue

Creativity as the Struggle to Remain Alive

—Creation, creativity is no Paradise no bed of roses. It's always a battleground. Like the stomping stallion or the stud in heat it beats the ground and tastes the blood and dust and ashes.

—Full of metaphor you are.

—Metaphor is the sword of Damocles, the hanging fire the suspension of the vision about to fall strike consume be consumed or dissolve. It's as diaphanous as a rainbow.

—You are plagued by opposites today. Harsh battleground dissolving rainbow. Which shall it be for you?

—I should like to talk of desire of the passion of the life within that smolders in the rage of the hatred of the death without that must be fully and finally conquered of its grey and grim dominion over us all, poet and politician alike.

—There you've lost me.

—I mean to say that creativity is a struggle to remain alive. It is not easy for any of us.

—Why so?

—Well for one thing we are born we deploy our autonomy establish our space of self-awareness crying of our momentary liberation from the womb. Birth Creation Shock Pain. A battleground of struggle. There is no other way to be born.

—True. But fortunately it's momentary. The adjustment is self-regulatory. The instincts reassure it of its being, of its acceptance. It becomes part of the known soon enough, this particle of the once unknown.

—What Wordsworth called the prison bars of life. The adjustment is a struggle not towards further autonomy but towards conformity and death.

—Then you feel conformity death? What a purist you are! Ridiculous!

—Why, by being a purist? We are all from the moment of life, of birth, moving towards death. Death is not a state of non-being. It is a process of becoming. It is sequential. It exists in time. And only when the duration of the self ceases does death stop or cease to be.

—What an arbitrary set of postulates. You're saying that life is not life at all. But death. Nonsense!

—Why nonsense? Look about you. What is the cause of the pain of spirit in our time? Why the weariness, the indifference, the unknown dread, the even temper of our boredom of days without end of hope and nights of wakeful sleeping as we count the hours to dawn and when dawn comes, we stifle the languid yawn and stretch, arrest our laziness, cold water-wash our faces into composure, put on our mask over the buried self, disguise and cover up our shame, frustration of the secret demon within us that is waiting for the walls of our guarded caution to weaken just that little bit for all hell to break loose.

—The way you talk you'd think we were all prisoners on the verge of rebellion.

—Well aren't we? Isn't so-called life a disillusionment a disappointment?

—Compared to what?

—Of course. Everything is indeed relative. And if you've never glimpsed heaven you don't know what you're missing. And I'm not necessarily speaking of religion.

—Well what then?

—Of the necessity of exaltation, really. Of exhilaration. Of at least the illusion of feeling we're alive and onto something we can call our very own like when we know the first infant cry proves it is alive.

—But you said yourself this feeling might be an illusion.

—Definitions and classifications and procedural trials and errors are utterly meaningless in organic relationships. It does not matter what you call something. As long as it exists. And you recognize the value to you of its existence. This is what I mean by life. By creation. The seizure of itself. Never mind its evaluation. If it exists. It has proven itself. It is alive. It escapes classification analysis abstraction definition. Because it is separate whole autonomous. That is what I am about as artist-creator. Working to generate. Not to regenerate. Using the essential particles of language. Whatever they are called. Noun verb adjective adverb preposition subject predicate and so on.

Destroying the sequence that has brought them to logic. And to grammar which carves out the line of the logic of the thing called the sentence. And which skeletals and destroys the flesh, the pulp, the seed, the gene, the cell, the flower, the perfume, the fruit of the Word. The grammar of the sentence is death. As the sentence is death. As it is not the thing itself but its package. Adulterated. Disguised. Avoided. Denied. Crushing the buried soul of the Word itself. Stifling its life its exhilaration of communicancy immediacy simultaneity synaesthesia and kinesis and ritual free abandon of magic and myth, invisible pulsation and visible music, that must violate annihilate, be cruel, to destroy the mummies and museums and mandarins of the living dead: traditions and cults and grotesques and logarithms and axioms of lingual lip-serving gargoyled grammarians and all the brotherhoods and sects and succubas of the formaldehyded sentence. Cast out the impurity! It stinks in every nostril of every poet. The sentence is after all the mummified skeleton of a language that died long ago. It danced to a tune we no longer play no longer hear. Its monotony of logic is the logic of death. Because death is continuity sameness. Grooving in its groove over and over. Repeating repeating over and over. Thing and idea as one and the same. Familiarity breeds familiarity and familiarity breeds itself one and the same. That is what death is. It is all around us. Comforting and familiar and therefore soothing. It mangles and destroys our sensibilities our imagination our hunger our thirst for change which is food which is life, in the vice the grip the casket-mold of Tradition. That which was becomes that which is. The dead breeding the dead! Long live the Sentence! Down with the Word! Long live Death!

Essay

Big Science and Big Publishing

Nova's "The World According to Victor Weisskopf" is an interesting survey of Science and our Times, posing the moral and intellectual dilemmas which have led us to the impasse today of Mankind as Divinity in both the Transcendental and Diabolical sense.

What is frightening today is that we can't turn back or annihilate the intellectual clock which is a Damoclean timebomb threatening our lives as human beings on the planet Earth and the future of Earth itself as an exemplary form of biological evolution in its most sophisticated highest most advanced expression.

What Weisskopf seems to have implied is that the exploration and development of atomic physics reversed or canceled out much of the physics of the past in terms of scientific knowledge or conceptions along principles of logic and causal relationships, heralding in a 20th century world of atomic unpredictability, random mysterious behaviour and paradox, so that intuition and the creative imagination became necessary to grope into a world of the unknown, a world not based upon the past, but upon the present and the future.

Weisskopf described this exciting world, discipled and apprenticed as he was, to mentors who in effect pioneered the new physics: Einstein, Niels Bohr, Heisenberg, Born, etc., and from whom he learned.

But suddenly that world of creative thought, of theoretical physics, was catapulted into the Faustian dilemma of spirit versus matter, of purity versus pragmatism, as Science deserted its innocence and idealism and was enslaved by the sins of the modern state, transforming the atom into a diabolical genii of military destruction.

Science, metamorphosed from its individual theoretical creative authorial mind into the collectivity of Big Science went from lyrical inspiration of idea to choric tragedy, where like Caesar's assassins, all partook of criminal guilt. As Weisskopf implied about the Los Alamos collectivity under the stewardship of the brilliant Oppenheimer, they were intoxicated by the momentum of the knowledge they were unfolding, and the results it was producing, both beautiful and harrowing. Repeating Einstein's observation that Science had changed the modern world but the modern world had not changed its way of thinking, one can draw an analogy here between the world of Big Science and the world of Big Publishing.

Big Publishing has also deliberately changed our reading and thinking in its manipulation of Literature, substituting the world of the Commercial where heretofore there had always been two worlds: the Literary, Intellectual, Creative, Theoretical and Investigative, versus the Journalistic and Commercial. The Pen is no longer mightier than the Sword, the Sword having ploughed under and buried into contemporary oblivion, the ploughshares, the bounty and fertility and seminal enrichments of the Pen, starving the Marketplace of the culture, tradition and civilization that Letters represent.

Whereas the Scientists, Physicists like Einstein, like Weisskopf and others, had renewed their moral responsibility and commitment to Pure Science once again, in an attempt to stem to control the momentum of the tragedy of the horror Science unleashed, perpetrated, upon us all, the Big Publishers do nothing to eradicate or to renounce the glut of trash of junk of commercialism, their overweening greed and immoral cynicism indifference to intellectual consequences, their behaviour has produced.

Literature's social responsibility cannot be realized unless its Art is supported by the Publishers. If Publishers continue to turn their back on Pure Literature, on the speculative, the theoretical, the new, then the holocaust of our intellectual and cultural annihilation will be as final and definitive as our physical annihilation of and on our planet.

March 7, 1984

The Crisis in Modern Fiction

When Heisenberg observed that "the laws of nature no longer deal with elementary particles, but with our knowledge of these particles—with the contents of our minds," he was referring to the way modern science views its world, through the evolution of the modern consciousness by way of the mind. According to the most recent studies, the human mind, consciousness and reflective thought can be explained by the biological structure and function of the central nervous system, and "can be totally understood in terms of atomic physics," which in its latest evolution into quantum mechanics, "must be formulated with the mind as a primitive component of the system" (*The Mind's Eye*).

By way of contrast, *Language* evolution in Literature, through exploration of the modern consciousness, is long overdue. That is essentially at the root of the contemporary problem of literary forms that have long since ossified into obsolescence and why a crisis exists in modern fiction and why the modern novel lacks an appreciable audience of readers and enthusiasts as against the audience it carried in previous centuries.

To blame this crisis on television's preemptive rifling of popular and classic fiction for its soap, sit-com, mystery, detective, romance-picaro-hero-rogue potboilers, is argument by way of cliché and rationalization without foundation.

Television is not the straw that has broken the camel's back in the demise of the novel. That it has aided and abetted its dissolution and marched in the funeral cortege, there is no doubt. However, that it is also an occasion, not for mourning but for rejoicing, there is also no doubt. For until Literature begins to investigate new language forms by way of the literary consciousness, Literature can in no way be regarded as vital, significant and meaningful in the realm of the human consciousness as science is in its consciousness of the structures of the universe.

Nevertheless, with the bombardment of images and image-making that assails us from the electronic tube, its narcosis of the mind and senses, reducing the human being to a pavlovian mechanism of stimulus response, the inner world of the self and the spirit we have always associated with Literature now escapes us.

It is, therefore, not surprising that confusion exists over the nature and place of fiction as art (and the novel in particular), in modern society. The distinction must be reiterated between the mundane reality of our everyday world and the art of transforming reality into a *new language* which only the art of fiction can accomplish. Why a *new language*? Because there now exists, with a clarion vengeance, two forms of the novel: *the novel of commerce, of the marketplace and the novel of literature.*

It is only Art that translates us out of the mundane, the topical, the evanescent, that which dies and is forgotten—i.e. the *real*—into the *super real, beyond the real*, a world of universal recognition emotion ideas, a realm of spirit that is not ephemeral but magical, refreshing, renewable, always new, the phoenix reborn, giving us new life from the ashes of the dead of the everyday world—what Kant refers to as that higher reality or Transcendence of the everyday—what Shakespeare's Ariel sings to us all: the transformation from death to life, into that poetic something "rich and strange."

Today, in the so-called anti-Novel, Post-Modern, or Post-Post-Modern literary movements, the recycling that is going on in terms of plot structure—what the new novelists call new language structure—is not new language structure at all: the "Gidian author" within the frame, commenting, observing, voyeuring characters through journal-diary imbedded along with lists, catalogs, popular songs, Proustian reappearances of personalities from book to book exclusive of and/or part of the author's persona, the tale within a tale or Hamlet mousetrap, etc. etc.

Not to deny any Technique which dissipates the over familiar into a coitus interruptus, nonetheless, any and all of these *are not* inventions of literary language, only literary structure.

As for *language*, how much longer will the trendy "new wave" modernist continue to mine and rifle Joycean territory. Likewise for outmoded *mythical structures*: how much longer will they parade castration fears of the "macho" male Hemingway misogynist sheathing himself behind his beer swilling football, baseball, big game hunting, fishing aficionados contra the female and her "devouring" vagina? Or contra the father Oedipus complex? New myths of adult consciousness are needed.

In the end, Literature is expressed in the structure of a language all its own—preferably a new language—a language within its most infinitesimal essence—the Word.

As for literary trends or waves, the Old South's aristocratic nostalgia final gasps trampled by the new rich redneck snopsian Yoknapatawphian vulgarians; the Hemingway/Fitzgerald deadended Lost Generation alcoholics; Virginia Woolf's expiring "Rites of Passage" cultural aesthetes; Joyce's polylingual explosive fracturing of the Western Industrial-rising Technological Age—have now been all but superseded by the "Meaning of No Meaning School" of the Literary New Wave's distortion-amalgam of William Carlos Williams' "No Ideas But in Things" and Concrete Poetry's no meaning radical guard verbal visualists.

All of which latter has resulted in the total erasure of the authorial voice and persona of the writer-creator—a rip-off whiteout in favor of the burial of the creative work by the largely Gallic-derived lapsarian Marxist radical extremist academic critics under a pseudo-literary guise of scientific scholastic jargon-clogged textural-structural mumbo jumbo criticism.

At the opposite end of the scale, Democratic mass society *distraction* and *trendyism* have displaced the vacuum once occupied by *authenticity* and *creative truth* striving to expand and elevate human consciousness along with aesthetic taste. Today it is not elevation but accommodation, satisfying what the *lumpen* majority are used to instead of tapping into unused, undiscovered regions of verbal expression. And so the exploitation of the reading consciousness in an already chaotic and fragmented society by proclaiming *story* based on *action* and *plot* as the proverbial categorical sine qua non of the *novel* whether popular or literary: taking the reader somewhere, anywhere, as long as it is away from thought, meditation, reflective space, away from new dimensions of human sensibility. And to think we have evolved through biological form and geological time from 600 million year old Cambrian Paleozoic single-celled protozoans through million year old African Australopithecus, 500 thousand year old Asian Pithecanthropus, European African

hunter gatherer Neanderthal, and artist cave dweller agricultur-
alist Cro-Magnon, to modern man!

If the novel as a literate art is to survive, it will not, if it
does not explore the evolution of the human mind, as science
has in its domain.

Story based on predetermined fabricated *action* and *plot*, is
the equivalent in fiction, of an 18th century Newtonian causal
framework superimposed on a 20-21st century fourth dimen-
sional relativistic random space-time world.

Story in modern fiction must exit from the linear cause-
effect finite circumscribed replication of the past 300 years of fiction and evolve into the consciousness of the spatial present. It
can only do so by rejecting age-old repetitious action and plot,
probing into a new territory of undiscovered sensibilities, discovering new inner realities of the hidden, the potential hitherto unexplored interior layers of thought, of mind, of idea—the
"waves" and "particles" of literary structure in the dimensions
of the verbal—the world of the *word*. In actuality, *literary structure* emerged only about a thousand years ago with the (1) un-
rhymed accentual oral poetry of Beowulf, followed by the foreign
grafting onto Anglo-Saxon of (2) Chaucerian Italian-French
rhyme, (3) Renaissance Marlowe-Shakespeare blank verse, (4)
Wordsworth-Whitman free verse, (5) early 20th century Joyce,
Stein, Woolf, Faulkner free association stream of consciousness,
developing into (6) contemporary 20th century "open structure."

Thus, in a thousand years, *six* major breakthroughs of literary forms by way of perceiving how we express the phenomenon of verbal sensibility across the chronology of human
communication. *Language* all through our literary evolution is
both an organ and organism of flux, of birth death renewal transformation re-creation, as much as any mutation from the past or
recombinant genetic projection of the future. We therefore cannot afford, for the sake of the creative imagination, which is the
literary equivalent of biological life, to be locked into the shards
and detritus, the stifling fictional junk heap of *plot, action* and
story that has buried us in the last 300 years of the novel.

Even in Chaucer's *Canterbury Tales*, what already
emerges is a journey *not of action, plot, story*, but *of frame*, in
order to present characters cast in images and metaphors of
words, the noise and hullabaloo of crowds, of individuals hus-
tling, hurling, pressing pell-mell onto a human canvas, striving
to explore and probe the consciousness of their own visions,

their own sense of being alive, by and through the structures of
speech, of language, of *words* giving voice to their own time.

In Shakespeare as well, what is insubstantial, cast aside, is
always, and perennially, what is gratuitous, the *plot*—a bor-
rowed scaffolding of Italian, Roman, Greek, Anglo-Saxon or
some such other fabrication—upon which to hang or frame the
words and characters as so much backdrop for the poet-artist's
vocal magic to play upon, to dance, to laugh, to cry, to whisper,
to shout, to love, to hate, to jest, to mourn, to meditate, and so
on.   The invention in Shakespeare is never in the story,   never
in the action, never in the plot—so much rigging—to show off
the real creation, the *pièce de résistance*, which is the *language*,
the Shakespearean *phrase* or *word*, the *image* or *metaphor* of the
consciousness, the vision, the poetry of the thought, the organic
life of literary creation.   It is those sounds, those visions, those
voices cast in unforgettable words, we remember, of Shakespeare
at his best.   Textural invention transpositions of sheds of speech
to make them organic, spatial with movement.   As Simeon Potter points out, regarding Shakespeare's conversion of *word as*
image, in his obliteration of *word as syntax*:

> Shakespeare was probably the first to use *window* s a
> verb in the sense *to place in a window* ('Wouldst thou be
> window'd in great Rome?': *Anthony and Cleopatra*, IV.
> xii. 72), and *to make full of holes* ('Your looped and
> window'd raggedness': *King Lear*, III. iv. 30). Shake-
> speare used adverb as verb ('That from their own mis-
> deeds askance their eyes': *Lucrece*, 637), or as substan-
> tive ('In the dark backward and abysm of time': *The*
> *Tempest*, I. ii. 50) or as adjective ('Blunting the fine
> point of seldom pleasure': Sonnet, lii).[1]
>
> (*Our Language*, 1954: 57)

Even earlier, Old English was less agglutinative, more inventive, creating its own images and ideas organic to its own
structure: *godcundness*, divinity (godkindness); *swegcraeft*, music (sound or melody craft); *sodfaest*, righteous (truthfast); *breostcearu*, anxiety (breastcare); *ealond*, island (sea-land).

Even in inflectional languages like Greek and Latin upon
which English grammar was arbitrarily pretentiously and inorganically based, *sentence word order did not originally exist*. According to Charlton Laird, there was "the strong suspicion that
classical grammar was not the grammar of any living language,
even in classical times" (*The Miracle of Language*, 1953: 143).
The inflection form or case ending was all that was needed. You

could mix or scramble the word (verb, adjective, adverb, noun subject or noun object) according to its emphasis in the context. And that is most likely how Vulgar Latin and its adaptation into French, Spanish, Italian and Portuguese came about. People would not put up with seven case endings just as today school children avoid the lingering vestigial apostrophe of the Latin possessive, the only case ending left in English. (See Stanley Berne, *Future Language*, 83-87, on the frustrations of teaching the possessive to incoming college Freshmen.)

Likewise with *ideographically* structured Chinese, which had even much earlier abandoned an inflectional case ending for the more economic, more dynamic metaphoric image of *distributive* sequence and position usage. *Ming* or *mei* as noun, verb, adjective: "The sun and moon of the cup" (the cup's brightness) or "The cup sun-and-moons," "Sun-and-moon cup" reflect the comprehensive simultaneous concretion of the images. (See these and other examples in: *The Chinese Written Character as a Medium for Poetry* by Ernest Fenollosa, translated by Ezra Pound.)

These are only a few of the myriad possible examples from the nature and structure of language as organic to the *word* and not to any superimposed arbitrary symbolic logic of syntax of grammar and the sentence.

Note

[1] See also: "Notes on the Neo-Narrative," "The Word as Creation and as Thought," Arlene Zekowski, *Abraxas* (New York: 1964), pp. 28-29.

Essay-in-Dialogue

Velocities of Change

—Velocities of change. Is the question bearing upon the roots of things.

—What things? Of our world? Or the Universe. Or Nature?

—Why always do we/you/they wish to separate? To disembody what we are from what we were and where we came from?

—Is not this the problem of our time?

—Not just now but of all the nows and has-beens and will-be's if we survive within ourselves.

—Within ourselves as what?

—As what we are. In the projectory of evolution. The "hero" stuff. Herculean of body mind spirit. And last but not least. Of will.

—The young do not believe or feel the hero stuff. In the sense of culture. Of reaching high.

—Then death is all around us.

—Is not death all around us? And despair. And loss of will.

—You mean the ease with which we armchair into consummated sleep of comatose absentia from the mind and consciousness of action and direction into realms and vistas higher and beyond us.

—There are no new frontiers or worlds of consciousness and hope to conquer even though there's revolution and counterrevolution all around.

—The war of will and terror and the new religious acolytes of death and suffocating conformity. Afghanistan Poland Iran South Africa and so on.

—And what about here. In the land of liberty. Of freedom?

—Surely not the same.

—Sameness is not the issue. Death is. The terror of collectivity. Of absence of will other than those who impose theirs upon the rest of us.

—We are not a totalitarian nation. An oligarchy perhaps.

—So you think cancer of the invisible is not cancer after all. What we don't know won't hurt us?

—The cancer of what?

—The cancer of consumerism. Feeding us. Eating up the world. The military-industrial political bureaucracy that orbits us into their satellites of power. That spreads its benign radiation-smiling embrace of messianic benediction of ersatz and consumptive engorgement of all that is stale flat unprofitable in terms of feeding us and them.

—But so many are satisfied with the way things are. At least in America.

—Satiated yes. It's not the same. We are impaled like Tantalus or Prometheus. With an unquenchable thirst. Of being eaten alive by our and other people's lust.

—Our great communicator asks if we are better off than we were before and we seem to be, judging by the consensus.

—The consensus. I like the census. Taking stock of what is the given and reporting on the numbers of the known. The visible. There is more to life. To the conscience. To the consciousness than the visible.

—Now you are being mysterious.

—Exactly. Without mystery. Without what is within and beyond us. In both the present and the future. Without facing the truth of the facts. And the facts of the truth. Whether hidden disguised buried. Invisible to the many. But not the few. There is no life. No culture. No human creativity. No human evolution upon this planet Earth. This biosphere that has produced the miracle of life and evolution Homo sapiens. It is our knowledge that makes us so. An unique of the animal branch of the cosmos of this our globe. Of the potential ahead. From the creation of ourselves. To what we can become. Is the question. And the hovering fragility that we are suspended by. Self-destruction renunciation or reaffirming our cyclic resurrection from the ashes of glut death and suicidal despair.

—All around me I see only drugs. Absinthe. Glue sniffing. Heroin Coke Crack and LSD. What's the use if the future is killing themselves off from the past of our culture our civilization our heritage of Western rationalisms.

—Western rationalism has brought us to this impasse. The logic of mind that stratifies separates schemes and strategizes. To divide the world. To suppress and deny the haves from the have-nots. Dividing and conquering. Death and destruction. Not evolution. But revolution. Terrorism of the Right. The Left. It's all the same in the end. So they've given in. Given up. The fatalists. The young. Softened into cynical reaction against any ideal of culture hero idealism belief or hope. Going after the buck. Buying selling enslaving themselves and others and their kind. Preening and parading their flesh cults. And ephemera of fashion and distraction. Waiting for the end. The Apocalypse which is to come. As surely as the surrender in themselves. To the end of Freedom.

—There are no more culture heroes is what you are saying.

—Relatively for those who've given up on absolutes to strive for.

—Is there absolutely no hope for ourselves? Our future? Our youth? Our society? Our civilization?

—Nothing can be absolutely the case for all of us. Relatively speaking.

—Relatively then there is an absolute of hope.

—Absolutely. There will always be some who refuse to succumb. If the World doesn't succumb to the despair and loss of will and lack of caring for itself and all of us. We have to care to believe in ourselves. As a species. To have a future.

January 15, 1985

Interlude

Populism TV-I

The "Good Morning Mr. Orwell" extravaganza aired on January first of 1984 was a curious melange of naiveté and pop trendy faith in art-video—an extension of simplistic optimism in the electronic technology of the future.

Outside of the satellite juxtaposition of simultaneous Paris—New York voices and scenes running double-framed, which gave a sense of the immediacy television is capable of, it was the content, largely rock-jazz that was vulgarly objectionable. Phillip Glass's *Act III* contribution was just as redundant noise, reverberative over and over, as the accompanying images were visually jarring. His flashy supernumerary superficial style is no modern Bach as it lacks a fugue-like discipline of development and is more populist and trendy than it is anything else.

Yves Montand's singing and dancing afforded a pleasant unpretentious simple elegance and relief to the attention-getting manipulations of Nam June Paik's entrepreneurial direction and his TV cello—more tongue-in-cheek novelty than anything else.

Allen Ginsberg's Rock Orchestral side kick jazz mouthings along with his side kick lover Peter Orlovsky's wails of Jamaican rhythms echoed old-fashioned sentimental Rod McKuen and diminished Ginsberg as a serious poet, reflecting a performance style enveloped in senility and sophomoric gestures.

The only elegance of avant-garde art that emerged was John Cage's performance of his music choreographed and performed in controlled and consummate movement by dancer Merce Cunningham.

It was unfortunate that Nam June Paik's program and its electronic rendition of Orwell's influence on 1984 were devoid of any genuine intellectual and aesthetic challenge or stimulation, reflecting as so much else on the present art scene, show biz superficial flash, egocentric sensationalism and narcissism.

January 5, 1984

Populism TV-II

Nicholas Nickleby as seen on PBS dramatized by Trevor Nunn, is again scintillating proof-positive that the 19th century novel will no longer be read but televised, the novel as we know it in its traditional linear language transposed as all linear language of long-winded excessive descriptive prose, into the spatial more functional language of television.

The show is operatic, episodic, brilliantly acted and tailored to exaggerative art as only the British can do when it comes to Dickensian melodrama and caricature with the occasional broad sentimentality that Dickens deliberately drew upon with his bow-wow grandiloquent strokes of populist appeal in the serial newspaper novel of his day, relying as it did on pre-cinematic cliffhanger plot upon plot effects. It is not surprising then that the plot novel of the past slides so smoothly into the non-reflective action-bearing sit-com TV soap operas and romances of today. For let's face it, *Nicholas Nickleby* is pure soap-opera melodrama, admittedly rendered by an artist of a showman novelist such as Charles Dickens, a populist writer writing for the populist masses of his time. Would he be writing for television today? Perhaps so. In contrast, what kind of writer was his contemporary, Thackeray, more subtle reflective elegant, hence less popular more appealing to the aristocratic educated enlightened reader.

January 5, 1984

Essay-in-Dialogue

April 1984 or Other Worlds of Being

—What's the difference?
—Does it make?
—A difference?
—Living. Existing. To become to be.
—In the time of *when* or *now*?
—Why not both. As well as in the *future*?
—It is. Or isn't it nonsense? To even try?
—Some all inconclusive. Non-conclusive moment.
—Then. And consequently. Subsequently. Avoiding endings. As in beginnings. As we probe.
—The search is on then. For other worlds of being.
—Yes. Especially within ourselves. As every all of us can go for it. The *tabula rasa*.
—The slate then. Naked. If not clean.
—Cleanliness is not the issue. Earth is. The dearth of earth. That grovelling. Scrambling. Delving. To satisfy the hunger. Not of food. But otherwhere and otherwise. The fate of finders keepers for awhile.
—Transitionally. As all of chance is?
—Somewhat. As desire holds our passions for awhile.
—So what the hunger?
—Is it made of?
—Yes. A *Shadenfreude*. A bittersweet. Illusory. Diaphanous. A silken spider web. The halo of a vision with no face. Or masqued from view. A floating air. Suspended. Gyroscoping on the mind. Flash-bulbed. A filament. A trace upon the film of memory. Lost without a trace.
—Undeveloped. So to speak?
—Somewhat yes. But there. Invisible to self. But there.

—As we are thrown. A *Geworfenheit*. Into existence. Such as it is. For being born. For all the trouble it is worth. To die.

—To die. The ecstasy of life. Conception or Dissolution?

—Both. As inseparable as they are.

—The one true fact our ego cannot displace.

—Indignities and Dignities of Pride of Self.

—All in one.

—Yes. All in one.

—Yet some would die. Enraged at being born.

—As many of us are. Who snort. For example. Burning the cartilage of their nostril—snotstrils. Gold and silver plated razor blades straws. Necklaced. Quarter inch spoons. Necklaced. Dangling from an ear. Cutting the cocaine to the powder of reality's memory-destruct. To levitate in revery forgetfulness. A walkout cop-out from the past present and future.

—Well some would seek no substance. Of the self to find.

—Exactly. As suppose. Not all are born to bear reality.

—Such as it is. And such as we are.

—Well then what is reality? What then *are* we?

—If we knew would we try. Would we probe? Would we struggle.

—I suppose not.

—Those who think they know. Presume upon us all. To save us. When in fact they smother and they kill.

—As which? Or whom? Or what?

—The murderers of the spirit the prisoners of the flesh and mind. The dictators of the social body politic. Those who shout their Jesus God or Hindu Moslem God or Marxist God or Jehovah God. And smother us with their evangelical pain and angst and call their cruelty and prejudice joy. And kill and torture and war and burn and pillage and ban and snuff out books and libraries and culture and science and truth. And foam and champ the bit against freedom and the rights and dignities of individualities of soul and person.

—And so there is always the terror of terrible Homo sapiens.

—The terror of those who live in fear of those who refuse their terror and their fear.

—What can be done for the few who only seek to find themselves? Who wish who demand nothing from others.

Who wish to confront or combat no gods. No tautologies. No shreds of garbage adolescent myths.

—Who wish to be left alone.

—Exactly.

—To discover new worlds.

—What kind of new worlds?

—Of the self. Of the consciousness. So its evolution can be vindicated. So in this sense. As human beings we survive. Prevail. Go on.

—To what?

—If I knew. Would I be trying to find out?

—So we go after *mystery* after all.

—But truth. *Aletheia*. To strive to overcome our temporal eternal *Dasein* of being in the world in the common world of the *Mitwelt*. Struggling towards the *eigenliche Existenz*, authentic existence of Being which is also a Becoming. *Sein* against the inertial intermingled *Seindes*.

—So. You are a Heideggerian.

—In the sense of the need. To discover. To fashion to form. To find the consciousness. And earth of my own invisible world.

—It *is* something.

—For me it is.

April 29, 1984

Essay-in-Dialogue

Hollywoodesque: Destroying the Picturesque

—Things Are The Agent Towards Our Disconnection. The Words themselves you grasp or anyone and all or even some.

—Why then must we be disconnected?

—Because we are and have and always been. As people non-historical. Americans are amythical. They don't exist in time. Except the present. There is no ritual no ceremony. "No way of daily living." (As Stein said of the British.) A way of life. Perhaps. Existence is an abstract of the space they occupy. It's all quite impersonal. "The American Way."

—Ours then is a spatial present is it?

—Yes it is.

—If that is the case it explains the "melting pot" as the metaphor that describes us. That we can't exist in layers. In ethnics. In wholes. In separate wholes.

—We'll never be whole. We don't want to be. We discard age. We discard infancy. We discard becoming. Only *being* counts. No past. No future. Only the present.

—Why no future?

—Because we live from crisis to crisis. We blunder. We do not plan. We live disembodied. In the space we occupy.

—Are we then different from all the rest of the world. Of the life of the planet?

—Yes and no. We yearn for roots. For the parent species. The nucleic family. Which with us is all but destroyed. Replaced by the non-camaraderie of our feudal work establishments. Echeloned chairman president emperor managerial supreme. Through the baronies and knights commanders of group-think and group loyalties collective. On down. The atlas load. Borne on the boredom pressures of the way and day. We call our lives. As we on the bottom rung of the ladder-corporate.

Sweat out our peonage. To reach the top. The things we live by and from. Are the myths and rituals of our lives.

—I'm bored and repelled. It's so well mechanized a picture of our way of life.

—The object is power. The power to reject and destroy. As well as to create.

—I see not much in the way of recreation.

—You are romantic. You want to be awed. To be American is to be brash. As Whitman said before he saw it as disillusion. In America the President doffs his hat to the people. Not they to him. God and King are not above the American. Nor is Satan below. They are among us. Always.

—(Sigh)   It's why I don't like living in the Twentieth Century. There's no magic.

—Oh I wouldn't say that. What you find painful is accepting being American. To be American is indeed to live in the Twentieth Century. All the others, from the Colonial on down. Were attempts to put us where we are now.

—Where are we then?

—Fully empirical. The first fully realized global empire the world has ever known.

—How so? There was the Alexandrian Greek. Into the Roman. And the Holy Roman. Not to mention the ancient Chinese. Or the Egyptian. And Babylonian. And Persian. And others.

—All other empires imposed the shreds and shards of their ethnicities and their religions and rituals and superstitions. They lived in the temporal sense of their own traditions. And rose victorious. By stamping out all others.

—Well don't we stamp out history? Or tradition?

—There is a difference. We don't believe in history. Or tradition. Or even myth. Or legend. Charisma for us is transient. We are always and only à la mode. Much more than the French. They have *la gloire*. From Charlemagne thru Louis Fourteenth and Napoleon to De Gaulle. Does any American still believe in George Washington as the father of our country? Or even Jefferson or Lincoln or Franklin or Kit Carson? We have no images or ikons. We are more radically empiric than the Russians even in this sense. They are corrupters of tradition. They use it as a scapegoat of their politics. But they don't destroy it. They wall it around. And isolate and ostracize it. So the past is there as an anomaly. Ours is not. Despite museums. And the cult of the sentimental picturesque. All the old towns and the Williamsburgs. And the Concords. We know are as make-believe as Disney World itself. In fact Disney World is more authentically American.

—How so?

—Because it is deliberately brashly artificial. A deliberate construction. Lumping all traditions all history myth as one grand guffaw of a perpetual put-on escape to a meaningless nowhere. An ersatz fabrication. An end to all myth. A hollywoodesque. Destroying the soul of the picturesque.

—Then in a sense. We Americans are the scourgers. Somewhat like the Huns?

—In a way yes. The Tabula Rasa is our thing. The clean slate.

—The nothing. Beginning from nothing?

—Somewhat. Except it is a going on. A movement. Not like a pendulum. More like an *assembly line*. Forward and continuous. Not back and forth.

—Then isn't it false or hypocritical of us. To talk of tradition in anything?

—There are always the Mandarins among any people. Not just the Chinese.

—You mean the lovers of culture of tradition?

—Yes. The paradox among us all. They say they are perpetuating all that is in the words of one of them Matthew Arnold all that is or has been regarded as the best. As worth preserving. As alive. But that is incorrect. It is just the opposite. What gets preserved embalmed if you will is what is dead. Not alive. Culture is part of history. The past. And the past is *dead*. Only the present is *alive*.

—Then all that we admire. Of beauty art culture tradition. Of the past. Is dead? Is meaningless?

—Yes. For the present. The past however beautiful or attractive or escapist or full of charm. Is dead. Think of Ulysses. How he lashed his men against the masts and stopped their ears against the sirens. Because he wasn't interested into being waylaid. Into death and destruction. His journey and destination was the present. He could afford no distractions. Think of the Renaissance. We call it the beginning of modern times. And so it was then alive and contemporary. Now it is dead. Part of the museum of culture. Of embalmed curiosity. Then it was the discovery of living in the continuous present. Of first worshipping dead languages. Latin and Greek. Finding it all so exciting. Like any archeological find is at first. The unknown is always exciting. Only at first. And then; familiarity breeds contempt. At least eventually. But for them the renaissancers found the modern way out: to draw inspiration as the model and the symbol of what once was alive: to create life new life by rejecting courageously the gods and the texts and the language codes and signs and symbols of the past. They did the Oedipal thing. Killed their fathers. Their Greek and Latin gods. Married their mothers. Committed incest. Performed the unclean thing. Took the offal. The fecal outcrop. The amniotic waste and effluence of their sea and air and local earthworks marine and vegetal stinking and sulphurous of day sweat and night orgy and copulation and sensuality and violence and Dionysian frenzy and chaos possession and dispossession and the salt and wit of every kind and cut and cloth and accentuated slur and curse fleshed syllable that lived and scalded their tongue.

And so came the curse of the Tuscan. Forged on the Promethean anger and fire of Dante. And so came the Chaucerian Anglo-French pollutant London dialect. And so came the Rabelaisian barnyard grovel and grit and manure flow of fulminating market-barking gutter and coarse earth snotting from the land of Cockaigne and the Abbey of Thélème. The French. Today they are languages. Fully grammared. Dictionaried. And museumed. Then they were dialects. Vulgar tongues. But alive. Verbi-voco-visuals. Of the present. Not of the past.

Interlude

New Story as Myth

**(Preface to *En Route to Auron Winter Ski Station,*
Volume II of the Trilogy: *Every Very Person's Future Forward
Journey of Return*)**

The true "story" of our lives is really on the order of
myth. By that I mean, as in traditional, historic myth, the hidden and forbidden taboos of the unconscious which surface from
the depths of our dreams, reveries, nightmares, fantasies clothed
and disguised in complexities, veils, cobwebs of fictions, symbol-
isms, metaphors or images that haunt and taunt us into neu-
roses, erratic, irrational behaviour, complexes of insecurities,
power struggles and fears.

We enjoy the caress of the typical story plot and de-
nouement of traditional fiction, however outlandish or untrue
because it does not disturb, penetrate or explain the mystique,
obscurity, befuddlement and confusion of our personal lives, the
terra incognita of our charted course from our moment of birth,
to which we return, partially, hardly or entirely unexplored, at
our death and dissolution: the so-called *unexamined* life.

How can we or why should we, we say—"leave well
enough alone"? Most of us do, except the artist of new fiction, a
rara avis who appears to disguise his tracks and flight path in the
language of new forms. I say appears, only for those who cannot
detect or who do not choose to, that something new has been
born: *a different kind of story* that displaces the myths and stories of the past and of other people's lives, for new metaphors of
our own, should we choose to chance the artist's beckoning to us
with a pied-piper plumage of sight and sound and movement
into new directions.

The new directions will play upon our lives and stimulate
and satisfy our hungers should we choose to be tempted. And

why shouldn't we be tempted by something new and unfamiliar? All around us we are molded and mauled by all that is mundane and over-familiar, numbed by the stridencies and caustic aggressive hawking of collective taste, collective ideas, tribalisms of family, society, nation, religion, politics, institutions of pedagogy and the shreds and shards of the fictions of old literatures.

The *new story*, the *new fiction* will therefore not be tied to any umbilical chord of past time. It will exist in a kind of fourth dimension of its own, a kind of time-space continuum of our interior sensibility, a sensibility largely neglected up to now, that seeks to explore and will explore the depths and dimensions, the waves and particles of its own entity of person and personality, event and world, connecting us all with the larger universe of our space upon the Earth, evolving us into all the modes and possibilities and potential of our human consciousness as global planetary human beings.

Interlude

Statement of the Author:
En Route to Auron Winter Ski Station

Where Matisse referred to his Polynesian "Oceania" as equivalent in Art, to Proust's "crystallization of reminiscences," I regard *En Route* . . . as a novella that introduces a new kind of narrative for the 20th century and beyond. Unlike all previous forms of the 350 or more years of fiction in the novel, in two respects, *Auron* reflects how we *see, think,* and *express* ourselves today, first, through liberation from the confinements of chronological time, replacing it with a more organic, more authentic backwards and forwards movement of past, present, future. Secondly, the *language* and *structure* of this new form of narrative—unlike our uninspired, overworked rigor-mortised 18th century derived present day expression—*restores* the *way* we think and feel by *combining*—no longer separating—*images and ideas formerly associated exclusively with poetry with those of prose.*

In fact, there are no more categories of poetry as against prose, fiction, non-fiction, novel, short story, drama or essay. In the *new narrative*, all, some, or many of these can be merged interchangeably in a *fission* or *fusion* comparable to the forms and constructions we find in nature, and like those scientists are discovering in contemporary physics.

That is what I have attempted in *En Route to Auron Winter Ski Station*, where a vast and varied array of European characters, personalities, events, from the '50s to the '80s, is universally accessible to our contemporary consciousness, for *all* readers everywhere, anywhere in the world.

Interlude

Salt From Sacraments:
A Neo-Narrative Prose-Poetry "Fiction"
after the Book of Genesis

Preface

In the end, that which exists has hardly to be proven, since acceptance is its end. In the beginning, however, the reality of its existence seems to weigh heavily, like a loud or ugly out-of-placeness, until justified either by popularity or some measure of approval. Popularity or acceptance in some form is what the "ugly duckling" of literature shall go on seeking forever and ever. As a fairy tale must end "happily ever after," this must be so. But before the knowing of the rightness of a thing to belong—that is, in the beginning strangeness of the view,—*it will not be believed*. It is so, and continues to be, hanging on, if only by a thread. The thread spins, the tale, again and again is told, and the web is formed.

The thread of prose has been lately lost somewhere in the web, and for this reason, must be spun all over in a new way, which I should like to call (for want of a better term), "neo-narrative," or new kind of story.

What will bother the reader in *Salt From Sacraments* is the use of so many periods. This is because, most probably, I wish to end, not any sentence, but the sentence, *altogether*, as it stands today. The sentence, as it stands today, does not stand for much more than a symbol of climax. What brings on the climax are the words. It is here, at this point, that we begin to suspect whether the words in our existing forms of prose really do what they are supposed to do, with that great economy and freshness, in the banging hit-back exciting way we learned to play at things when we were young.

Art is to enjoy, and to enjoy is to play. When we were young, play branched out carelessly in many games of forms. If youth is wasted on the young, as has been said, then so is Art— for the business of life, for the creative nature is to convert the energy of play into growth, and to make that growth, which is the art form—*a living to be exciting.*

Words are my game, my joy, my enticement. The artist, in a sense , is the child grown up *how to play.* Art is the highest form of play. For this reason it is both civilized and free. In the game of prose, the players are verbal. But the point of any adult game (lest we forget), is *thought* . If our verbals prove stale in the old formations, then we must devise new ones. And that is what any artist must do to make the play exciting and worth-while. It is what I have done. Devised a new method to "play" the *thought,* to make it bounding and beautiful, ugly when it must be ugly (for play is also cruel when it becomes a matter of survival)—as serious games *must* be.

I came upon this new method by practicing thoroughly, with love and ruthlessness, the old, for some fifteen years, learning everything about my game there was to learn, in order, first, to find out what I was about, in order for now, to really *know.* To really *know,* that is, the beginning. The beginning of the broken sentence, as it appears to be.

But a look can be deceiving. It is when the eye rests or skims casually, a kind of sidewise glance, a taste, a sniff, a touch, and then slowly more, more and more across the page, that the sea of words and periods merge out of the jig-saw and puzzle with the added dimensions,—which is what the "new" strangeness really is.

Essay-in-Dialogue

Artifice and Art

—We are really necrophagous you know.

—How so?

—As lovers necrophilous and eaters necrophagous, homo *mechanicus* et *consumens*, is hardly *sapiens* or *percipiens* or *sentiens*.

—No longer knowing perceiving feeling?

—Exactly. Consuming is as mechanical and meaningless and lifeless as dying. We know more about dying really than living.

—In what way?

—To live is not to waste, to function utterly, to transcend death to perpetuate miracle. We can't all be saints or angels or poets.

—No. But why should we be lovers and eaters of death? Isn't there a paradox here somewhere?

—You mean when Socrates said we don't know what death is he was really speaking of himself.

—How?

—Being non-material uncaring about *matter*, caring only for *spirit*, tending it, against jealousy fear ignorance, the matter of matter, of the crowd, of death.

—He always said riches come from spirit. And not the other way round. His riches then were not material.

—Look around you. Thoreau said: "Lives of quiet desperation." Lives? I say "deaths." In "life:" we die many times. Over and over again. We live many many deaths. Over and over as long as we "live." And some of us if we are lucky like the caterpillar. Experience transformation, metempsychosis. and die finally. Into life.

—Life then is a greater mystery than death?

—Indeed. As precious as it is rare. It is easier to describe
the signs and symbols of death than it is to describe those of life.
—Isn't life, being born?
—Yes. But how many can perpetuate creation? Look
around you at the universe. A universe that "believes in
progress." A going forth. An energy of systems codes signs symbols formulae categories languages institutions theodicies eth-
nocracies oligarchies autocracies technocracies . . . going nowhere. All alike.
—Why going nowhere? Why all alike?
—Well look you. It's a question of which prejudices dominate at the moment. To prejudge is *a priori*, before the fact or
act before existence, before being. We humans are always judging a priori or a posteriori, before or after, never a *momenteriori*
or *simul* never now or simultaneously. We live for death. For
the mound of garbage of death, that is the history of the centuries and millenia of art science politics religion philosophy
laws mores culture if you will, of the planet, of the eons of time
the now six million years it took to form the creature we now
recognize, and identify with as Homo sapiens. Man knowing.
     Knowing what? Knowing death and disease and de-
struction. The lover of death, not life. It thinks it is superior to
the cannibals. Civilized man. Montaigne didn't think so. He
saw their purity. A natural life. Even when they killed and ate
their fellows. A ritual of death bringing forth the spirit of those
they ate. They are spirit. And we? What do we eat? Matter.
Artifice. Manufactures. Products of every form and kind.
Things. Objects. Machinery. Chemicals. Representations. Imitations. Substitutions. Approximations. Simulacra and simili-
tudes. But never any more the elemental purity itself. This is
the 2nd Middle Ages. The 2nd Dark Ages. Our alchemists are
better than those of the first age. We can change everything to
gold. To profit. To consumption. There is no limit to what we
can consume. Just look at us. Everywhere and anywhere over
the planet. Children of the industrial age: technocracies
necrophagous. Lovers of death and artifice of all things made,
not created.
—How can you distinguish between made and created.
Isn't it a matter of semantics really? Art? Artifice?
—Semantics means what you know is believed at the
moment to mean. Now. All art becomes artifice eventually.
Capable of imitation of reproduction. But at its moment of cre-

ation it is invisible arcane unique whole indivisible, elemental,
hallucinatory,   incantatory, mysterious miraculous and divine.
In a word. Spirit. It glows. Because it is alive. With no past.
New. Genuine. Unrecognizable.   An essence.   Not a copy.
Alive. As only *being* is.

Essay-in-Dialogue

Visions as Appearances of Things

—To live long is to see that visions become the appearances of things.

—Whose visions?

—Indeed. That is the question.

—And where the appearances die?

—Then that is death.

—But there are those who live without visions. Then are they dead?

—In some such form perhaps no longer recognized. Except for nightmares dreams fantasies.

—Rejected. Buried. In the consciousness.

—As yes until they surface beyond the will or passion to deny.

—And then the cauldron burns. The body quakes and trembles. And the mind surrenders to some ecstasy or horror. And the wars begin.

—Private or public?

—Either or both.

—The fears of feelings instincts. Nostalgias of sentiment. Of love. Of sentimentality. Of hate. Of envy. Of bitterness. Repression. Regret. Of hungers and frustrations after power. Of dominating subjugating the other. Of cruelty. Of self-flagellant and self-inflicting vertigos of pain delight. Upon the self. Or other. In the jealousy of cold command. And heat of twisted and aborted life. All these pathologies of human consciousness. Of acts and days and moments of our lives of being and nonbeing. Swimming in primordial seas of our beginnings. Biologic. Fetal. Or otherwise. So grates our confusion upon ourselves. Stabbing like some stubborn hangnail. Or fungus itching athletes foot. Society's plays and counter plays. Judgments. Misjudgments. Wrong calculations. Flimflam flounderings. In the shouts of action of derision and applause. The maudlin stereopticon of image frozen images. Upon the medium of the Media. The Media impose upon the body culture. Of the body politic. It itself can scarcely be accounted to be depended on. Micro and macrobiotic sponges jellies mouths. Anal and digestive stomachic intestinal crud and clotted dung of feces slimed and slathering. Regurgitant responsive tail-wagging dog and bootlicking ass-mooning farts and belches. Smiles/applauses handclasps fists and fisticuff salutes and unison uniform goosestep bootmarch parades of order in disorder chaos ceremonials eulogies perorations salutations and lecheries of lubricious heehaws dogbarking shouts shimmying belly and backthumping thunderations to their laying on of thorns and whiplashed flailings of the enemy in self-proclamation to their Christian no other God the father son great communicator political priest lawgiver and lawtaker away shaman medicine man bite the dust and military commander God militant all Provider for them that provides the gelt for themselves and brick-asses and crushes the hands and empty bellies of the handouts the sick the lame the elderly the poor the ignorant the starving as so much offal in the dust and to be carted away and off and buried in urns and ashes and garbage bins in memorials of hollow plainsong and dirges of the failures that they themselves became the self-proclaimed victims of through no fault of society's but their own of course. The skeletons of pariahvilles across the mountains and the prairies and the villages and towns and cities from sea to sea of this blessed oh so fortunate and fortune making land of the rags to riches chicanery tycoonery genus Americanus.

Thinking Spatially

The spatial sense is the nearest approximation to the cosmic in our geographic or earthbound limitations of mind. What the spatial sense does is liberate us from the immediate, the contingent of our here and now environment of preoccupying tensions that distract us away from, but not out of ourselves. The human being is a mysterious animal capable of great thoughts and great deeds, as well as evil thoughts and evil deeds, residing in us one and all, often in the same person. What sets us off to realize, to set in motion, to make choate what is inchoate, to throw down the gauntlet and challenge the world, to rise, to rebel against *the here and now* for the *hereafter* and thence *forward* and *from now on* is a kind of *fate* in which we are both puppet and puppeteer, playing and being played upon the strings that make us dance the drama, the tragi-comedy of our lives in the world.

In art as well as life the spatial enlarges our possibilities of thought, of creativity, of magnanimity, of soul, of spirit. The spatial is also a paradox. While it tunes us in to the music of the spheres of our most grandiose dreams and fantasies, and clues us in to a simultaneous sense of the world, it also interiorizes us away form the vulgar, mundane, meretricious and sordid vileness, the criminality, corruption, greed, hypocrisy, selfishness, trivia, tawdriness and trash of the social chaos and destruction of our time: the Moslem versus Moslem Iranian Iraquian; Lebanese-Syrian-Moslem versus Christian versus Moslem Sunni Shiite Maronite Druze Maronite Franjiyeh versus Gamayel dynasties both murderous, etc., Israeli Jew versus Palestinian Arab; Irish Protestant versus Irish Catholic; South Afrikaans White versus Black African; Nicaraguan-Sandinista Guerillas versus Centrists and Rightists in El Salvador, etc. The fascistic hypocrisy of the prayer in the schools evangelicals and

Supreme Court Nativity Scene decision judgment to lump Christ in public Christmas observances with the secular Christmas National Holiday, eroding our separation of Church and State Constitutional principles and tradition.

These and other phenomena of our time are emblems of the mental sickness and madness that prevails in *linear* versus *spatial* thinking. What is *linear* is narrow, ungenerous, limited, a myopic perspective or one with blinders upon the human vision, a kind of rear-view mirror, shackling, enslaving the human being into fear of majority or minority consensus, preventing the human being from reaching out into the universe of potential that is both within and beyond, preventing the heroic thrust that humanity is capable of, if it but chooses.

It is left then only to the artist, to take on, to create, as Yeats said, out of his quarrel with himself or with the world.

Only the artist can rise above the linear into the spatial, move beyond the plebeian narrow confines of the public reality into the protean possibilities of the aesthetic domain: enlarging the possibilities of the literary consciousness in new forms of language and expression, providing that special communication of sensibility to a largely unregenerate but hungry-souled world. Only with new attitudes, new programs, new solutions to human thought and potential can humanity in the long run, survive itself, in fact, *be saved*.

Sunday
April 1, 1984

Art as Psychic Rebirth

In a mass society, with a mass technology such as ours, the only saving grace for the individual who believes in and indulges in the sense and sensibilities that surround his own consciousness, is the development and evolution of that consciousness to its most liberating and satisfying point of expression. This means struggling in every way to free oneself from the nullifying and debilitating influences, blandishments, temptations, distractions, above all, tyrannies and emperies and oligarchies of power that seek to enslave and separate us from the potential that resides within us, and our own human consciousness to set us free.

What are these tyrannies? There is not one that we cannot recognize from which we have not suffered and been hounded and driven by and been denied and deprived the treasure of the self, our individual consciousness of being: family, tribe, institutions of education, society, politics, government, above all religion, race, sex, money and all the contractual prejudices, beliefs, opinions, fears, loves, passions and hatreds that *enslave* us to these ghettoes of environment and behavior from our first drawn breath into this world.

Does this mean that we reject or try to separate ourselves from it all? Yes and no. Depending on how far and to what extent we wish to become free and to enjoy interaction with others on this basis.

There are hazards and liabilities. It's a lonely trip. Most individuals cannot pay the cost, the price of discovering and developing those inner resources of self and consciousness which provide the greatest enrichment of our lives and which we are capable of sharing with others.

Sharing is the key since the purpose, the raison d'être of the progress of the self is not withdrawal but expansion and communication with others, knowing there are other human beings who have stumbled upon this startling fact that we are enslaved from the moment of birth and that the umbilical chord from which we think we have been set free is still there invisible, dangling like a ghostly damoclean sword pulling us puppet-like on a string which others pull to make us dance to and perform according to the ways of the world.

The one individual who refuses, who eventually more or less and to the degree to which he or she is capable, finds his own tune, attunes and develops his/her own harmonies and accommodations with his own surrounds—the various hells and enslavements that wish to deny and stifle this individual evolution—is the *creative artist*. All my life as a creative artist I have pursued 2 goals: the discovery, evolution and rebirth of the self, the consciousness, and the parallel discovery pursuit and evolution of a *language of art*, to express and reveal that consciousness to others.

The purpose is not self-serving solipsistic or narcissistic. As in any art of ultimate value, the magic of discovery is both *reflexive* and *transcending*. It reveals not just the discovery of the self of the artist to himself or herself, but the discovery of the self of the reader, the participant to himself or herself. It is a sharing of that human consciousness and its freedom and potential for creative birth and rebirth that only the language and literature of Art can provide for now and the future in this human world of ours.

Art of any value to us is a psychic rebirth.

July 20, 1985

Neo-Narrative Interlude

Serving in the Uses of This World

It is better to be lost in dreaming.
Than in thought.
The dream that opened like the petals of a chrysanthemum.
Burst open and was remembered as a sunflower.
Do I remember what is meant?
No but I felt the joy.
It was warm. It glowed as a log fire of piñon. And reverberated heat like a rose.

To say what of the origins of the self.
On this small planet shriveling to putrid.
In its ooze of pressure of the life to bursting.
Filling in the spaces once left to chlorophyll.
Even the Amazon bleeds and chokes itself.
As its jungles and its natives die.
For progress shantytowns of tin for engineers and beer and steaming heat that roars and beats the head and eardrums into lunacy beneath the sun the tropical sun.
Oh well what of less oxygen for the earth's inhalation.
The exhalation of the forests of the Amazon are to blame.
Or is it the Brazilian G.N.P.?
The colonies of jungle hacked to death.
For the colonies of towns. Super suburbias fighting fever malaria torpor sweat fungus heat uprooted indians roused to murder fighting for the umbrella of that green world in the green shade, its shadows falling under the sun and bulldozer.
The giant machetes that beat down their own. The green canopy that was. The canopy of their death that is.

If now oh world the money exchanges in Brazil enrich your money changers and you clip more coupons and smile with pleasure.

Remember that the air you breathe has become more rare and precious and you will feel it more and more on days of inversions and of smog and of stationary non-turbulence.

And will hardly remember ever to give thanks to the sacrifice to progress.

That the gods of the jungle forest and the jungle Amazon natives died for.

For your G.N.P.

The closures that we make and settle for.

On this small planet of the sun's hegemony.

Are as apocryphal as that eon as the one the astrophysicists proclaim.

5 billion years and poof!

Some shriveled stardust.

And we the Daniel Boones Kit Carsons Coronados Pizarros Columbuses Cabots Magellans, Highwaymen, Bushwackers, Billy the Kids and ghosts of Tombstone and their kind.

Will lariot our spaceships to some galaxy or outer satellite on Copernican charts in Einsteinian time.

And find another moon of a satellite courting a reasonably mineralized watery haze of a blob of a planet boomeranged into zones of our life zones.

And maybe who knows? Another sun to warm us. Another atmosphere and stratosphere to penetrate.

And colonize. And kill and die for.

All the sons of the fathers of the lovers of the sisters of the brothers of the mothers of the daughters of the prostitutes and pimps that ever pandered for the flesh or danced and pantomimed and bowed and scraped at the dust to hear and see and touch the ounce of fire in the hand that clasped and fisted, worshipping each insult as a lover embracing groveling enslaved by what he loved. The beauty ugliness and death in life of sweat of years that shrivel into aging into aches and agonies, frustrations of the dream that haunts the brothels of the working world we occupy and serve and dance to tunes that others play the ones we close our ears to if we can and listen to the crippled voices of the visions of our dreams that clamor clamor always and forever beating their pulp of life and fervor against the walls that verbalize their pain. And so we twinge awhile and the fever and the rash and sore and itch and palpitation sweat and nightmare overtake us in our islands of solitude we build and stake like fortresses against the make-believe of the burying and the selling of the flesh and person and yes sometimes of soul they would so claim if we would put down our fight to surrender to a cause not ever ours even though those so many years of our lives of our non-being are spent in the fields like peons draining the ditches and digging the canals and working the rows of sustenance and manning the factories and sweatshops and officers and boards of education and commerce and politics and juries bowing bowing bowing standing like martyrs St. Georges St. Sebastians Saint Teresas, St. Joans St. Cecilias burning beheaded stoned arrowed, impaled, lashed, hung knived nailed gored raped smothered disemboweled shot mined poisoned exploded and above all used in the uses of this world serving in the uses of this world.

But though we are used and though we serve in the uses of this world, we do not forget the manure that feeds the rose.

And like the phoenix we can and do rise from the ashes and from death.

And though we prostitute and pimp and serve like soldiers and like slaves in the world's work. . . .

The spirit of the flesh and the flesh of the spirit is ours which no body owns but our own.

To dedicate is to serve like no other—emperor or slave.

The riches we serve and we earn and we own—pearls rubies emeralds diamonds sapphires—jewels of the flesh of the blood of the sweat the struggle the pain the joy of our sacrifice of our will to serve the dream, the vision and the hope beyond each circumstance that crushes to the wheel. We rise like fire. Like water. And like stars. Like sun that warms us all. Our visions must and do prevail. We win in the end though we seem to have lost all our lives. We win the life that survives. In the art. The work of art.

Interlude

Interview with the Author Arlene Zekowski
on Her New Book:
Histories And Dynasties

Questions and Answers

Q: What is *Histories And Dynasties* all about?
A: It is about the deterioration of the American Dream.

Q: What do you mean by that?
A: I mean that as a nation and a people we have failed ourselves in that our ideals and our hopes have not materialized. We have found ourselves suddenly floundering in mediocrity, our sense of excellence in both work and culture has collapsed.

Q: You are a novelist. How do you deal with these ideas in a novel?
A: It has been necessary to write a new kind of novel, one that can come to grips with real people, real thoughts, real and important feelings, feelings and ideas shared by all Americans!

Q: How did you do that in *Histories And Dynasties*?
A: I have tried to deal with the drama of a great nation such as ours is, wrestling with complicated issues: our European past, our religions, our diversity of peoples, our sense of the frontier, our great capacity for production, our young people: whom we see today acting out their lives with alcohol, drugs, and with a sense that America no longer has a destiny worth achieving.

Q: As an author, and a woman, how do you view the woman's movement?

A: Well, I write as an individual first, but women have not voiced their opinions, or made their impact upon civilization. Their opportunity as artists has been limited until this century. Now, I feel that it is necessary for women to be heard from. We have something very valuable to contribute, a view of life that has a different angle of vision from men, but one that is vitally necessary in order for a balance to be achieved. We must hear from the most gifted women, as we must hear from the most gifted men, in order to have an accurate sense of reality and of life.

Q: You seem to indicate in *Histories And Dynasties* that one of our problems in America is the denial of intelligence. What is meant by that?

A: We have neglected intelligence in America because of our standards of measurements. That is, our country was founded on intelligence. The most intelligent people of the eighteenth century, men who knew history, who dreamed of the possibility of a new enlightened democratic society in a new world came forward and set up democratic standards conceived by intelligent people working together. Today, we have entirely departed from that ideal. Our measure today is money, greed, and popularity. As a result we have neglected intelligence and we are in deep trouble.

Q: What do you mean by deep trouble?

A: I mean that man's and woman's creative intelligence is the means by which we realize higher standards of living, meaningful productivity, a healthy culture. For example, in publishing today we entirely depart from intelligence and allow moneymaking popular junk to dominate the marketplace, with bad books actually driving out good books for the sake of a supermarket "best-sellerdumb" mentality which literally prevents our best writers from making their appearance on the shelves of bookstores to which most people have easy access. The theory of the publishers who are exclusively obsessed with money is that the public is stupid therefore, the more stupid the books, the greater the profits. No authentic American author or poet shares that view. We write at our highest ability and excellence because we are the ones who believe in the American people, and in America as an intelligent nation, not a stupid one.

Q: You suggest in your book that Americans feel betrayed by their own country and by the way we are today.

A: Yes, there is no question about that. That explains the alcohol and the drugs and the delinquent youth, and the wave of crime that is washing over us. We are portrayed in *Histories And Dynasties* as dehumanized, computerized, mechanized, "lost to number." We Americans resent being treated as numbers. We are traditionally great individualists, full of human strengths and weaknesses— we have always prided ourselves on being individuals. But our human quality can only be recaptured by applying intelligence once again to American life and culture. We cannot continue to live with violence and egalitarian mediocrity to the neglect of civilization and *excellence*.

Q: You said excellence. How do you mean that to be understood?

A: I mean that excellence, which was the ideal of our founding fathers, must be restored if we are to survive as a great nation. For example, in the industry I know best, publishing excellence is abused and neglected. Our best authors are not published or distributed. That means that people have access only to junk, work produced only to satisfy corporate greed for profit. I believe that feeding people corporate swill to satisfy their hunger for imaginative thought, which is what good books do, makes pigs of the consumer, and pigs of the supplier. So, we have a culture devoted to swill. Don't you think that rubs off on people and embarrasses us as a nation? In Europe, where I lived for several years, they do not trust or admire our judgment because what we export to them in the form of "Culture" is generally thought of as common and vulgar. We don't act like leaders.

Q: Is *Histories And Dynasties*, then, all discouragement and pessimism about America and its future?

A: No, not at all. I love this country. It has given me birth, it
       allows me to write and create freely. I think we have a
       great future ahead of us. This century is "The American
       Century." The world, though it criticizes us, would like to
       be like us, in many ways. For too long a time we have
       been unhappy and confused about our values and our di-
       rections. In this book I have attempted to confront these
       issues and to show how great our potential is, how much
       better it can be for our family, all of us, the family of
       America.

                              * * * * *

       "Because we are a topsy-turvy people. Gulliverian
       and Alice-In-Wonderland. The child-in-adult builds
       Disneyland and Hollywoods. To perpetuate the dream.
       Of all that future that is blatant with success. As we
       sing our odes and benedictions to our many gods. All new
       and shiny in their artificial molds. The pepper-upper.
       And the pill to sleep. The mouth breath freshener. And
       the underarm deodorant. The shampoo that doesn't fib
       its dye. The un-cola. And our degermed cereals and
       breads and cakes. But we can limp to health with the
       vitamin bottle. And chase away the pressure and the
       pain. With aspirin or mary jane."
                                    —*Histories And Dynasties*

Neo-Narrative Interlude

Sidelights

In a recent critical discussion on "language," from my brief essay: "The Crisis in Modern Fiction," I commented.

> *Language* evolution in Literature, through exploration of the modern consciousness, is long overdue. That is essentially at the root of the contemporary problem of literary forms that have long since ossified into obsolescence and why a crisis exists in modern fiction and why the modern novel lacks an appreciable audience of readers and enthusiasts as against the audience it carried in previous centuries.

I should like to cite some of the major causes for this lack of "language evolution" by referring to "Notes on the Neo-Narrative: 2nd Series," which appeared in *Assembling*.

> Newton. English Grammar. And the sentence. The mechanics of Newton. The mechanics of grammar. Laws of science. Rules of noun verb adjective adverb. Are products of 18th century arbitrary linear inertial systems. As well as: Letter writing. Newspaper novels. And horse and buggy communication.
>
> Literature existed. People read literature. Before grammar and grammarians. Policed language. Imprisoned. Circumscribed. And proscribed. Stamped discipline rote drill upon language. And substituted logic for thought.
>
> After grammar. People wrote. Parsed sentences. Dreaded writing. Forgot Literature. And hated to read. Novels especially.
>
> The neo-cortex. Our newest brain. Rejects logic. Accepts. Receives. Conceives. Patterns. Invents. Not in sentences. But in images.
>
> Our Neo-Narrative writing (I refer to the books of Stanley Berne, as well as my own) is an image-compatible language. Of the word. 300 rules/elements of grammar. Swept away. Clean. Reduced to 2: the

"long" or "short" of the image. Clusters of comma (Kommatic) Stanley Berne. Or period (Periodic) Arlene Zekowski.

For over 30 years. In Novel. Story. Poem. Play. Essay. Our neo-narratives of poetry/prose open structure. Have been based on the word. The image. As the matter of language/literature. As matter is waves/particles in modern science. Words. Corresponding interchanging substituting. Sound color form movement taste touch smell hearing song silence speech. Creating. Destroying. Foreshortening. Accelerating. Decelerating. Real/Expanded/Compressed/Time. The word. The words. Only the word. And the word. As the consciousness. Of its time.

Or, as I have stated in an earlier volume:

The combinations in any art are as multiform and mutable and infinite as Nature itself.

If it is true of the medium of all forms of creation it is true of words in language. . . .

Thus, in art, the sentence must be destroyed because it never existed. Only words exist. And words engender thought.

("Notes on the Neo-Narrative:
The Word as Creation and as Thought")
Abraxas, 1964: 29

Just as Time in the modern world is relative. To position place situation of person. So is Word. Relative to position place situation relation in writing.

The moving "space-time" of changing simultaneous relationships. Experience in multi and sensory dimensions. No more absolutes. In Language. Art. Or Science.

In literature. The old novel drew picturescapes. A series of surfaces. Before invention of the "visual." Photo movie television video satellite.

To see is "surface." To perceive is to seize feel sense "structure."

The new novel rejects *picturesque* for interior organic *inscape*. The New novel no longer tells surface (old fiction). Tells penetration (new story). The interior of human consciousness. Abandons *visual* for *perceptual*. There are no limits to human consciousness. Just as there are no limits to reality.

The mind. The consciousness. Expanding. Unlimited. As the universe. Of which. And by which. The brain. Tells us all.

For now. And the future. In Literature. Language.
The *unknown*. The *new*. The language of to-
day/tomorrow. A language of images/perceptions. Of
curved organic structures. No more flat visual surfaces.
No more 18th century linear sentences. In 20th-21st century immediate simultaneous geodetic space and time.

Just as the old structure of language in its linear form has
become antiquated, so the old novel, the old story, the old fictions in their arbitrary predetermined traditions no longer serve
the literature of today.   As elaborated in "Questions and
Answers" from the 1969 volume: *Seasons of the Mind*:

Story means simply a telling of something. The
concept of story has become cliché because the telling of
something has been reduced in the novel to an arbitrary
form known as plot.
Plot as we know it must be destroyed because in this
form the reader does not experience anything new. . . .
Story then simply means exposure to a new frame of reference in the form of a narrative which does not follow
any familiar recognizable sequence but which creates
its own.
Every man and every woman who constitute the
readers of the new narrative become, if you will, the
'characters' where the responsibility of being exposed
to an experience is no longer at last a fiction but the
truth. . . . Only with the New Narrative will the old
saw take on its true old and new meaning: 'Truth is
stranger than fiction.' And only with the encouragement of what is true, can literature breathe authenticity now and in the future.

The new narrative, as I have described it in *Image Breaking Images*, and as Stanley Berne has in *Future Language*, as well
as in our co-authored volume of essays: *Cardinals & Saints*
(1954)—will in the future take on a life of its own, a kind of rebirth in the phenomena of new forms and experiences—a genuine evolution in literature which, in its liberation of the imagination, the mind, the senses, the unconscious, we now refer to
as "Trance Fiction."

Living Only in the Thing Itself

—Myth is well and away the dream stage. Of all that is as disembodied. Sensation in itself as being.

—Why disembodied?

—Disembodiment is pure being. As language never is. Language circumscribes imprisons. Regulates as mind and order. Destroys the spirit. And brings on death.

The shaman once before the word was written spoke the magic of the sound and was the agent-shaker of the spirit. And the theatre in the circle lived the sounds. And no one asked about their meaning. Everything and everyone was action. And those souls before the word *was* then sick and silent now as the words spoke themselves were released and the former sick no longer passive found their souls again and answered in the voice they found. Now the magic is all but gone.

—The magic of words. The magic of sounds?

—And the magic of spirit. Of being. The Navajo no longer erases his sand painting. He angers and insults his gods. For the god of mammon. He reproduces what is already dead. He uses the language that belongs to others. And not his own. Just as we have for long long centuries. Locked in our magic genii. Our spirit-beings. Denied and renounced and swept them under the rug. Marched to the martial ritual of grammar and logic. And worshipped our priests of grammar: of sentence of paragraph of story in the temple of Fiction, of noun, verb, adjective, punctilios of punctuation as separate and exclusive, and have not realized they've been dead for ages.

—We are lovers of the familiar and the recognizable. The *status quod* can never be changed. It is how we are.

—How we are. Is how we have been trained to be. Nothing more.

—How can language be released from form. That is ridiculous.

—I did not say released from form. I said from grammar. Grammar always has destroyed the spirit of Letters. And always will.

—It is fear I think. Of the unfamiliar.

—Of letting go. Of freedom. The paradox of the American tradition. A democracy? Hardly. Collectives of our will. So willingly enslaved. Our oligarchies of establishments. The language imprisoned and corrupted as are our laws. All truth in spirit truth of spirit. Violated and destroyed. We've always secretly admired the rapists. The bushwhackers. The adulterers. We can't leave spirit be. Trees. Grains. The vegetative or the animal or marine. The spirit of air or earth or river—sea. We want to improve. And so abuse. And bring on death. Americans as the greatest conformists of all. With the power of individuation liberation at their fingertips. Raté. Failed. A failed nation. A failed spirit. With the potency within them of all Spirit. Of all that is human available to them. Every form of myth of dream of space—extension of passion feeling aerated hope and excitement and energy of the imagination of dignity and trust and angelic beauty of community of humanity of freedom from prejudice and ego and hate and repression and pettifogging brutality and lying and corruption. They themselves denied themselves. And so the death mask. The dance of death in sameness and conformity. More dead from the dead of the vestiges of repression they ran away from. They are more violent too than all of these. When archaeologists from the year 2500 unearth our kitchen middens. They will find us all not basket weavers but casket-makers.

—How so?

—We are lovers of death and nature-improvers!

—What is a nature-improver?

—The same as being necrophilous. Kidney machines and heart pumps and crutches and mechanical limbs are better than kidneys and hearts and legs and hands and arms, as vehicles are better than walking as boxes and cans and chemicals and insect killers and insecticides are better than natural foods and grains and vegetables and wasps and praying mantises and birds and lady bugs. Just as plastic trees and flowers are better than the real ones. Artifice and death are the same.

—And Art? What about Art?

—How can Art exist when we live by the familiar and not the unfamiliar? Art is the spirit disembodied. Living only in the thing itself.

—What then is the thing itself?

—The word. Nothing else.

—Nothing more?

—No. Because you'll take away its disembodiment. We have done with nounizing and verbalizing and polylinguisizing. To say "angelsaxon" is still a Renaissance pun like "Look for me tomorrow and you'll find me a grave man" or "*Que beau ce*" for the land of Beauce. The spirit is in the word. And always has been. It is not the words that are dead. It is the language that we strap them into. Treating the human soul as if it were sick and deranged. Needing control and the corseting of grammar. Adulterating and violating their movement and essence. Telling them and writers what they can and can not do. Telling us literature is the poem or the story. When all words being spirit are poems. When all story. Is destruction of truth. When all language all narration that moves in a straight line because it follows logic because it is continuous is truth. What is organic is true. And nothing else. What is organic is true to itself. And not to language to logic to common sense, to literature, to grammar, which are all false artificial and sick and dead. And corrupt. As the tradition of anything is corrupt and dead. Because it represses life.

—To civilize then is to fossilize?

—Yes. And to stop movement. To dam up the spirit like you dam up a river. To repress and discourage invention creation individuation. To destroy person and personality. To civilize and collectivize all in the genre and the species. To make literate.

—What a paradox! And I thought culture civilization were the preservation of life.

—The perpetuation of someone else's life. Not your own. We are all taught to plagiarize and be parasitical. When we relate to others we are borrowing other people's lives.

—Isn't this because we are afraid of the self?

—Because the self is unfamiliar. As life is unfamiliar. Only death is familiar and recognizable safe and secure. Who said death is unfamiliar? It is all around us. The substance of our daily living of the collective life of the race. If we ever hope to retrieve our souls we shall need new forms that demand nothing less than the adventure of probing within ourselves to find the lost spirit that is in each of us.

—Do you truly honestly believe that we are possessors of individual spirit?

—As surely as we believe in life and don't practice it as surely as we allow others to possess us and play others games and not play with ourselves our own games I do. There is nothing that stops us from possessing ourselves. The right of ownership comes from the moment we cry out, from the moment we breathe.

Arranging Flowers from the Garden

—Arranging flowers from the garden?
—No. But yes. As thoughts. In colors. Form. The petals. Forced by bees. To gorge. To open. Perfume. Pollinating air.
—Hopping to a way for centering. To balance. In the takeoff. For the flight.
—Precisely. As for us to marvel at exposure. In the nude. Of colors and of forms. Each variegated kaleidoscoping star or sunbeam. Or lotus. Arrowshaft. Orb or sphere. Formed by the color. Or the color in the form.
—The infinite of minuscule. As worlds contained in whorls which nature nurtures.
—As we in finite largeness. Crudeness of our space. As occupiers. Trespassing upon the universe. In small or large. The micro-macro cosmos mystery of the soul the flesh the self the creature kingdoms that surround for taking of our usurpation greed and fabricated would-be hungers. Killing for the sport of kings. Antelope Lion Elephant Buck. Or Mafia revenge seekers. Or jetsetters. Setting the pace for gawking copycats and mimicries of fashion-favored fools. Flaunting jests for jesters and punk freaks. Wail shouts and body struts. In peacock colored silk satin rags tatters ribbons chains belts bracelets earclips flashing gems and diamonded stones.
—Video shout tracks. Wailing and popping eyeballs through the sick night flights of hashish coke sniffs and stonings. On the street. Off the street. In dives and dens. In discos. Pads. Flats. And shacks. To and from. By sea. Air. Flight. Highway. Mountain pass. Canyon. Off road desert dunes. River run barge. Freighters. Cattle cars. Trucks. Speedboats. Copters. Yachts. Planes. Burros. The underground transcontinent transhemisphere country island commerce of the world's low and high life reject turn on turn off death-in-life life-in-

death buyers and sellers of self and strangers hookers and hooked addicts leechers parasites hawkers seekers suckers succumbing to the jungle rot going for the jugular of the artifice of existence as suspension in the nothing nowhere limbo of its kind.

—So life as limbo for some.

—More in number than we know or bother for the count.

—While yet a little longer. In the light of time. Of the planet's course of starburst stardust life we linger on the edge.

—Of what?

—Of moments. As eons of the second of what we are. The arrow of our flights of chance to choose. Or call it as it lays or plays. The wheel of cell growth soul merge self sense rise and fall. The swells and surges waves of struggles rolling up the hill and fall back of the stones of weights of trials and tribulations balancing out the scales of our existence such as it is.

—Or such as we hope for it or like it to be.

—So be it. Or wish it to be.

—So be it.

May 6, 1984

Essay

Art versus Reality: Spirit versus Matter

Everywhere we look, everywhere we turn our lives, our thoughts, our tastes, our commitments to ideas, our islands of privacy are being invaded.

The world of Reality and the Reality Principle—have become our prison. This means the divisive and corrupting influences that separate us from Authenticity and Truth—the transforming and transcendent generative level of the Spiritual versus the Material.

Religion, Politics, Money or should we say the Politics of Religion and Money have become the servants of the new Consumerism with Consumerism as the bandaid for an ailing Capitalism that sucks us deeper into the vortex of a junk society trashing us in every breath with pollutants of the dead, the useless, the obsolete, the tawdry and the meretricious. Junk food, junk cinema and TV, and theatre, junk music (rock and punk), junk industries, junk roads, highways, bridges, junk evangelical religions, junk education and, last but not least: junk publishing, have become our world of Reality.

Is this America's legacy to History, with nothing left over to Art or Spirit, Truth or Authenticity? There seems to be a constant erosion of the promise and potential of what we, as exemplars of a Free Society were dedicated to offer the world. Nothing lately but ashes, embers, dust, instead of any fire or flame or outreach of great and human commitments to inspire the vast majority to rise from its kneeling, cringing, crouching haunches to any standing or elevating or soaring reach.

Only one dimension can do this for us—not Politics, Religion, Money, Family or Tradition can remove us from the prison of the everyday life and its surrounds, of all that is painful, mundane and vulgar—and that is Art.

In America today we confuse and corrupt Art with Reality as we confuse and corrupt Politics with Religion, Education, Government, Industry, Publishing, Money, and so on.

We are losers for being confused over the nature of Art. The Creativity of Art, Literary form in its highest expression, is not Reality. It is a distillation, a Transformation or Transcendence, a special kind of Truth, of authenticity into Spirit. Contrary to the ideas of the vulgar, of the herd, of the Publishing Conglomerates, it is not an escape from Reality or from Life. It interprets. It distills. It creates. Gleaned and mined from the impurities and sweat and labor of its surroundings. Faceted by craft into the uniqueness of itself. Literature in its highest form is born from the roughness pain and labor of life into a special and unique creative experience that we cannot do without.

For unlike Religion, Money, Family or Tradition which feed on prejudice, material greed, hatred or repression and are divisive—the highest form of Literature as Art is magnanimous, humane, compassionate, loving, liberating us from meanness, pain, fear into hope, excitement, courage and dreams for the future. Art above all, is our comfort. It caresses us always as a loyal friend that never lets us down. It is generative, producing food for thought and beauty of spirit.

Sunday
March 25, 1984

Interlude

Tide Pool Beach Walk

Beach Number Four
Kalalock
Olympic National Park

Our walk begins.
        At 6:30 of the ante-meridian.
        By a minus two foot tide.
Down to the littoral past the beach walk.
        First we brush past.
        The event the happening.
        A breach of the marine protectorate
                Its eco-system cracked.
                        By adolescent thievery.
                The kidnapping by the bucketful hauls of starfish.
                        Pail after pail of them, the chubby hands.
That in our time built castles of sand and dreamed with the sea
    embracing.
        Now have advanced childhood into adulthood crime.
        To own, oneself, what belongs to all.
                By seizure and glee and carols of infant-devilish
                        laughter that boom out.
                        Echoing, cannonading every beach rock and
                                boulder.
                        These starfish are mine!
                        In non-surrender adamant and proud.
                        Carried by the wave of their own gratuitous
                                impulse.
                        They've subtracted a piece of the ocean, of
                                the future—of the Universe of sea.
                        That formerly momentarily to all belonged.

After the death-ritual parade and show of these infant killers.
Multiplied in tin pails.
Shriveled and dead.
    We descend, nursing hurt and shock.
    Silently into the green drizzle and haze.
    Groping towards miracle as fact, of the green world.
    Before a future transforms it to nostalgia after death.
    Sea anemones symbiotically algae-greened, nestled in
       their flesh.
    Or jasper-agated red by others of the same species.
    Barnacles, tubeworms minuscule to mammoth in colony.
With limpets.
    Acorn and gooseneck barnacles.
    Hermit crabs tenanting.
    Periwinkle, mussel, chiton-lined
razor, horse clams.
    Starfish red ochre regenerating their central disk.
    Red feather dusters.
    Sea weeds, sea kelp,
    Olive-brown leathery "wrack"
    Pale green lettuce of the sea.
    Red-purple pepper "dulse" sea-sack.
Rock-coitused in eelgrass brown, eelgrass olive, eelgrass red.
    And the shipworm clam burrowing immortal sculpture
      in the tidepool suburbs and friendly communes.
    The sculptured rock skeletons
    Proclaiming presently marine graveyards of the future.
Because the children of men learned the ways of the rapist and
    the bushwhacker.
And discovered too late.
What is death and destruction for all.

The Portales Notebooks

A Reply to George Steiner's:
"The Retreat from the Word"

Friday, October 27, 1967

As a writer, I feel at this moment in historical time, hauntingly alone, awed by the overwhelming and superhuman responsibility to which we have dedicated ourselves—the pure investigation into new modes of thought and the exploration of being, of *pure* being which we call the Neo-Narrative, a language of our own creation.[1] To follow some purpose unswervingly and inevitably without becoming eroded, tainted by the shouting blandishments and easy corruptions associated with ulterior motives of profit, exploitation, the pursuit of the commonality's definition of success—is not every man or woman's "cup of tea." The only security one feels (for being human, there are frequent moments of doubt, frustration, impatience, disillusionment) is the security (if one can call it that) of knowing that the dedication, the mysterious dedication, is not one of one's own choosing. It is at once involuntary and fated.

The silence that surrounds one must be comparable to that vast, mysterious, awesome, frightening silence of outer space with its new worlds, new universes to be explored.

The silence that surrounds us is akin to the intergalactic one since our position involves the slow and painful as well as often exciting discovery of new worlds, new universes of *being* inside man's psyche hitherto unexplored. Why new? Because the tools of language were not available until we found ourselves inventing our Neo-Narrative. And now it's all out there, in spite of the silence of virtual non-recognition thus far, on the part of the critical and literary community.

I find that Man's most prominent feature is his habitual tendency to imitate, because he is not a god, only thinks he is.

For example, Man's first powerful stage of imitation was the Renaissance. The Renaissance period prided itself on resuscitating the Greek and Roman cultural world from oblivion. This period established modes of behavior and thought that are still with us today. Along with learning about letters from their classical mentors, Renaissance man also copied the classical perspective, the classical way of embracing experience.

At first Renaissance Man was like a child gorging on the glories of the written word (printing was to the Renaissance world what our electronic world is to us today—our world of Radio and Television)—reading books (such a novelty in the expansive proto-commercial world of the 16th century). *Words* became exciting and entertainment was even verbal in the lyrical explosion of madrigals, ayres, and so on.

By the time we arrive at the 17th century there are "rules" for writing odes, couplets; the sonnet is not only frozen, but parodied in Drayton, and cynicism with Donne expresses its reaction against the idealistic innocence of the Renaissance born of great discoveries in the humanities.

We have idol worshipped the Renaissance mode with its emphasis on Greek proportion, mathematical and logical balance until now. (I have written an essay: "Man as an Idol Worshipper," which explores this subject and concept, included in *Seasons of the Mind.*[2])

As a result of this dominant Hellenic perspective we are left with no resources to view the revolution in science (completely anti-logic with its preoccupation with accident and probability) which has affected painting and music and also literature (the existentialist drama of Ionesco, Beckett, Pinter, etc.) the illogical yet valid nightmares of Kafka's world of anti-justice which were later to become a Middle-European reality, etc. (Kafka is the most significant influence on Brecht, Ionesco, Pinter, etc. Aren't they translating into theatre what Kafka envisioned decades before it happened?)

Now with the rise of electronics, bad TV and bad Radio have engulfed listeners and viewers who were formerly readers.

But literature, the future of letters, the product of man's creative instinct must survive if man is to survive.

George Steiner's article-essay: "The Retreat from the Word" (*Kenyon Review*, Spring 1961), is an example in point, of a brilliant intellectual scintillating fireworks display by way of an exploration of the low estate of the *word* and its problematic

survival in this age of computers, electronic news and informa-
tion data retrieval systems.

His examples are all based upon anterior and not contemporary philosophical investigations when he speaks of the Zen
and Trappist ideals of silence—the withdrawal from a speech-
cloyed, dead-letters world.

The ideals of silence and tranquillity which he says one
associates primarily with Eastern experience are not at all Western. Because we are all like Pascal, struck to terror by the vast-
ness of space.

I beg to differ. I am living in a state (New Mexico) with a
population of 1,000,000 people (New York City alone embraces
12,000,000 in its metropolitan area).

When first being exposed to the vast mesa butte and
mountain and plain and desert country of New Mexico, on our
first trips with not a gas station, village or just a cluster of
ranches for some 50 or 60 miles, I confess at first to a feeling of
strangeness, even of agoraphobia. But it did not take me long to
love and cherish as something precious and unusual in this
ever more crowded world, the sweep of space and geological
changing vista which I now prefer to almost any and all lo-
cales—for living, for stretching, reaching out one's thoughts in.
Space is contemplative Mr. Steiner. But its appreciation is not
limited to a Chinese or an Indian or a religious monk. To con-
clude categorically that Western man cannot appreciate cosmic
space is wrong, unless of course, you have become inured to
your environment of Western Europe (crowded Western
Europe) and to the classical view of letters.

Yes, it is true, we would agree that our traditional language for literature in English cannot cope with modern science
and its "space-time continuum of relativity, the atomic structure
of all matter, the wave-particle state of energy, [as] no longer accessible" in terms of the literary tradition.

That is precisely why without being scientists ourselves,
we began to atomize words, to make them work like particles of
energy, like light waves with electrical charges of interacting
force, bridging time, space, past, present, future, in an explosion,
a series of explosions of new forms and combinations of the
Word in the Neo-Narrative.

Words may function in any manner or means according
to the way they operate in a given situation, is a paraphrase of

what I explored in: "Notes on the Neo-Narrative," from my book *Abraxas*.[3]

Mr. Steiner thinks words give only other words. (In the traditional language of cliché they do.) But words engender thought (as I stated in the *Abraxas* introduction referred to above) if they are rearranged in a new creation, a new structure, proto-organic, a tabula rasa of the abstraction of the sentence. After all, the Greeks discovered the atom as they taught us to worship letters (humanities). It is only now that scientists are learning of the contradictory and unexpected nature of the atom which the Greeks attempted to harmonize into a system that we now find untrue. Because logic, like grammar, is only an abstraction, and only works if you accept the abstraction. But abstractions lead to dead ends as *logic* (which is now discounted in science, for probability) and *grammar* (which forms the basis for literature up to now, but must be also discounted, overthrown) are today.

Mr. Steiner, you will not find your new writer for the age in a Lawrence Durrell, as you propose, since you are using measurements that are classical and myopic. You wish someone "to keep literature literate." Ridiculous. This is the same as saying let's keep literature the way it has always been—Hellenic-inspired, logical, harmonious but untrue, fictional and mechanical and recognizable and *dead*. You can't have your cake and eat it too.

A new form such as the neo-narrative proposes to destroy the old "logic" of "grammar" and fiction with a "story," in an effort to restore to the *word*, its power of eliciting human, not fictional responses in the reader, to discover and build upon truth after truth in a new organic approach to the words we use, so that they become as exciting, as new, as breathtaking as a trip through outer space, enlarging our capacity of penetration into our own psyche as we penetrate into inner and outer worlds. Or as Albrecht Unsold's *The New Cosmos* (New York: Springer-Verlag, Inc., 1969) so aptly concludes: "Whether we penetrate into the depths of the universe or whether we search the mysteries of the human mind, on both sides we view a New Cosmos."

And the music that we'll hear from the Word will not be silence, Mr. Steiner. It will be a music of the spheres, as all great literature ever was, is, and shall be.

Notes

[1] See *A First Book of the Neo-Narrative*, Arlene Zekowski and Stanley Berne (George Wittenborn, 1954), available from American-Canadian Publishers.

[2] *Seasons of the Mind* (with the correspondence of Sir Herbert Read). New York: George Wittenborn, Inc., 1969. The volume includes: related essays, radio interviews, legends, a preface and manifesto.

[3] *Abraxas* (New York, George Wittenborn, Inc., 1964). The volume features Sir Herbert Read's last essay on literary aesthetics: "The Resurrection of the Word," later republished in *The London Magazine*. He regards the neo-narrative, as the culmination of the language breakthru from Mallarmé, Valéry, Joyce, to Zekowski and Berne.

Essay-in-Dialogue

The New Cosmos?

> "Each individual is also the child of a people."
>
> —Hegel,
> *The Phenomenology of Mind*

> "Whether we penetrate into the depths of the universe or whether we search the mysteries of the human mind, on both sides we view a New Cosmos."
>
> —Albrecht Unsold,
> *The New Cosmos*

—Why is to find what is *new* so necessary?

—It is a question of *survival*. All around us. Everywhere. The planet's girdle. In its states and countries. Little petty kingdoms and fiefdoms of power and assertion. Islands of escape from brother enemy friend lover mistress spouse children sister father mother relations governments bureaucrats ruler and ruled. The miasma of the stench of our pollutants upon one another. And our world and other's world. On land and sea and river and mountain. In bedroom boudoir and school and church and office and library. In the streets and alleyways. Parks and garbage dumps. Slaughterhouses and fish stalls. Apartments houses bungalows cottages condominiums health resorts mineral spas mountain cabins fishing camps ski slopes forests and trail heads ghettoes in purgatory and the 9th circle of hell swamp forests of guerrilla fighting guerrilla prisons of the apartheid village or otherwise death rows of the lost abandoned crime and sex and thrill killers and the hallowed and hushed World Bank temples and Consortia of the money changers and money lender and blood price pound of flesh usurers breaking the backs and necks and ribs and starving the bellies and sucking the blood of consumptive dying Third World countries groveling with broken bones and knuckles to climb upward into the light of day and life from their sinkhole of poverty and disease and unconsciousness. All around us. From the mountain. To the prairie. City Village Cave Jungle. Desert Ocean. Life struggling against life. Death around us in us. Always hovering to claim its own. Against the synapsed current of the biomass energies of discontinuities. The quanta leaps of movement motion change. The universe of life ourselves within. And life the Cosmos Nature without.

—Is there no peace? Is there a meaning to it all?

—Peace? Are you kidding? Are you serious? Death is Peace. And even then the cycle of dust of garbage of putrefaction decay rust and rubble a la Truk lagoon where the sea grave of Jap rusted sunken ships fossilized into coral of sea legumes and fisheries and mangrove swamps filter eroded sludge beaches and tropical downpours into new barrier reefs of life.

—What's the meaning? Where is the world life going? It repeats and repeats. The more it advances. The more it retreats.

—Human? Or animal vegetable mineral?

—Are they the same?

—Yes. And no. A mystery hardly to fathom. Since we as humans are a part of it all.

—So there is nothing. Nothing to fathom.

—I did not say that. The more we fathom. Penetrate the planet and ourselves. The more it all has changed. From what we were or knew before.

—But the meaning? The value of it all? Are we liberated in any way? Or into further mystery and conundrums?

—I do not know. Except the feeling that like Adam first tasting the fruit. Found that it was good. Pleasurable. Satisfying. Knowledge is a feeling of security against fear. All around us. From animal to man. We are imprisoned by fear. Fear of the other. *Das Man*. In men as in nations. And so we war. Or saber rattle. Like rival Shamans trying to outscare each other. We bluff. Battering rams or bull elephants or trilling warbling birds. To assert our territory. Our power over one another. When it is all a charade. A comedy of atomic law. A universe God of Physics and the constellations from the Cosmos of our cells and atoms and molecules and DNA-RNA sensorium structure of our body-mind stream as the fissure fission explosives of our nuclear indifferent Hermaphroditic Yin Yang Sun infant star of our miniscule constellated planet system ringing days nights millenia until the black hole moment in time and space when it will be sucked in sucked out again to nova pulsar pulsate into beginnings and endings as far as we can know or see or understand at this moment in the time-space continuum of our lives.

January 8, 1985

The Jiggle Jangle Juggle of the World

—As from out within which. Flying to the demands. The inner commands. Of bells that buoy. Or that chime. Their bronzing exhortations. To look alert. To look without. The salutations of the world's work and thrust upon the self. Against the struggle. Against the tide and swell and surge and shouts. To drown us. Each and every soul and shred of soul. The inkling of the tinkling from within. The still small voice of opposition. In assertion. Of whatever is authentic in our lives. Against the cut and thrust of other people's rub and grain. This is the challenge and the raison d'être that we trial our innards against.

—Is the world's work then demeaning? Do we absent ourselves from others? Do we run from the overheated kitchen? Shall we hide in our closets when or if all hell breaks loose?

—There is no running to retreat. But there is running. Yes. There must be running for survival.

—Survival how. In a hell's bells helter-skelter world?

—You must run after what you need.

—At what price?

—At whatever price to pay the price for its own sake. Everything must be for its own sake. Or otherwise we perish. We sacrifice whatever authenticity we struck or sucked at in our mother's milk.

—And do we escape from the lynchers and leechers. The killers and parasites. We imbibe society. We imbibe the world.

—And so we do. As always it was is so. And so we must live as best we can. And best the animals and engines of destruction. From family squabbles haggles over dead meat vulture kills of money and wills and legacies over who gets what and how much and gimme gimme gimme for car rentals and repairs

and dental bridgework and food supplements to welfare checks
and child and brother and sister and mom support and plane
and train emergency travel and house repairs and tornado wind
hail fence and roof insurance and medicine and pharmaceutical
prosthetics orthopedics and doctors and diet health farms and
hospital care and nephews guitar lessons speech therapy leg
braces wheelchairs taxis to clinics therapy vacations first and second mortgages city state federal excise luxury food and income
taxes, losses from thefts burglaries, collision and life and fire insurance, pensions and social security, annuities dependents typewriter and computer repairs, gas and oil and car tune ups trailer
repairs, heating and cooling telephone water and utility costs
plumbing refrigeration washer and dryer freezer heater and
jacuzzi well pump breakdowns, grass cutting watering, lawn and
tree feeding upkeep, and then there's the government.

—What about the government?

—Whether. After and during and through the struggle to
emerge and not to submerge. To survive through the hassle of
it all. To play the heaves and swells and surges and bureaucratic
behind the back knife thrusts of power climbing over the wreck-
age of the costs of another's challenge another's defeat. To
smother and not be smothered. To swallow insult and argument and gossip and rumor rangles of lies and fabrications and
jealousies and fears and hates and machinations in the world of
work in the deadly outer reefs of family quarrels and succubus
importunate oedipal wailings and beratings of you don't love us
him or her ungrateful child we brought you into the world and
is this what we get in return. And so on. And so on. And if we
survive all this and more. Then it's the government that ulcer-
ates.

—Yes. What about the government?

—Governments are like families. And employers. They
are not soul builders. They are people destroyers. In the jungle
of the world. You jive to their jiggle. It's the dance of life. The
challenge.

—What challenge?

—Why the challenge. The jest to foil the jester that is
you. To survive. All around you. Obscenities of destruction.
To destroy a world that wants to live and let live. Against power
structure emperies. Pitted one against the other in the ring. The
poker game play bluffs and braggadocios. Confrontation instead
of accommodation. Child's taunt power plays on and on. Ob-

scenities of wealth 5 million a year executive stock options in a free oligarchic capitalist empery where one in seven souls exists below the poverty line. And so on. Where in another totalitarian socialist empery. Armies and battalions and military booby-trapped walls. Surround and imprison client states. Muzzle souls minds bodies thought into silence or conformity. Where ethnocentricities of plural tongues races civilizations. Once and former outposts of culture. Are genocided into a racist programmed state political religion of Authority. And so. And so. The jiggle jangle juggle of the world. Our life and times.

May 10, 1984

Inevitability

—As the delve down will of circumstance provides. Contingency draws as the blood and marrow of the bones. Articulation calling for the words. The essences of things.

—As ideas or as feelings?

—You cannot separate one from the other. No more than you can abstract God.

—Is not God an abstraction?

—We'd like to think so, wouldn't we?

—Well. Yes and No.

—Exactly both. The all encompassing. The pain and suffering and sorrow and joys and fears. The order and chaos of the world. And of this our lives. To blame it on. To shake our fist at. Clench our sweating palms. And cause our lot. Of no or little luck. The happenstance of fate we call the God. Determinator and terminator of our lives. When all along it is ourselves we must create. As self-substantiated beings from the morass of our flesh and bones and blood and mind and spirit.

—That would be Nietzschean in the extreme.

—Art is extreme. Life is extreme. And fate is the fart of a bad joke. That others perpetrate upon our lives. And the odor and the breath of it. The methane stench is gas gas gas.

—Not to believe in any of it then? In Art. In Life. In Fate?

—The Art. The Life. Shaped by ourselves which is the Fate?

—And Luck?

—Luck is of the time and tide. The ebb and flow. Flotsam and jetsam. And of how we see ourselves in the surrounding waters of our struggle to maneuver. To keep alert. To shape and plough. And run with the current. The rhythm of our lives.

—We can't always be on top. What about the storms?

—The rages. The storms. Are generally from within. We say we try to do our best. To reassure. And wait a moment for the weather of disturbances to pass. Which it generally does.

—If we have the patience.

—Yes. If we have the patience.

—The images of others. The icons of their fears. To smother and to lash us to the mast. And flagellate us with their hates and passions. Are what we all must suffer from. One way or another in this world. Their configuration versus ours. Is what the struggle in Society is all about.

—We cannot always go it all alone.

—Yes and no. When to pull and let go. When to listen and be silent. When to speak out and assert. Are the issues of our lives which no one can resolve but ourselves.

—In America we work by consensus. The politics of the herd. Of the lumpen majority.

—That's why America is going nowhere. Frenetic movement to stand still. The status quo.

—The quid pro quo. You lick mine and I'll lick your ass. While the shit flows round and round. On the merry-go-round of our trash society.

—And if you back away from it all. And reject the recycling of our *modus vivendi* of *mediocritas*. The consumerism pragmatism materiality ne plus ultra of our lives. You're branded as elitist.

—Excellence. Individuality. Creative thought. Ideas. Global versus national concern. All subversive.

—So what to do.

—Do and act and say whenever however whatever you can. To the best of your abilities and beliefs. And hopes and convictions.

—Even though you appear to be losing?

—Was the Emperor less naked even though the majority believed he wore new clothes? Do family skeletons exist even though they're kept hidden in the closet? Are the facts less true even though they're reported as lies?

—But the majority can always be manipulated.

—The concerns of conscience and of soul of spirit of art of truth of mind of ideas of evolution of the facts of life on this planet of each and every one of us in our time and in the destinies of our future cannot be eternally and perpetually withheld denied rejected and refused.

—So there is hope?
—There is inevitability.

December 22, 1984

Essay

Literature and Language for the Year 2000:
Poetry-Prose Neo-Narrative Open Structure

*(A survey of some new
twentieth century views and approaches to literary forms.)*

In a taped interview Memorial Day 1979 at the Municipal Building studios of WNYC-FM, with Professor Walter James Miller, broadcast Monday, February 11th on "Reader's Almanac," I suggested that the *innovative* literary artist writes literary criticism as an "apologetics" to his/her art, largely because of falling prey to the socio-political crotchets of the general run of literary critic (bereft of a knowledge of contemporary forms of abstract art, music, psychology, anthropology, biology, physics and their bearing upon modern aesthetic and linguistic philosophies)—in our mundane culturally warped reviewing scene.

Consequently I speak here *as a critic by default*, after the fact and practice of a life-long literary art.

In my own writing I have chosen to pursue a "tradition" not yet recognized as such—of breaking away from the *linear temporal grammatical* mode of the last 250-300 or so years. Today this mode has reached an impasse, a blockage of thought and expression, rudderless in the sea of possibilities that loom like awesome icebergs to those who fear necessary inevitable *change*, which they view like seismic shudders of quakes on the Richter scale.

The "tradition" that is as yet no tradition, is the direction the English language has taken thus far in the 20th century in the writing of James Joyce, Virginia Woolf and Gertrude Stein, with adaptations by William Faulkner and others.

What do these three writers share in common, despite or because of their literary "idiosyncrasies" that distinguishes them from most other writers and writing of the 20th century?   In their work, for the first time in 250-300 years, there is a total rejection of a *linear temporal* language as a vehicle for structuring reality and the human consciousness.

Whether you refer to James Joyce's *Portrait of the Artist as a Young Man, Ulysses, Finnegans Wake* or Virginia Woolf's *To the Lighthouse,* or *The Waves* or Gertrude Stein's *The Making of Americans, Operas and Plays, Ida,* 20th century language in these literary works is no longer an extension of an established tradition but of a new "tradition" which most of us are unaware of or do not recognize at all.

It is a *new tradition* because a tradition is an instinctive acceptance of something, consciously or unconsciously realized. And all of these writers regardless of their distinct and individual characters *no longer accepted the language of the previous three centuries as a vehicle for twentieth century literature.*

Regardless of the language used (Swahili, French, German, English, Chinese, Russian, Arabic, Navajo), there are three components of expression which all writers reflect in all times and places: *spatial, temporal, grammatical*—and these are all related to our visual or perceptual way of viewing what we choose to call reality.

Today, "grammar" is greeted with general revulsion by the vast majority who have been successfully brainwashed against literature by successive generations of forced-fed English composition. Nevertheless, even if secretly detested, everyone thinks that grammar, like spinach, vitamins or health food, is good for you. In *Against the Disappearance of Literature,* I characterize this phenomenon as follows:

> Freshman college students, for example, experience a 'Time-Lapse' and 'Jet-Lag' that is biologically as well as psychologically and intellectually unnerving and disturbing when their imagination and sensibilities are not engaged because of being strait-jacketed into writing and reading according to grammatical structures which are really *analytical* and *scientific* rather than *esthetic* and *literary. Beauty* and *form* which are a part of nature as well as literature are thus denied them. They do not know for example that language soars from the printed page in its metamorphosis into sound rhythm tone accent emphasis—elements of voice, speech, music, etc. As a result they are tone deaf as well as tactually inert to what words say and mean and feel like and their sensory power is lost, buried in the

> jargon of grammar and composition surgery performed
> upon, what is for them, already lifeless matter.
>
> (Page 27)

But essentially *what is grammar* and *who are the grammarians?*

By broadest definition, *ars grammatica* is the art of written structure, nothing less and nothing more. Structure by whom?

In the last 300 years, grammatical art has been no art at all, not being practiced by artists of the word, of the language, but instead by invading autocrats who have preempted the inherited role and legacy of the written language (formerly belonging to the literary craftsman), to themselves, imprisoning, circumscribing, bureaucratically controlling, distorting our instincts about language into frozen artificial forms that they call "grammar." Or, as I have described this in *Notes on the Neo-Narrative—2nd Series*, originally published in *Critical Assembling*:

> Literature existed. Before grammar and grammarians.
> Stamped discipline rote drill upon language. And substituted logic for thought.
> People read Literature. Before grammar. After grammar. They wrote. Parsed. Sentences. Forgot Literature. Hated to read. Dreaded writing.
> Writers. Innovators. Liberators. Inventors of language. Despised. Grammarians. Policed language. Imprisoned. Circumscribed. And proscribed.

Thus we have latterly come to associate *grammar* with the way it has abused language and made it unpalatable, making it an uphill struggle for innovators like ourselves and others, whose fate it is to be practicing an art largely despised and unappreciated by the majority who instinctively blame the creative writer for the sins of boredom, constipated rhetoric, pomposity, intellectual aridity, committed by their enemies: the grammarians! Whereas before the era of print and publishing when language was still free floating and organic, close to speech, plastic and resilient to its time, reacting to moments of change, to the *feel* of the word and its structure in its true relativity of application and circumstance, free of proscriptive definition analysis or mundane vulgar "conformity," nobody questioned or doubted who the true, the genuine authors or authorities of language were: the writers themselves, the crafters of the art of the language. So that if we choose to be purists, the makers of the "grammar," of the structure of all language were Homer, Dante, Chaucer, Rabelais, Shakespeare, Milton and their modern counterparts: Joyce, Stein, Woolf. And all the other artist innovators in between the earliest and the latest, across the centuries.

In sum, what we call grammar today is a *perversion* of the art of language, and the grammarians, *corrupters*, *slanderers* and *thieves*, who should be driven, flushed out of language and human consciousness, swept away in a great burning of all the tomes of rhetoric that have been conceived, force-fed and eternally undigested in an unhealthy tumulus of verbal detritus and degenerate pseudo mathematical logic-oriented boot-camp jargon of rules, definitions, regulations, speech part shreddings, purged out of us at last and not too late before we lose all sense of the love, art and beauty of human communication in language.

From the late Renaissance on, *language*—which before printing technology had never differentiated between the written and spoken word—suddenly became *linear, one-dimensional*, where formerly it had been *plastic* and *multi-dimensional*. Line by line, sentence by sentence, subject verb predicate order virtually destroyed the free floating spontaneous images of speech into abstract rational analytic frozen and fixed standardized discourse. The *metaphor* or *image*, the *neural* source of all creative thought (poetry or prose) was gradually buried and forgotten through the dominance of science, the rise of positivism and cause-effect "logic" that suddenly superseded truth.

As Time was gradually blocked and circumscribed into units of cause and effect, so *language* became limited to what the cause-effect sentence could do. No one questioned why sentences were said to express thoughts or whether logic was really true until our way of *seeing* changed again from *words* as synthetic pseudo-scientific abstractions back to *images*. This new way of seeing occurred first with the invention of the instantaneous photograph that revolutionized the classical traditional "grammar" of painting from reproduction of the *visible* linear flat plane, to creation of the *imaginative* multi-dimensional plastic interior-exterior world of the artist's own perceptions. Subsequently *the sentence* in literature, was gradually rejected in part, or modified by Joyce, Woolf and Stein and their followers, for *the image*. As a result, *cause* and *effect*, invented by an earlier more deterministic age, became no more valid for post-Newtonian science than for painting or literature. *Exploration* and *possibility* became once more *limitless* in a finite but unbounded 20th century Einsteinian universe.

Reviving the pun of the earlier Elizabethan Shakespearean era, Joyce simultaneously created a polyglot neologistic almost private language as his solution to the staleness, rigidity and mundaneness of English: "There's the Belle for Sexaloitez!" (Angelus bell and female, Latin six for the angelus rung 6x.)

Virginia Woolf united poetry and prose in the embrace of the metaphor, hating what she called the ponderous unnatural masculine sentence:

> But it is still true that before a woman can write exactly as she wishes to write, she has many difficulties to face. To begin with, there is the technical difficulty—so simple, apparently; in reality, so baffling—that the very form of the sentence does not fit her. It is a sentence made by men; it is too loose, too heavy, too pompous for a woman's use.... (*Collected Essays*)

Gertrude Stein thought a more simplified grammar and time sense would revive a dying language, developing the principle of the *eternal present* and *repetition* with theme and variation as a cosmic pattern organic to life and speech:

> Always from the beginning there was to me all living as repeating. . . . Sometimes it takes many years of knowing some one before the repeating that is that one gets to be a steady sounding to the hearing of one who has it as a natural being to love repeating that slowly comes out from every one.
> (*The Making of Americans*: 264,
> *Selected Writings*)

But Stein, fortunately to her credit, created as much out of and beyond old grammatical structure as she did simplifying it within an eternally present Steinian time.

Although both Joyce and Stein experimented with language beyond grammar, they did not pursue this possibility as a solution to the dilemma of the artificial linear structure imposed upon English literature for the last 300 years. Virginia Woolf in emphasizing the eternal unit of the metaphor, somehow managed to skirt the ultimate ogre glaring in the distance of 20th century literary expression cutting off circulation: *the sentence itself.*

* * * * *

Sooner or later *the sentence* had to be confronted. This, I decided, was what I would have to do. Not consciously, deliberately or arbitrarily as many seem to think, but instinctively inevitably, as it turned out to be.

I was fascinated with the play of language, not just in an intellectual and scholarly linguistic way, as was the case with Joyce's scintillating vision, or in the brilliantly analytical enigmatic way of Stein, or in the haunting, musical, poetic-prose of Virginia Woolf. I was concerned more with getting at a language that would extend the possibilities of both the *mind* and *sensibilities*, the multi-level consciousness of feeling, dreaming, sensation, thought, the areas of buried mystery and potential—a language that would speak to every human being regardless of time, place, circumstance, ethnic, social, mythic, psychological milieu—of reaching into the immediate, simultaneous, spontaneous present as into the unknown potential of the future, as unbounded as defiant of encirclement as possible.

Exploring and experimenting with a more *geodetic* spatial form, more in harmony with the space-time dimensions of the twentieth century, I had to discard more and more, the traditional syntax of linear one-dimensional grammatic structure. In addition, *the sentence*, that vestigial anachronism of 18th century narrative vision, would likewise have to go. Just as there are roles we all must play, *there are different forms of language to meet different circumstances.* As far as I was concerned, *in art, a sentence was not a thought.*

In the introduction to *Abraxas* from "The Word as Creation and as Thought," in "Notes on the Neo-Narrative," I rejected the whole tradition in language, of speech parts, in addition to explaining the role of the *word* in art:

> There are no different parts of speech for the creative maker of the future just as there is no particular musical scale for the composer, no particular combination of colors for the painter as there is no particular combination of forms for the sculptor.
>
> The combinations in any art are as multiform and mutable and infinite as Nature itself.
>
> And words are all and everything according to the way they function. *They can paint they can make music they can sculpt they can dance they can sing as well as speak.*
>
> If it is true of the medium of all forms of creation it is true of words in language. . . .

> Thus, in art, the sentence must be destroyed because it
> never existed.
> Only words exist. And words engender thought.
>
> (*Abraxas*, 1964: 29)

About twelve years after the introduction to *Abraxas*, I
wrote a book of literary criticism: *Image Breaking Images: A New
Mythology of Language*, elaborating my thoughts on language,
art, religion, feminism, psychology, science, literature, education,
etc., with frequent passages expressed in neo-narrative open
structure dialogue form. I had gradually come to realize that the
artist in language affects not just the art form but eventually
other forms of usage and application as well, and had to arrive at
the inevitable conclusion that *the sentence was no more meaningful in everyday communication than it was in literary expression*:

> Why is it difficult to teach the sentence in grammar?
> Because in reality the thought continues. The unit of
> 'thought' of perception, if you will, is not a 'sentence'
> but a cluster of clauses or images. When does it end?
> Certainly not mechanically or arbitrarily with a pe-
> riod. The period is merely a mechanical device in-
> vented by the grammarian's fanatic sense of logic and
> warped sense of truth. The thought, which is a series
> of percepts, or clusters of images concepts constellating
> or elaborating upon or enlarging or exploring or probing
> or accentuating in any way or manner contributing to a
> state of being or motion or emphasis, what the totality
> of all these parts of which the sentence is a part, con-
> tributes to the entity or whole.
>
> (*Image Breaking Images*,
> 1976: 115-116)

A companion book of literary criticism by Stanley Berne,
expressed the following, regarding *the sentence*:

> The enforcers of the Sentence are the enforcers of
> thought control: teachers, and the police. Both are no-
> ticeably little thought of.
>
> The Sentence is not organic to language. Only thought
> is.
>
> The Sentence has become, unhappily, an industry or
> factory wherein youth are manufactured, if they allow
> it, into exact replicas of the demonstrated failure that
> the humanities have become.
>
> They do not speak or write Sentences on Mars.

> The Sentence is the argument of Dictators to read arbitrary law to the impenitent political prisoner about to be sent to the camps.

> The airplane defied walking, as the imagination defies the earth-bound Sentence.

> Thought will not be confined, private conversation is never conducted in Sentences.

> The Sentence is the 18th century brush stroke of Sir Joshua Reynolds: all portrait, drapery, and horses.
>
> *(Future Language,*
> 1976: 26-30)

Even in inflectional languages like Greek and Latin upon which English grammar was arbitrarily pretentiously and inorganically based, *sentence word order did not originally exist.* According to Charlton Laird, there was "the strong suspicion that classical grammar was not the grammar of any living language, even in classical times" (*The Miracle of Language,* 1953: 143). The inflectional form or case ending was all that was needed. You could mix or scramble the word (verb, adjective, adverb, noun subject or noun object) according to its emphasis in the context. And that is most likely how Vulgar Latin and its adaptation into French, Spanish, Italian and Portuguese came about. People would not put up with seven case endings just as today school children avoid the lingering vestigial apostrophe of the Latin possessive, the only case ending left in English. (See Stanley Berne, *Future Language,* 83-87, on the frustrations of teaching the possessive to incoming college Freshmen.)

Likewise, with *ideographically* structured Chinese, which had even much earlier abandoned an inflectional case ending for the more economic, more metaphoric image of *distributive* sequence and position usage. *Ming* or *mei* as noun, verb, adjective: "The sun and moon of the cup" (the cup's brightness) or "The cup sun-and-moons," "Sun-and-moon cup" reflect the comprehensive simultaneous concretion of the images. (See these and other examples in: *The Chinese Written Character as a Medium for Poetry* by Ernest Fenollosa, translated by Ezra Pound.)

A similar conversion of *word as image* obliterating *word as syntax* Shakespeare observes throughout his work. As Simeon Potter points out:

> Shakespeare was probably the first to use *window* as a verb in the sense *to place in a window* ('Wouldst thou be

window'd in great Rome?': *Anthony and Cleopatra*, IV. xii. 72) and *to make full of holes* ('Your looped and window'd raggedness': *King Lear*, III. iv. 30). Shakespeare used adverb as verb ('That from their own misdeeds askance their eyes': *Lucrece*, 637), or as substantive ('In the dark backward and abysm of time': *The Tempest*, I, ii. 50) or as adjective ('Blunting the fine point of seldom pleasure': Sonnet, lii).

(*Our Language*,
1954: 57)[1]

Even earlier, Old English was less agglutinative, more inventive, creating its own image and idea organic to its own structure: *godcundness*, divinity (godkindness); *swegcraeft*, music (sound or melody craft); *sodfaest*, righteous (truthfast); *breostcearu*, anxiety (breastcare); *ealond*, island (sea-land).

Navajo is also a neologistic language incorporating few European words, preferring its own verbal structuring: tomato is "red plant"; elephant, "one that lassoes with his nose"; automobile (*chidí* or *chuggi*), in imitation of the sound of a car; gasoline (*chidi bi tó*), car's water. And like Shakespeare's English, Navajo is a language of the verb, with nouns as nominalized verbs. Its unique poetic precision economy and conciseness is described as follows by Clyde Kluckhohn and Dorothea Leighton:

Because so much is expressed and implied by the few syllables that make up a single verb form, the Navaho verb is like a tiny Imagist poem. . . . One Navaho word more often than not turns into a whole sentence in English: *haadinsh'aa*, I hand it over to him by word of mouth; *shíí'iid*, He gave me a piece of his mind, *híínáál*, You are shuffling along sidewise; *ná'íldil*, You are accustomed to eat plural separable objects one at a time; *hanicóós*, You take a fabric-like, object out of an enclosed space.   (*The Navaho*,
1962: 269-270)

The image-making power of Hopi also demonstrates the life of the *concrete* essential to all language resilient to the plastic organic energy of the *word*: *Apónivi*, Where the wind Blows Down the Gap, place name; *chosposi*, bluebird eye, turquoise beads; *Lepénangtiyo*, Icicle Boy; *Ponóchona*, One Who Sucks from the Belly, the Dog Star; *sivaki*, iron horse, train; *tasupi*, before the sun has pulled down all the light, twilight; *simocho*, squash flower before it opens; *túoinaka*, stack of corn, ear jewel (Frank Waters, *Book of the Hopi*, 1970: 416-423).

These are only a few of the myriad possible examples from the nature and structure of language as organic to the *word* and not to any superimposed arbitrary symbolic logic of syntax of grammar and the sentence.

* * * * *

It is time to kill a narrative that you know everything about, and create new stories out of new forms, and new forms out of the sensory experience of the modern world.   (Arlene Zekowski,
Cardinals And Saints, 1958)

The new language must have a texture of its own that seizes all our senses so that with it we can feel the poetry in every pulse beat of the prose, and vice versa, . . .
(Arlene Zekowski,
"Rhythm, Texture and Communication,"
Seasons Of The Mind, p. 139).

. . . the Neo-Narrative involves a use of language (words, phrases, which change their functions from noun, verb, adjective and back again, etc.) familiar to all of us but arranged differently in order to express experience, knowledge, extension of being or multiple and simultaneous dimensions with multiple and coexisting frames of reference. It is using language finally in a contemporary sense, in a post-Newtonian way, non-geometric, non-Euclidean, non-linear, anti-absolute, spherical, organic in depth, with length, breadth, width, time, intermingling in new combinations and new discoveries, allowing ideas to suspend and immerse themselves in exploratory dimensions never conceived of before.   (Arlene Zekowski,
"Relativity and the Neo-Narrative,"
Seasons Of The Mind, p. 162)

Soon after the appearance of *A First Book of the Neo-Narrative* with excerpts from *Bodies & Continents* by Stanley Berne and *Grounds For Possibilities* and *Hemispheres* by Arlene Zekowski, our *neo-narrative* was described by Roger Martin Adams of *The Hudson Review* as: "A device for responding directly to reality without the clumsy intervention of grammar," and referred to thereafter as the *grammarless language*. With the appearance of *Future Language* by Stanley Berne and *Image Breaking Images* by Arlene Zekowski, our second books of literary criticism, we tended to incorporate as theory what we had heretofore largely only suggested in our earlier collaborative work of 29 essays: *Cardinals & Saints*, but of course demonstrated in separate and individual creative works of short story, novel, poetry and drama (*The Dialogues, The Multiple Modern Gods, The Unconscious Victorious, The New Rubaiyat*, Stanley Berne; *Concretions, Abraxas, Seasons of the Mind, The Age of Iron*, Arlene Zekowski). That is, *the reduction of 300 or more rules of English syntax in a work of literature to no more than two*: the *period* and the *comma*, each of which we had adapted to our own particular style: the *periodic* (Zekowski) and the *kommatic* (Berne).

In our *periodic* and *kommatic* expression we have acknowledged the legacy of Joyce, Woolf and Stein, perpetuating a new, a more open 20th century structure of writing which not only supersedes 18th century grammar and the sentence, but furthermore—in a language based on the *word* as *image—no longer separates poetry from prose*.

* * * * *

There are many variations of both the Berne *kommatic* and Zekowski *periodic* in each of our works, with combinations of both forms.

In his "Foreword," Berne describes *Bodies and Continents* as follows:

> *Bodies and Continents* is a novel that uses the body itself as a point of departure from which to examine the external world. The novel attempts to show that body and external world are one, interacting on each other in a way that cannot separate one from the other . . . seeks to express the simultaneous existence of all things, as they exist to our perceptions, and as they lie hidden also, but are part of our consciousness.   (Stanley Berne)

Sight, sound, touch, feel, smell, all seem to converge upon the exultant aliveness that transcends body into soul and back to body again as mind and spirit soar and transpose person and place, as in this opening passage from Chapter II of *Bodies and Continents*:

> *Awake*
> To sing (hours stolen).
> Are fill. Hear.
> What cries are far as ferret.
> Eye round. Slow to feel there lie and wait as all grace
> and pay and for their area of veldt as mountain high

are to swing to, . . . soul, that hunger throat that moves
of feel and nest as hair and short are fall and spread as
all the sea shakes and feels of liquid moving as the
tempt, out, smell, shall rise, vast, shall reach, as eye
the doze and shape.   (Stanley Berne,
Bodies and Continents,
A First Book of the Neo-Narrative, 1954)

The theme of *Bodies and Continents* continues in *Legs and Crevices* (Berne), with the body in coitus, defeating death by copulating into immortality:

I seed, I fat, I grow and enter at the moments of her
limbs and lips and spread and dancing and hollow of
her parts and music as the wind that spread and legs
and entrance there with my points unthinking to enter
and spit and leave and soak and withdraw, defeating
time, invigorating life, catching death, *defeating it*!
(Stanley Berne,
The Fault, 1975)

With *Teeth and Tongue* (Berne), the human body and the body of earth finally merge as one:

Short as I am.
I need the well.
The water of blue color. (Beneath the earth. Gur-
gling round and licking over the rocks.) I have never
seen, but want for the lips. Want fall and ask and
around and envelop and warm. Want as the love of the
plants that deep as their roots are people living.
(Stanley Berne,
Intermedia, 1976)

As Berne states in his "Note About the Title," in *The Unconscious Victorious And Other Stories,* life and history coalesce in the ironies of the unconscious defeating the conscious of man's will:

And beyond this, is the future, always hidden, somewhat menacing, . . . yet approaching, inevitable, unin-
vited 'unconscious'—and always victorious over man's
will: always devastatingly victorious over his dreams,
prayers and hopes.   (Stanley Berne,
"*The Unconscious Victorious* is the future")

In "Brown Earth as Medium," from *The Unconscious Victorious* (Berne), the Roman wars become the principal theme:

of Alva who loved to kill, . . . of 45,000 in battle
slaughter lying for the men to come at night and steal
the money, jewels, swords, . . . killing for ideas mis-

> taken, for leadership by deviates . . . the feeling that it
> is hopeless, that the mad world is right, . . . small ex-
> periments sweated, perfected, given to the world as a
> bouquet of flowers—   (Stanley Berne,
> *The Unconscious Victorious*
> *And Other Stories*, 1969)

Berne's recent work: *The Great American Empire*, published in 1982 develops Roman themes as the major mirror images of today's America:

> The vogue for hair was well on then, before the next
> phase of shaving, shaving of the shagpot, so to speak,
> the scalp now carefully cut and shaved and polished,
> both men and women, the whiskers gone, sideburns,
> mustaches, even eyebrows for both sexes, smooth as bil-
> liard balls and very smart and modern indeed, quite
> suitable to the people whose style of life had brought
> them colonies on the moon and on mars—
> (Stanley Berne,
> *First Person Intense*, 1978)

* * * * *

Though in my own writing the unit of thought has always been the liberated *word*, which is structured in clusters of
images basic to all literary form, past, present and future, there is
a difference in the style of the writing from the fifties against the
writing of the sixties and seventies. In *The Sudden Testimony*,
Salt From Sacraments, *Lazarus: Book I*, written around the time
of *Grounds For Possibilities* and *Hemispheres*, the images are
radically compact, the emphasis a multi-facetted reverberation
where the shock of language seems to exult in a wild almost intoxicated abandon from traditional more conventional patterns.
The following, from Chapter XXVII of *The Sudden Testimony*,
published in *Kayak* 26 and *Delirium* 4/5, emphasizes the rich
marine decay of the barrier reef its symbiotic life/death aspect
where nothing is wasted:

> Who tastes. Who sends to seas. And weeds. And
> salt. And fatted globuled seaweed. And the jellied
> muck. The fired sting of arms. The fish in star. The oc-
> topus in rain. And streamered bone. And wired eel. All
> these. All wastage. Wampum. To the reef which
> grows. And stones. And offers lime. To stay. Secures
> the kill.   (Arlene Zekowski)

also, where each structure and moment of art, of nature, of the universe, has its own season, its growth maturity and purpose, as in this final motif of the work:

> A loom looms. Blankets. In a cloud. A mountain gathers snow. Each thing to seasons. Seasons what it grows.
> (Arlene Zekowski,
> *Kayak* 26, 1971 and
> *Delirium* 4/5, 1979)

Lazarus: Book I, excerpted in *Intermedia* (see earlier passages in *Measure*), was conceived as a composite portrait a kind of moral allegoric fable of every sentient person's awakening to the conflicts tensions shocks surprises of mind body experiences, the murky confused hovering awareness of the self, family and others, shadowy reflections of fate and struggling spirit:

> The strands he straddled. Then now when. A boy man. His fin ribs. Fishing for the rib that quaked and caulked. Caked with his salt fears. Bobbed over in the bob-cut hair. Buster-browned as his shoes. As his suit of ulster. Blue. Collaring the cut keel of his sail-end tie. Shadowing the man.
> Winded now. His horse prance whistled. By the brine-lapped railings. The railings railed.
> Down his spine. Lazars one by one derailed. Rattled single by single latch. And gutter cornice. Stone and rubble. Rabble shutter. Gabled gravel slate and tile. And shuttle. Wood and soot and chimney. Filings.
> Tar scarred. Mullion millioned mildew. Light died in the drib-drab. Smell. Cracked in the shell. Where glass shimmered. For the last time.
> Each landing. Nestled in a nave. Upright. The secrets preyed. Storey by storey. Hymns rushed up. And scolded. The house kneeled down. (Arlene Zekowski,
> *Lazarus: Book I,*
> *Intermedia,* 1976)

At this time absorbed in the reading of the Book of Genesis I found myself writing a neo-narrative prose fiction in which I tried to recreate a kind of 20th century verbal orchestral lyrical choreographic topographic bas-relief of those remote times people and events. Here is an excerpt from *Salt From Sacraments*, Chapter XIII on David and Bethsheba, published in *Kayak* 18:

> As music moved. Slowly. By difficult shootings. The ways of its own. Proved. Rain as age. Of life. Long hidden. Cry. Singing sang. Dry to wet. The same. Joy rang. Was.

> Lays were. Wherever fruit fell. From the mother.
> Under side. To mouths. Youthing. Their hunger. Fed.
> Off spring. Of kind. Warblings. Where the brook
> trout swam. Bathsheba breasted. To the window.
> From. Where David saw. And feasted. Drinking. Af-
> ter.
> As before. The waiting. To be known. Makes.
> Made. Where music was. As rain beat days of rain.
> And other days. To be.
> Moves the cloud. The burst. The rain. Bowed out
> from under. On the colors. Is. As positive. To hue. And
> cry. The God.   (Arlene Zekowski,
>   *Salt From Sacraments*, Chapter XIII,
>   *Kayak* 18, 1969)

There is also a spillover, in Chapter V of *The Sudden Testimony* (published in *Delirium* 4/5), of the energy and preoccupation with those remote times, the harmony of people and nature:

> As so. A chapter falls. To tombs. Lie hidden. Cov-
> ers between. The pages of the written afternoon. When
> there these every very ones to say. Said all. A monu-
> ment in mausoglyph encyclopedias.
>
> As full. They lived. These ours. Ancestried. To
> none except themselves. The first fruits. From no first
> fruits. Fallen. Angels were. The only. After. Towards
> reward. A seeming. Necessary for. Necessitied.
>
> To try to read. Where sun was. And the rivers.
> Why they gave. As open. Mouthed in belly oceans.
> Jarring generous. At sometime. One time holy. All the
> way then. Tried. Easy as a whisper. On the windside.
> Blowing was. As climate a caressing. As time all space
> in outwardly. A bounce above below the never in. No
> pressing of the beam. Light. Lighting. Sound. Less
> stars their singing. The velocity to near as far. As was
> is. Always and forever for. No rushing. Needed.
> Rhythmed. The all. Of a piece. Whole. Was.
>   (Arlene Zekowski,
>   *The Sudden Testimony*, Chapter V,
>   *Delirium* 4/5, 1979)

In our most recent critical volumes we decided to write a small critique of each other's writing as well as our own. This is an excerpt from Stanley Berne's descriptions of the following segment from Chapter XIII of *Grounds For Possibilities*:

> All the blazon. And the flags.
> That summers. Birds. And feathers.
> In their under. Leaves. The tree.
> (Zekowski)

In this small sampling we have the very essence of the summer season described, the birds in their feathers or plumage, landing on the full leafed trees which are like flags of the season, and the birds are naturally part of the trees. . . . What Zekowski is saying here is that original language was a picture, not an abstraction. 'Birds.' is a separate picture and does exist apart from specie detail, while, 'And feathers.' returns that knowledge of the structure of birds to its separate common characteristic. But the conclusion, 'The tree.' gives us the on-going process in which it, the tree, 'summers' the feathered birds: and all taken together, the birds, their plumage, the full leafed tree, and the shelter afforded by the tree to the 'Birds.' are the flags and blazon of the glorious moment 'That summers.' or IS Summer. *(Future Language*: 61-63)

Conversely here is my commentary on Stanley Berne's "The Man in Space" from *The Multiple Modern Gods And Other Stories*:

> From Stanley Berne's 'The Man in Space' in *The Multiple Modern Gods* I've selected a portion of what looks like a minimal poem where the only punctuation is the period instead of his more characteristic comma. Remember again punctuation is used as organic relation in our writing. This is from page 78.

> Narrow hall.
> Few books.
> No art. No God.
> God of the old man.
> He alone spoke.
> God as his best friend.
> He spoke little.
> His conversation was prayer.
> A store was his church.
> A box was his altar.
> His law, a Hebraic roll.
> Love was God.
> Curse was wife.
> Wigs and piety sincere.
> Simple annals of the poor.

In keeping with the theme of the book's title: *The Multiple Modern Gods*, there is now juxtaposed the 'No

> God./God of the old man.' who is we find a jealous ex-
> clusive selfish all-consuming yet piety producing mod-
> ern sterile god. All of these impressions are suggested
> by the stabbing ironies of the hail of words which pen-
> etrate into the reader like arrows hitting their target.
> The poverty of fanatic spirit is complemented by the
> pathos-irony poverty of the church site, 'a store' and of
> shock-effect poverty of the altar: 'A box. . .' The wor-
> shipper and priest is no more than an animal in a
> pavlovian cage existing on the stimulus-response level
> of 'Love was God./Curse was wife.' The shock of this
> bestial fanaticism is redeemed by the half-compas-
> sionate half-ironic 'Wigs and piety sincere./Simple
> annals of the poor.'   (*Image Breaking Images*:
> 141-144)

Abraxas, a work symbolizing the all-embracing Mind-
Word-Multiple Heavens Sun God of the Egyptians, also invokes
life and death, religio-mythic enslavement, cyclic nature and
dreams:

> The lowering of hours to the grave. Or higher re-
> gions of the mind. The iron portals which Egyptians
> called the doors of sky. The amulets. Abraxas. And
> the gnomic names. The Elohim. And Ra. And Adonai.
> The serpents we must crush beneath our powers of com-
> mand. As yet they ride. And still our voices. In the
> vice and grip. And nature of what is. . . . The pollinat-
> ing earth and sea of earth and sea. . . . As phallic.
> Thrusts its urge to grow. To generate. In names and
> numbers. And in forms. The meat. And cushioning.
> Which fleshes over. And which feeds. As windows on
> the world. And on our dreams.   (*Abraxas*,
> Arlene Zekowski,
> 1964: 108)

At the beginning of *Abraxas*, the settling of the American
continent emerges as a composite of the myth of nature and
human history as well as America:

> All that after purple. Clogged.
> In seas of dreams of struggle. As
> by far to move. America.

> Here we have a series of images which call to mind
> the animal-like fecundity of the sea from whence
> emerged the original source of the purple worn by the
> ancient Phoenician, Greek, Roman, and later Egyptian
> kings, that is, the Murex dye extracted from the species
> of mollusk which bore it.

To muse over the source of the most royally symbolic color is indeed to dream of the past and to evoke
the 'seas of dreams of struggle' which the wearers of
royal purple often lived through literally all their
lives.

These human struggles of the Old World past, are
suggested as part of the very marrow sea and landscape
of the New World, since even America is moved by
those very same titanic dreams of ambition: 'As by far
to move. America.'. . .

America is ever so friendly as we say here, ever so
ironically:

> America.   What burst of
> praise.   The handclap.   To the
> vulture. In its sea of sins.

America's grasp is friendly but amoral. It embraces
'the vulture' which is predatory and full of destruction,
a veritable 'sea of sins.'. . .

We are like the winds Western and dry that surround us and symbolize our struggle. We merge and begin to resemble our own harsh landscape:

> The large past.   Never stop-
> page.   Of the winds.   That
> crackle up our skins. Like burnt
> pig. Brown and smoky sweet.
> We burn. We surge. We gasp.
> We wonder. And we die. To
> dream. The birth of million fa-
> thered blooms.

We are rather low and porcine-like in our stubborn
mindless thrust and struggle. But the view is double-
prismed, much like Pascal's view of man, noble in relation to his ideals, ugly in relation to the material
world. Thus: 'We burn. We surge. We gasp. We wonder. And we die.'

Our whole human struggle, ambitious as it is has
something both titanic and ridiculous about it. And certainly melancholy. And perhaps immortal and as creatively marvelous as a flower with its blooms, since '. .
. we die. To dream. The birth of million fathered
blooms.'   (An Exposition of Chapter VI,
                                             (*Abraxas*: 46-50)

* * * * *

Some of the themes in *Seasons Of The Mind* contrast *Man thing* versus *Man thinking*: "My country 'tis of thee!/Sweet land of profitry./'Let junk-heaps pile!"; Western druidic kinship of peoples: Anglo, Spanish, Navaho, Zuni, Hopi, mingled with adventurers, fur trappers, hunters, scouts, pioneers, conquistadores, against modern man's buried ancestor-indifferent soul; History and Religion as "fictions" and "lies" versus Art as . . . "life-loving and life-giving"; Knowledge consisting not of Platonic recollection of pre-existence, but of moving on into the future; and Reality, the "evolution . . . flux and flow of our feeling moments, the one true progress of the soul":

> And so we say goodbye to all the past. To all the pain and hate and horror and confusion. And wait in never resting. Restless expectation. For the flux of life within us. Each and all. Continuous and becoming. To be part of. In all our courage. And our fear. The glory of it all. Unknown. As all true glory. Of the true life. Always is. But must be in its full aliveness. Being what it is. In full becoming. Flowering and alive.
>
> (*Seasons Of The Mind*)
> Arlene Zekowski,
> 1969: 111)

Seasons Of The Mind, and the two works of the 1970s, *The Age Of Iron And Other Interludes* and *Histories And Dynasties* all explore and further develop one of the motifs introduced in *Abraxas*: the settling of the American continent as a myth of nature and of human history. Here is a selection from *Histories And Dynasties*, a book published in 1982.

> So blessings on you. Wild Bill Hickock. Calamity Jane. Kit Carson. Coronado and Cortez. And Buffalo Bill. The friend of kings and presidents. Pony Express Rider, Buffalo Hunter, Frontiersman, Army Chief of Scouts. America's and the worlds' greatest huckster. Barnum of the West. And your Wild West Show. . . . And the whole darn breed of America's bummy seedy dustgrit greedy seething whiskey-bellied cowpoke huckstering lily-livered puritan hell-fired purgatoried god-fearing bible-toting man hating indian killered bushwhacker mine and cattle stealer desperado, hired-gun vigilante justice rough and ready roistering bite the dust, hangman railroad gangman and the whole glamor bag of smart-aleck frontier get-with-it success or succumb philosophy of exploit or be exploited. And carry the white man's burden. Which happens to be a bag of

gold. And not his sins be hanged. Be hanged if you do.
And be hanged if you don't.

("Chapter XXI,"
Histories And Dynasties by Arlene Zekowski
Published in Voices from the Rio Grande, 1976:80)

In *Seasons Of The Mind* and in Stanley Berne's *The Unconscious Victorious And Other Stories*, we included, along with
transcripts of several radio interviews, Herbert Read correspondence, our most ambitious essays to date on language rhythm
and texture, poetry and prose, the novel and short story, literature and science, high art and low art: above all, a *new kind of
story*, a "fiction" based on the authenticity of experience, not on
the old traditional literal "fiction" of a predetermined plot, constitutes our view of *literature for the year 2000*:

> But it can never be the function of dedicated author-
> ship to allow the genius of words to be the servant of
> another art. . . . The critics of literature seem to set
> their jaw in the stubborn direction of forcing writing to
> serve the cinema, by insisting there is but one kind of
> narrative, and that is cinematic narrative.
>   . . . the short story can do the things that only lan-
> guage itself can do, which the camera cannot do, . . . op-
> erating within the frame of the action of language it-
> self.   (*The Unconscious Victorious
>   And Other Stories*,
>   Stanley Berne, 1969: 158)

> Story means simply a telling of something. The
> concept of story has become cliché because the telling of
> something has been reduced in the novel to an arbitrary
> form known as plot.
>   Plot as we know it must be destroyed because in this
> form the reader does not experience anything new. . . .
> Story then simply means exposure to a new frame of ref-
> erence in the form of a narrative which does not follow
> any familiar recognizable sequence but which creates
> its own.
>   Every man and every woman who constitute the
> readers of the new narrative become, if you will, the
> 'characters' where the responsibility of being exposed
> to an experience is no longer at last a fiction but the
> truth. . . . Only with the New Narrative will the old
> saw take on its true old and new meaning: 'Truth is
> stranger than fiction.' And only with the encourage-

ment of what is true, can literature breathe authenticity now and in the future.   (*Seasons Of The Mind*,
Arlene Zekowski,
1969: 158-160)

Note

[1] See also: "Notes on the Neo-Narrative," "The Word as Creation and
as Thought," in *Abraxas*, 1964: 28-29.

References

Berne, Stanley. *Future Language.* New York 1976-1977.
Berne, Stanley and Arlene Zekowski. *Cardinals And Saints: On the Aims and
Purposes of the Arts in Our Time.* New York, 1958. (Distributed by
American-Canadian Publishers, Inc.)
—. *A First Book of the Neo-Narrative.* Sections from three novels. *Bodies &
Continents* by Stanley Berne. *Grounds For Possibilities* and *Hemi-
spheres* by Arlene Zekowski. Stonington, Connecticut, 1954.
(Distributed by American-Canadian Publishers, Inc.)
—. *Grounds For Possibilities* in *Future Language* (1976-1977): 61-63.
—. *The Unconscious Victorious And Other Stories.* Including the
correspondence of Sir Herbert Read; three radio transcripts on the
Novel and Short Story; six related essays and a Preface. New York,
1969, and 1973, Horizon Press.
Fenollosa, Ernest. *The Chinese Written Character As A Medium For Poetry.*
Translated by Ezra Pound. Washington, D.C., 1935.
Kluckhohn, Clyde and Dorothea Leighton. *The Navaho.* New York, 1946.
Laird, Charlton. *The Miracle of Language.* New York, 1953.
Marckwardt, Albert H. and James L. Rosier. *Old English Language and Litera-
ture.* New York and Toronto, 1972.
Moore, Samuel, Thomas A. Knott and James R. Hulbert. *The Elements of Old
English.* Ann Arbor, 1955.
Potter, Simeon. *Our Language.* London, 1954.
Stein, Gertrude. *Selected Writings of Gertrude Stein.* New York, 1972.
Tindall, William York. *A Reader's Guide to Finnegans Wake.* New York, 1969.
Waters, Frank. *Book of the Hopi.* New York, 1970.
Woolf, Virginia. *Collected Essays.* 1967.
Zekowski, Arlene. *Against the Disappearance of Literature.* Troy, New York,
1997.
—. "Notes on the Neo-Narrative," "The Word as Creation and as Thought."
Abraxas. New York 1964. (Distributed by American-Canadian Pub-
lishers, Inc.)
—. "Notes on the Neo-Narrative: 2nd Series." *Critical Assembling.* New
York, 1980.

—. *Image Breaking Images: A New Mythology of Language.* New York, 1976.

—. *Histories And Dynasties.* New York, 1982.

—. *The Sudden Testimony. Kayak* 26 (1971): 47. Reprinted in *Delirium* 4/5 (1979): 95-98. Other chapters in *Intermedia* of Vol. 2, No. 3 (Spring 1979): 25.

—. *Lazarus: Book I. Intermedia* Vol. I, No. 4 (Winter-Spring 1976). Other chapters in *Measure* 5 (1974): 13-18.

—. *Salt From Sacraments. Kayak* 18 (1969): 44. Other chapters in *Center* 6 (1975): 64-65.

—. "An Exposition of Chapter Six, *Abraxas.*" *Abraxas.* New York, 1964. (Distributed by American-Canadian Publishers, Inc.)

—. *Seasons Of The Mind.* Including correspondence of Sir Herbert Read; Three radio transcripts on New Influences in the Novel and Short Story; Ten related essays. New York: 1969 and 1973, Horizon Press.

Also see *Interstate* 5: Chapters 7 and 11 of *Histories And Dynasties; Interstate* 6/7: *Seasons Of The Mind,* Chapters 7 and 8: *Image Breaking Images,* Chapter 7; *Kayak* 49: *The Sudden Testimony:* Chapters 3, 4 and 5; *Center* 11: *Histories And Dynasties:* Chapters 7 and 26.

For publications by and about Arlene Zekowski; consult "A Selected Bibliography" pp. 165-171 in *Image Breaking Images.*

For publications by and about Stanley Berne; consult "A Selected Bibliography" pp. 145-150 in *Future Language.*

The Portales Notebooks

A Visit with Georgia O'Keeffe

Tuesday, November 14, 1967

We are approaching another Thanksgiving holiday which reminds me very much of how we spent last Thanksgiving in a visit with the American artist Georgia O'Keeffe.

There was first an exchange of correspondence back and forth. The visit was actually precipitated by our sending Miss O'Keeffe copies of *Concretions*, with illustrations by Milton Avery and *The Dialogues*, with illustrations by Matta. (Both of these books, incidentally are now, unfortunately virtually out of print.)

We drove out of Española over a rutty thoroughfare which in New Mexico passes for a main highway, passing hamlets of adobe houses, the red chile drying in festoons like some exotic jewel pods, from the roofs and hand-carved wooden pillars of the porticoed porches both Spanish and Western in style. Each adobe house had its own small farm of corn, cotton, sorghum, or raised a small herd of beef cattle. The cottonwood trees were still covered with their autumn yellow leaves and they would be seen clustered around a stream bed with the backdrop of the golden pink sandstone mountains and hills covered by juniper and pine and forming a brilliant orgy of color contrast as we rode by.

The country towards Abiquiu where Georgia O'Keeffe lives is both lonely and intimate. It is what we call in New Mexico, contemplative and meditative. The hamlets are few and far between and if one is driving, one fills the gas tank full, either in Santa Fe or Española before starting out, because the gas stations are as few and far between as the hamlets, and some villages do not even have gas stations.

The buttes and mesas in this country are the strangest and most spectacular, the shapes, the colors, the textures unfolding before one's eye like a series of small Grand Canyons, one more surprising than the other.

It is sculptural and painterly and old. Time goes back a long way and nothing seems to have changed and in fact has not changed. The villages' inhabitants are most of them descendants of the early Spanish Indian and Anglo settlers a few of whom have intermarried so that the genealogy after a while becomes blurred.

The country is also Catholic and Penitente which means that a certain medievalism and mystery pervade the region with its old-fashioned Spanish courtesy.

The name Abiquiu derives from the Indian Pueblo Abechiu because the Pueblos were living in the region when the Spanish came and took it over first for Spain and then for Mexico sometime prior to the mid 18th century. There was caravan traffic between here and the markets of Chihuahua Mexico with rejoicings and fiestas of celebration when the caravans returned safe and unharmed.

In the mid 19th century the region garrisoned the Americans who protected the area against Indian attack. The Ute, Navajo and Apaches threatened the region from 1747 on.

There was also the famous santero painter Molleno of Abiquiu who painted saints on hand-hewn boards. Known as the Chile painter, his *santos*, with their chile decorated corners and designs, are easily identified in the churches of Trampas, Ranchos de Taos and museums of Southwestern art.

The river Chama runs through this fertile valley making it possible for the region to both grow and stay the same with its fertile valleys of corn, chile and fruit trees.

It is this region which Georgia O'Keeffe has adopted as her own for the last several decades. Today one cannot think of Abiquiu without its past history, without its geologically fantastic vistas or for that matter without Georgia O'Keeffe. Abiquiu is Georgia O'Keeffe and Georgia O'Keeffe is Abiquiu.

Wednesday, November 15, 1967

As we approached Abiquiu from the highway leading out of Española, we were surprised to find nothing but a gas station whose attendant informed us that the town itself was located on the mesa above the highway. He pointed to a secondary road with a fairly steep incline which skirted the mesa and served as the only access to the town.

As we climbed we could see a series of adobe outcroppings resembling from that distance the early 11th, 12th and 13th century Indian cliff dwellings, along with Taos Pueblo, their prototype, still being lived in by Taos Indians to this day. We were later to discover that these adobe buildings were part of Georgia O'Keeffe's home which commanded from its mesa location the whole sweepingly magnificent view of the Chama valley below and the near and far sandstone cliffs and mountains.

When we arrived at the top we found ourselves in the town plaza which included the ancient Spanish church, old by several centuries. Children busily engaged at stick ball were chattering away in Spanish playing around the church walls.

We parked for a moment to ask an old dignified Spanish gentleman who was chopping wood, if Miss O'Keeffe lived somewhere about. He pointed to a grand manse surrounded by cottonwood trees and evergreens and a walled adobe enclosure as the home of "la señora O'Keeffe."

We took the short dirt and gravel road leading to the house and parked outside near the cliff escarpment.

Two rather vicious looking dogs barked at our approach and the cook and general housekeeper (who lived in a cottage with her husband, the caretaker, alongside the main pueblo adobe enclosure) told us that Miss O'Keeffe was taking her accustomed "siesta" after her lunch and would we please wait. We sat and waited for some three-quarters of an hour, impressed with the stark simplicity of the living room in which we were seated. There was not a painting to be seen, just art books and phonograph records, the art books carrying the titles of such presses as Skira, Phaidon, Abrams and others, the best of their kind. Many of these art books dealt with Oriental, Polynesian, Indian and Asiatic as well as African and other art. The records were complete scores of Bach, Beethoven, Brahams, etc.

The floor which was of Indian mud (typical of a genuine adobe dwelling) was covered with throw rugs here and there.

There were velvet covered pillows of muted earth-warm beige which served as cushions and backrests against the adobe stone and mud banquette that extended on one side as a natural addition from the wall itself. This too was traditional or typical of the earlier Spanish and Mexican Colonial interiors of the region. At the far end of the room was a floor to ceiling French window which looked onto a patio of cottonwood trees in their golden fall coloring.

The effect of the room was calming and meditative. Everything, the design, the sparse furnishings with its velvet cushions, a cane rocker and few chairs communicated the austere yet consummate taste of the inhabitant and designer and architect who was Georgia O'Keeffe herself. She later told us that the house had been abuilding for 20 years; and one could see how much it constituted an organic expression of its owner and the Chama region.

We got impatient waiting and so returned to our camper and took ourselves a siesta. To our surprise a tall thin slender grey-haired lady wearing a long simple black skirt and white blouse with just a trace of a flare or flounce, came out to greet us. First she seemed flustered, irritated, prima-donnaish, explaining that she had not expected anyone, that she was expecting company (some strangers later in the day, prospective buyers of her paintings). We patiently explained how we had not made a mistake, how we had followed the instructions of her last letter (there had been several intervening ones) which invited us to meet with her on the day we came.

She eyed us shrewdly with her calm deep gaze, noting how nonplused we were over her prima-donna temperamental expostulations. Noticing our handsome Royal Coachman Camper, peering in but not going into it in spite of our welcoming invitation, she commented on the fact that "We certainly knew how to live!"

She showed us the dogs which were her companions but above all watchdogs to scare off any intruders. We walked thru the front patio where the dogs gambled revealing their rather vicious teeth (I believe they were part wolf), and entered the salon where we had waited before.

We told Miss O'Keeffe how much we admired the later paintings (her paintings of the late '30s to the present where the emphasis was no longer on flora and still life, but on the texture of the New Mexican landscape) which conveyed a trance-like transcendental haunting quality of the timeless geology of this land, that exuded as well, something as classical in its own special way, as the most representative Oriental nature scene. Paintings like "Cliffs Beyond Abiquiu—Dry Waterfall 1943," "Red Hills Beyond Abiquiu 1930" or the tiny almost postage-stamp size marvel "Red Hills with White Cloud 1937" or "Above the Clouds" and "The Winter Road" both 1963, we had viewed with unqualified admiration at the September-October 1966 showing in the University of New Mexico Fine Arts Museum.

She sat in the rocker reminiscing about people and places and events. First she reminded us that the best of the more contemporary work had been sold during the earlier Southwestern showings at the Houston Museum of Fine Arts, for example, where her friend James Johnson Sweeney, one of the greatest aficionados of O'Keeffe, managed to channel the paintings to the best buyers.

O'Keeffe is about the shrewdest and most demanding of artists. Her straight-backed posture whether sitting or standing is symbolic of a certain commanding amour-propre and pride in herself as both an artist and a woman. With her long iron-grey hair tied behind her handsome head with its strong features of prominent chin and nose and piercing penetrating gaze, you know you are in the presence of someone accomplished who does not allow too much self-satisfaction in her obvious success to sway her from the necessary self-discipline she imposes upon herself. She reminded us of the fact that she walks several miles each day, out into the butte country to which she has become so attached and which now forms the backbone almost literally of her present (and to us, best) work. When Frances Steloff of Gotham Book Mart (who has been our mentor and friend for years as well as a friend of O'Keeffe) visited with her, Georgia scolded her for wearing dancing slippers instead of sturdy walking shoes. "Poor Frances," sighed O'Keeffe, "no sooner stepped out of the car to admire the country when she stumbled and broke her ankle!" O'Keeffe snorted huffily that Steloff was "strange" being a vegetarian (who can live on lettuce?) that she was senseless in not wearing the right footgear for walking in the country. O'Keeffe however was quite chagrined that Frances (bedridden during the whole visit) would not touch anything served her but vegetables and was too polite to inform O'Keeffe then and there that she was a vegetarian.

Of the UNM Art showing she informed us of how disappointed she was over the way they hung the show. Whereupon she herself took everything down and rehung it to her satisfaction. That is Georgia O'Keeffe imposing her will upon things the way she insists things must be. For they must be right.

When she complimented us on the beauty of *Concretions*[1] with the Avery illustrations and *The Dialogues*[2] with the Matta drawings, she wondered why we were not better known. We explained as best we could that the only answer we could give was the one the late Waldo Frank proffered some years ago when we visited him in the friend's apartment he occupied in the Village whenever he visited New York. (His actual permanent residence was in Truro, Massachusetts on the Cape.) He said that to be an artist, a writer, today, was much more difficult than in his day when the intellectual and creative élite consisted of a much smaller circle of people who knew and bolstered each other much more than it is possible today. Then the center of things was New York with the Stieglitz Gallery as its headquarters. Today artists, writers, composers, sculptors are scattered everywhere in Europe, in America, in large urban areas like New York, San Francisco, Los Angeles, Chicago, in university centers where they teach, etc.

Whether she understood our anomalous situation and our greater and harder struggle to impose our esthetic on a mass society, to appear in the several few magazines that count in the plethora of the hundreds that are born, proliferate and die on the constantly changing literary scene of today, we do not know. At any rate she listened quietly and thought her own thoughts. She told us of the time Frank Lloyd Wright, then utterly unknown, would come into the Stieglitz Gallery with a book and just sit silently reading, speaking to no one. It was only later that they found out who the distinguished looking silent gentleman was, who used the gallery as a library.

To our question of how well she, an anglo, got along with the rest of the community which was exclusively Spanish-speaking American, she presented us with an amusing story which revealed her consummate shrewdness in human relations.

During her first year upon arrival some twenty years ago, she wondered what she could do to help the children without hurting their pride in receiving any gift of charity. So she outfitted the local school football team with completely new uniforms and in this way perpetuated eternal good will throughout the town. La Señora was then and thereafter one of them. And so the children come to visit with her on Halloween and other occasions thereby virtually eliminating any mischievous pranks occasioned by idle curiosity, etc., etc.

She is also happy about the fact that the Federal and State government at long last recognized the needs of this otherwise bucolic but somewhat impoverished town by building them a free water installation pump and purifying plant. O'Keeffe was particularly pleased since the one she had built on her own property finally ran dry.

Although she could not in all sincerity see herself working in black and white and thereby potentially offering us illustrations for some future books she nevertheless urged us to visit with her in the future. And I do believe she meant it.

Notes

1 *Concretions* by Arlene Zekowski.

2 *The Dialogues* by Stanley Berne (George Wittenborn, New York, 1962). Available from American-Canadian Publishers, Santa Fe, New Mexico.

Interlude

Mapping the Neo-Narrative and the
Grammarless Language:

An Interview Conducted by Welch D. Everman[1]

For twenty-five years, Stanley Berne and Arlene Zekowski have been producing innovative texts which illustrate and articulate what they have termed Neo-Narrative writing, texts based upon a grammarless language. Their earliest efforts were championed by William Carlos Williams and Sir Herbert Read, and, over the years, critics such as Richard Kostelanetz and Henri Peyre have continued to follow and praise their works.

This interview was conducted on the occasion of the publication by Horizon Press of two new and definitive statements on the Neo-Narrative and the grammarless language: Berne's *Future Language* and Zekowski's *Image Breaking Images*.

Everman: One criticism which is often lodged against innovative literature of any sort is that it isn't literature at all. It has been said that experimental literature is written only to illustrate aesthetic theories and not for its own sake. Now both of you have often articulated the aesthetic theories of your own Neo-Narrative works. With Neo-Narrative, did the theories precede the works or were the theories outgrowths of work you were already doing?

Berne: Welch, let me say first of all that the work that Arlene and I did, first published back in the 1940s, that creative work came before any theory and the theory developed indeed much later.

Zekowski: We did it quite instinctively, and of course at the time we probably didn't think in terms of calling what we were doing a grammarless language. That probably would have frightened us. But in reality that is what has resulted.

Everman: In your Manifesto of 1962, you stated as a principle of Neo-Narrative writing that: "Thought is its own excuse for being." Exactly what did you mean by the statement? In other words, what is the relationship between your theories on Neo-Narrative and the autonomy of human thought?

Berne: It has always appeared to me that language such as we have it is limited and permits only a certain amount of thought to be exited from the mind. It always appeared to me that I had other thoughts that couldn't find means of expression in the language of ordinary logic and grammar. So my feeling was that I wanted to explore the meanings between words, the meanings around words, and the thoughts in my head for which no acceptable language seemed to be permitted.

Everman: So language as we have it is not sufficient to deal with the entire scope of human thought.

Berne: In a sense, I think this is something like Schoenberg's development in music. It's always appeared to me that grammar and language were something like the ordinary notes of the scale. When Schoenberg came along, you remember, he wished to examine the sounds between notes, and those sounds between notes and before the scale and after the scale are just as respectable as the absolutely lawfully limited number of notes in the classical scale. I felt that language was in that condition, and I wanted to explore every thought which any human being has in his or her mind for which no language would be acceptable. For me, the grammarless language or the Neo-Narrative was an attempt to explore those forbidden areas. And those areas are the areas which yield to the unconscious and the subconscious. Of course these areas do not necessarily respond at all to logic-oriented, mathematically-oriented artificial grammar formations.

Everman: Thought, then, is agrammatical?

Zekowski: I think perhaps what we want to distinguish in terms of explaining what we mean by thought today in the 20h century is that we are using a language to express thought by way of verbal communication that was formalized for us back in the 18th century. It seems to me that we went about doing something about the necessity of changing the structure of language.

Everman: Necessity? Why is changing the language necessary?

Zekowski: The reasons for a grammarless language or a new structuring of a language for literature and for all kinds of transcendent communication is of course in the realization that we cannot use an old structure to communicate 21st and 20th century consciousness. Thought really escapes from structure if it is going to do anything in terms of inventing ideas, expressing new sensory and intellectual relationships, and making people feel that they are not only living ideas and experiences but that they are also creating them as well. That to me is very important.

Everman: You mean that you see the reader as participating in the creative act of literature through the process of reading.

Zekowski: Writing has always been, and certainly is in our Neo-Narrative, a dual process of involvement both for the writer and the reader. Every form of literature has always been a form of communication, not just as expression of the writer himself or herself. If you are going to liberate thought, then it should not be restricted by any form of rigid limits to movement. The thought continues beyond the sentence.

Everman: Why is it important for thought to be as unlimited as possible?

Zekowski: Well, first of all, the *imagination* should not be in any way restricted. The imagination can be straight-jacketed, and of course, has been, not only for the reader but for the writer. In order for the imagination to probe and invent, it seems to me that the structure of the language should be as open as possible. That is what we mean by saying that thought is its own excuse for being. It should be permitted to exist and to flourish and to grow and to develop and to mature and to flower. Only in that way are we as human beings going to enjoy existence, to create new existence and new ideas for the present as well as for the future.

Everman: So the idea of Neo-Narrative is involved in the freeing of thought through the opening up of grammatical structure, right?

Berne: The idea of the Neo-Narrative is *new story*. We thought it was time for a new story since, in our view at the time in the 40s and 50s and 60s, the old story was by then exhausted. Everyone was repeating himself. But if you are going to create a new story, you are going to have to have a new medium. So we had two problems to solve: to create a new story and to have a new form. We didn't know it at the time but the new form is the grammarless language. We identify it as such today.

Everman: Your works began to appear at about the same time as the emergence of the New Novel in France. What is the relationship, if any, between your efforts in fiction and the writings of Robbe-Grillet, Butor, Simon, and others of that camp?

Berne: We were happy with the anti-novel movement, although it didn't seem to affect any novelists but ourselves in this country. We felt entirely alone. There were very few critics who understood what we were trying to do. We attempted to interest Gallimard in Paris in what we were trying to say. The American editor there introduced us to Butor, and we became friends. This still didn't help to persuade Gallimard that American literature of a new sort was at all worth their attention.

Everman: Are there any theoretical relationships between your work and the New Novelists'?

Zekowski: Both we and the French are concerned with getting away from the whole positivistic framework of language and thinking, in other words, getting away from the subservience to logic. Robbe-Grillet went about doing this by emphasizing something that he felt was anti-romantic, anti-symbolistic. I believe he wishes to emphasize the fact that there should be no meaning whatsoever in the content of the subject matter of his novels and stories. This, I suppose, is because he is emphasizing his interest in cinematographic, mechanical, visual detail. In fact, one

of the aspects he deals with in terms of novelistic inspiration, if
I'm not mistaken, is that the novelist should find inspiration in
the now classical techniques of cinema, that is flashbacks, cutting, montage, freezing of the photo, mixing, and the use of the
oral and visual. What I object to in Robbe-Grillet's approach is
that I have always been under the impression that literature was
an art in itself. Although literature can use influences from
other arts, in no way do I feel literature to be subservient to any
other art, such as cinema. But Robbe-Grillet practices this point
of view and in fact recommends that the novelist take inspiration from the oral-visual techniques of cinema. Now if you are
going to follow along these lines, you are going to depart from
what the Neo-Narrative is all about. We feel that in our projection of the use of textures, there should be no sensory limitation
whatsoever to the possibilities of the power of the word. Robbe-
Grillet is almost rigid in his relegation to the oral-visual camp.

Everman: So, in other words, you think that Robbe-Grillet has
only discarded one kind of limitation for another.

Zekowski: There is a very flagrant and startling difference between the French anti-novelists and us. That is primarily in the
fact that none of them has created a new form of language, a new
language. They have dealt with a new content which is anti-
linear, but we have created a whole new anti-linear approach
not only to the content of fiction but to a total new verbal form
of structure.

Berne: I seem to remember a piece of criticism some years ago
in which it was said that Zekowski and Berne seem to unite the
inner and the outer in a new combination. We have always
tried for that balance. It appears to me that the New Novelists in
France concentrate on the outer reality, whereas we have tried
for the integration of the inner and the outer.

Everman: It is true that Robbe-Grillet seems to be concerned
with the detailed description of the objects of consciousness, following his own variation of the phenomenological method developed by Edmund Husserl. Neo-Narrative works, on the
other hand, seem to take the direct *acts* of consciousness as the
objects to be described. Does that seem right to you?

Zekowski: Robbe-Grillet, in his theory, seems to argue for the exclusion of such attitudes in literary criticism as interpreting literature or incidents or ideas from novels and descriptions in novels in such a way as to exclude the so-called anthropomorphic or anthropocentric tendencies found in the pathetic fallacy, symbolism, and the moral interpretation of characters, ideas, and situations.   He does not seem to emphasize the purpose of attempting to exclude everything human from the presentation of description and characters and any form of plot that he wishes to project.   But it would seem to me that his attempt to be non-rigid and non-classic in literary critical interpretation causes him to fall into the very strait-jacket that he abhors.   He does, of course, emphasize phenomenology and he seems to insist that it is possible that objects can be described without any human reverberations, attitudes, interpretations or overtones.   In essence, I would think that since all forms of creativity are human, it would be very difficult to exclude any form of interpretation, even if you are going out of your way to enlarge the area of creative communication.

Everman: So you would not agree with Robbe-Grillet's basic aesthetic?

Zekowski: I understand his purpose, and it is laudatory, but I don't think we can go to the extreme of saying that what is important are the things themselves and that there should be absolutely no interpretations, no meanings, attached to those things.

Everman: I gather, Arlene, that you would have no objections to interpretive analyses of your own work.

Zekowski: If people want to attach interpretations to what I write, let them do so. I would not attempt to rigidify in any form of scientific philosophy any theory that limits any individual to an exposure of Neo-Narrative.

Everman: Well, given that Neo-Narrative differs from the New Novel, what is the difference between Neo-Narrative and the kind of stream-of-consciousness writing practiced by Joyce and Woolf?

Zekowski: Neo-Narrative is a further development of some of
the experimentation of Joyce and Woolf. There were times
when Joyce did deal with, shall we say, grammarless sentences,
but he did not develop that particular direction; he decided instead to deal with a polylingual frame and to create according to
his own particular expertise in languages a kind of polylingual
phenomenon involving, of course, the age old classical and
highly Elizabethan form of the pun. As far as Virginia Woolf is
concerned, what she did is probably closer in a pattern of direction to our work.

Everman: How so?

Zekowski: The reason I say this is that Woolf instinctively attempted to destroy the classical rigidity of separate genres of poetry and prose. She did this both instinctively and, I think, deliberately. At least one is much more aware of this attempt in
works like *To The Lighthouse* and *The Waves* than one is aware
of such techniques in Joyce where you have largely the vivacity
of conversation, the voice, in handling the polylingual techniques that he developed. In Woolf you will note that the prose-
poetry aspect of narrative finds the greatest emphasis, especially
in the use of certain transcendent effects that one finds in music
and other sensory and verbal ideas.

Everman: Stanley, do you find a similar link between your
own stories and the stream-of-consciousness techniques?

Berne: I want to answer that by condemning an element
called story or narrative, and this on two grounds. It seemed to
me that, after 1940, all the stories had been told. Now what I
mean by story is the orthodox novel-story of the 19th century,
the Victorian novel, if you will. As a writer, there were no more
stories that I could invent; every story invented had been told.
That is, the geography, the outlines of that story had been told
before by some other writer, and I was simply repeating techniques. The second point is that story today is false; that is, when
I looked at my life, I could find no part of it a story. In this I
agree with Woolf who indicated quite clearly to me that there
were no stories, only incidents, one layered on top of the other.
My life seemed to be this for me. As I began to study the mind,
and I did this in normal fashion, I found that the mind had cer-

tain universal laws, that is worked by sensory impressions coming at it from every direction. The two main directions were the
objective world and the inner world that the individual reacted
to or thought about. When I began to write seriously, I wanted
to do something which would move literature forward one step.
To do what had been done so well by my predecessors would be a
waste of strength. I began to try to explore the layered mind of
incident and objectivity. It was very clear to me that these elements layered one on top of the other came at one in a flood,
and it was that kind of flood which interested me. My work became a flood simply to try to be truthful to the way data was
coming at the mind.

Everman: So stream-of-consciousness writing, and Woolf in
particular, offered you something in the way of subject matter.

Zekowski: As far as the subject matter of Neo-Narrative is
concerned, this is the curiosity that I think you might find rather
unique in our work. We do not really take direct inspiration
from literature, and I think this is a dramatic departure from the
literary work of previous centuries. By that I mean, we have
taken all human consciousness, all human knowledge in every
area to be part of the province of Neo-Narrative. For example,
in previous works, you will find that some works deal directly
with geology, history, myth, and other areas of science as well as
more obvious areas of the human consciousness.

Everman: Both of you have mentioned Gertrude Stein as a
fore-runner of Neo-Narrative, though there are obvious differences between your works and hers. Would you elaborate on
some of these?

Zekowski: One area of psychology that Stein seemed to exclude
from her consideration was the area that followed William
James' explorations into the stream-of-consciousness mode.
James defined the stream-of-consciousness as a conscious and
logical development. Of course we have learned since, after the
explorations of Freud, that the mind does not think logically;
this was Freud's great breakthrough in his free association
technique. This particular technique was the one that literature
seized upon beginning with Joyce and continuing with Woolf.
Although Stein did instinctively play with words as non-linear

forms of exercise, she did not liberate herself from grammatical structure. I would say that Stein was in conflict in terms of what her instincts as a creative writer caused her to do with her magnificent experimentation with verbal cubistic imagery and her analytical training as a doctor and as a student of psychology where, of course, she followed the techniques of William James. Now James' techniques are totally alogical; I think that is why Stein did not focus her attention upon the autonomy of the word.

Everman: Well, she did experiment with the autonomy of the word, didn't she?

Zekowski: True, she experimented brilliantly with the autonomy of the word, but she did not theorize on the autonomy of the word. She was interested largely in grammar; she says so time and time again in her critical writings. As a result, her experimentations involve, of course, a kind of post-naturalistic technique called the continuous present. This was a newer and fresher handling of the present tense and other tenses, in participial forms, to give the feeling of simultaneity, of presentness to her writing. This, of course, is laudable and magnificent, but it eventually reached its own dead end, because the necessary liberating technique, it seems to me, in the 20th and 21st centuries is to take the construction of the word and give it all its plastic, liberating, reverberating potential and possibility. Consequently, that is why we differ from Stein.

Everman: Because Stein was still involved with grammar?

Zekowski: If you are going to accept consciousness as your point of departure, then you accept grammar; the two go hand in hand. But if you are going to accept all the potential and vibrant and unlimited areas of the consciousness in all of its visible, invisible, subconscious, and extra-sensory forms, then you cannot accept linear structures like grammar and you must create a non-grammatical language if you are going to allow new forms of consciousness to generate and to create.

Everman: You've mentioned the autonomy of the word several times, and that makes me think of the Tel Quel group in France and other younger writers who are placing a great emphasis upon the literary text as text, that is, as a purely verbal construct. Do you feel sympathy with their work?

Berne: I am in great sympathy with the Tel Quel group in France. We met with Sollers in Paris when we visited there several years ago and we told him so. I am very much in sympathy with the concrete movement in poetry and with visual poetry as well, because anything that frees the word from its old rigid connections in the sentence will go forward as a monument to human progress.

Zekowski: Tel Quel means, in French, "such as it is," and, of course, we have to understand that the philosophy behind the Tel Quel group is one based upon a close adherence to textual matters of literature. I've just read recently in a fascinating article in *Boundary* 2 about the rise of a new group, the Change Collective, which poses itself in direct opposition to Phillippe Sollers' Tel Quel group. The point, as I understand, in the Change Collective is that they object to them because the Tel Quel group is largely rigid in its approach to language, literature and structure, whereas the Change group is far more heterogeneous and is interested in all the possibilities and transformations of language and consciousness and does not want to limit itself to any kind of rigid pattern of theory or approach.

Everman: So Tel Quel and its treatment of text as text and word as word is also too limiting?

Berne: It appears to me that insofar as using the word as word is concerned, it must remain the province of a very talented group of people who are very aware of the implications of what they do and who have the strength to entertain and to play with words.

Everman: Well, Neo-Narrative theories don't impress me as being quite that elitist.

Berne: Yes, insofar as open structure and the grammarless language are concerned, it has been our concern to open up language to everyone. The reason for this is a dire necessity. Our minds are now filled with events, feelings, and ideas for which there are no possibilities of words if we use the sentence, the

classical sentence of the 18th century. So using the idea of concrete or word as text, we are anxious to open up the technique to
larger access in order that *every* mind may be free of its heavy
burden of reality. That heavy burden of reality is hemmed in by
the sentence structure. There has been criticism of our view by
young people who find it to be too psychological. They speak of
bringing about a revolution and that we should be writing something which will bring about a revolution in society. But to
bring about a revolution which is going to be successful for the
future, it will have to be an integrated one. We cannot have one
based on the machinery of outward objectivity or outward life,
because it would leave out the human. But we cannot exces-
sively depend on the psychological. And so we argue in our literary works that there ought to be an integration of the societal
and the psychological, not the way the Victorian psychologists
saw psychology, but the way we experience the drives and the
inner pressures of our human psyches. This is always going to
be with us, no matter what kind of society there is.

Everman: One inevitable question: Is Neo-Narrative fiction
really fiction? What about character, plot, and the other elements of traditional fiction?

Berne: Yes, I think Neo-Narrative fiction is really fiction. Fiction is an exercise of the imagination: that might be one definition, and of course, the Neo-Narrative answers to it. Insofar as
the elements of traditional fiction are concerned, there is today a
very great problem with that. The elements you mentioned,
character, plot, and so on, seem to be more elements of the cinema or of television than of fiction per se. As a matter of fact the
problem of fiction is immense, in the sense that if there will be
about 40,000 titles published this year, only about 1500 or, to give
a conservative figure, only 2000 will be fiction titles at all.

Everman: Oh, so then, when you talk as you have about the
death of fiction, the death of the story, that death isn't only an
aesthetic one but an economic one as well, is that it?

Berne: This brings up the whole question of the economics of
publishing, actually, and they have undergone a tremendous
change since, let's say the 1940s. Publishers seem less interested
in fiction as a literary form and more interested in fiction as a

property of the cinema and television. I think that it is possible that fiction will be like poetry; it will become very difficult to sell; it already is that. Year by year the number of titles of fiction are falling. Here the publishers think in terms of character, plot, and the other elements of traditional fiction. Of course we have been talking about the death of the novel, and I believe that we were the first to say so. In the 1950s, the idea that fiction could be dead was greeted with a great deal of discouragement. Since then, the number of fiction titles has fallen dramatically, from somewhere around 10,000 titles.

Everman: Both of you have written fiction, non-fiction, and poetry. Now, Arlene, you mentioned the breakdown of the distinctions between poetry and prose in your comments on Woolf. For either of you, is there still a marked difference between poetry and fiction?

Berne: That is a very interesting question, but for me, I think that there is still a marked difference between poetry and fiction. Yes, I have written poetry in a book of mine called *The New Rubaiyat of Stanley Berne*. I attempted to write poetry, and I enjoyed it very much. But, in spite of the dictum of Wordsworth in his 1800 preface to *Lyrical Ballads* where he suggested that there was no difference between good poetry and good prose, well, for me, there *are* categories of literature.

Everman: Then you'd also say that there was a difference between fiction and non-fiction.

Berne: Yes, writing a book like *Future Language* was clearly an exercise in non-fiction. I set myself the problem of reaching as many people as possible with an argument, an idea; it is an idea book which attempted to solve problems of reading and writing. It presented the argument that language is such a problem today for most people that it must be solved or literature will die, all language arts will disappear. So *Future Language* is clearly non-fiction. The book that is not yet published which I wrote before *Future Language*, called *The Great American Empire*, is a prose epic of some sort in which I trace the life of an individual, a young man who has grown up in America since the 1940s. In this we have presented a rather clear picture of this young man and of the epochal period in American history from the 1940s to the 1960s. That, to me, was clearly a problem in fiction. So there is a difference between poetry, fiction, and non-fiction.

Everman: I think that Arlene probably wouldn't agree, am I right?

Zekowski: I can only speak for my own usage, my own handling of Neo-Narrative, but I tend not to wish to draw a distinction between poetry and fiction. I feel that the textures in the post-modern forms of literature combined various degrees of poetry and fiction. I would say that largely speaking it is a matter of degree, intensity, and emphasis, a matter of deliberation on the part of the writer. One of the most difficult and challenging questions in terms of definitions today is: what is poetry and what is prose? Gertrude Stein did it in her critical essays and commentaries, and I must say that, as brilliant a literary critic as Stein is, I think that her attempt to define the difference between poetry and prose was a failure. Other writers have done this as well. I think for the most part to try to define the nature of fiction today would involve perhaps a contradiction in terms of the sensory universe that we are dealing with in the last part of the 20th century. This particular universe is a multi-media world. We are living in a global, geodetic kind of universe where logic and linear structure no longer obtain.

Everman: I can see how your ideas apply to non-fiction as well. In fact, your own non-fiction in *Image Breaking Images* is very poetic and perhaps fictional, too.

Zekowski: My own tendency in *Image Breaking Images* was to experiment with literary criticism, to use the framework of a dialogue and, within that framework, to answer in the framework of Neo-Narrative. Of course, Neo-Narrative involves the grammarless language, and in many passages of *Image Breaking Images* you will also detect poetic expression. If you were to ask me whether I did this deliberately, I would say no, because even in writing a work of literary criticism the point of departure is almost the same as writing a work of fiction, poetry, or even a dramatic work. That is to say, I plunged into the expression and did not pay much attention as to whether it came out as straightforward prose, which most of the time it does, or occasionally as a kind of poetic grammarless language. So you see I tend not to

make rigid distinctions between poetry and fiction, the old classical categories that have existed for over three centuries.

Everman: O.K., so then, Stanley, you would want to retain the
traditional categories, while Arlene wants to be rid of them in
favor of a single category, literature.

Berne: I think the single category, literature, is in question, the
whole category is in question, and that is due to the economics of
publishing rather than to the writers themselves. The people I
have met in the upper reaches of publishing have little or no interest in literature, little or no interest in poetry or ideas insofar
as non-fiction is concerned, too. The people I have met are spill-
overs from very large corporations, those who have run the
bookkeeping departments of very large corporations which have
incorporated under their umbrella publishing houses. The people running it are not the same kinds of people that we had before the 1940s. Before the 1940s, it seems to me, there was still
some interest in the category, literature. Today those in the upper reaches of publishing are interested not in literature but in
properties, and by properties they mean the kinds of titles that
they can sell to other media, to the movies and to television.
Indeed, the great television networks own publishing houses,
their own publishing house, and the idea there is to develop
properties. Literature has absolutely nothing to do with it.

Everman: In terms of your own fiction, you seem to place a
heavy emphasis upon the rhythm of the prose, though in different ways. Arlene, you favor a short staccato line while, Stanley,
you tend to use a line which is long and flowing. Is rhythm a
way of structuring language which is no longer confined by the
rules of grammar?

Berne: Arlene has approached grammar through her style,
which we have come to call the periodic style. The periodic style
is simply what is being used today a great deal; that is, to have a
word or two words or three words forming a single concept. Let
that simply be what we might think of as a sentence. Each of
these appears to be an image or a thought which conveys emotional and intellectual meaning. In order to get around the problem of structure, because these concepts lie in the mind in an
unconscious pattern, not in a conscious logical pattern, in order

to become more truthful to the pattern in the mind, it is necessary to emit them as they actually lie, and so she has evolved what we have come to call the periodic style. In my case, I have taken the longest possible attenuated structure to exit from the mind a series of images in a flow. In order to make them a literary object, it was necessary to give them some shape and form, and yet, to keep it simple, I have used the comma, and so has evolved the kommatic style.

Everman: Are there other structural possibilities?

Berne: Of course. In between these, the long of it which is the kommatic style, and the short of it which is the periodic style; these are the parameters of a new possibility which we call open structure. Somewhere between the very shortest possibility and the very longest possibility anybody can find a home.

Everman: This would seem to imply that the theories of Neo-Narrative do not make up a strict program for literature but are open to exploration which could result in many kinds of literary works.

Berne: Both of us have made it a point not to erect another strict form of structure. We're leaving it open. What we want to do is to show where the parameters of possibilities lie.

Zekowski: We are not rigid in following these arbitrary styles. They come out as they come out in various combinations and forms. We are constantly experimenting, and the form and structure of each work is dictated by the work itself. Naturally in the earlier works the forms are highly emphasized and highly distinct, but as the work develops over the years you will find all kinds of combinations; just as Stanley has said, the long and the short of it involves a spectrum of variety of structures of grammarless thought. Between the periodic style and the kommatic style, there are many many structural possibilities.

Everman: Throughout this discussion, both of you have demanded a radical change in the use of language, not only in the aesthetic realm but in every area of life. Obviously literature is to be a primary instrument of change. But where is literature going?

Zekowski: As we have both said on several occasions, our literary generation in America was blind to all writing that was not sociological, post-naturalistic socialist-realism oriented, or generally traditional in form. It was closed to all innovation, investigative contemporary exploration. We struggled alone until the cultural, technological explosion of the underground alternative scene in the multi-lith offset revolution of the early '60s. Until this happened our Neo-Narrative grammarless writing was known amongst a select, sophisticated, culturally and largely European-oriented readership. Now the present generation are often brilliantly and certainly courageously innovative, anti-linear, and multimedia-oriented. They have caught up with the 20th century. Not as many as we would hope, but the number is growing.

Note

[1] Welch Everman's essays have appeared in numerous literary journals including *Review of Contemporary Fiction, Salmagundi, American Book Review,* and *Contemporary Literature.* His latest volume of criticism: *Who Says This?,* was published in 1988 by Southern Illinois University Press. He has served on the Wisconsin Arts Commission, was the recipient of a National Endowment for the Arts Fellowship, has a Doctorate in Philosophy and a second Doctorate in English (*SUNY,* Buffalo) and is now teaching at the University of Maine.

Interlude

America at the Crossroads

Lecture and Discussion Sponsored by
"Santa Fe Public Library Famous Authors Series."
Santa Fe Public Library,
Thursday Evening, December 2, 1982

In a sense I suppose I have been writing *Histories And Dynasties* over the last two decades or at least brooding it through many of the thoughts and feelings developed in previous books of mine.

Essentially *Histories And Dynasties* explores the crisis of America today, what we are feeling as individuals, as human beings in an America that seems not to know what distinguishes it from other nations and other cultures of the past and the present, and what will be its role or fate for the future.

The characters in this novel are not fictional fabrications but you, I, all of us probing the *illusion* and the *reality* of being American—our original and traditional hope and ideals and our present disillusionment anxieties over whether we will or can reach our goals. For clearly we are presently experiencing the *deterioration of the American dream*: floundering in mediocrity; our sense of excellence of leadership in both work and culture collapsed; the democratic ideals of equal opportunity buried under the power of the affluent; the arts, the humanities in our institutions of learning all but disappearing for neglect of books and ideas that are alive and contemporary.

In all sectors of our society, in government, in politics where we elect "the best Congress money can buy"; in industry; in mammoth conglomerate best-seller-dumb Hollywood blockbuster celebrity-oriented book publishing; in college and university education; in television and pop entertainment, we have forged a new American religion of money and power: *Consumerism*.

Unlike most colonial Empires of the past (and we *are* an Empire of Commerce consuming 3/4's of the world's raw materials) our philosophy of culture is "Business."

I do not believe that the "Business" of America can continue to be just "Business" if we are to realize—as all great nation empires of the past have done: Greece, Rome, England, France—our greatest potential, our memorable place in history. Our cultural image in the world, as we stand now, is raw, primitive, vulgar, mediocre: materialist/money-oriented vs. humanity-oriented, exporting Fast Foods; Hollywood Blockbusters; Punk Rock; Blue Jeans and Pop Entertainment.

I think the reason for this distortion between our ideals and our disillusionment over the realities is born of our own confusion about what America represents to us all: does America really mean the Americanization-Technolization-Dehumanization of the world? Or does it mean the hope of fulfilling the legacy of Greece—the world's first fledgling democracy—of fulfilling America's own promise of becoming the first great full-fledged Democracy of the world?

As Rome's mission was to civilize the European-Asiatic world, America's mission according to the ideals of its founders was to Democratize at least itself and to exist as the ideal and real example of what a truly Democratic nation can and should achieve.

Where have we gone askew?

From our very beginnings we have traditionally reviled the concept of aristocracy and the tyranny of Europe from which our immigrant ancestors fled. But somewhere along the line of our great democratic rebellion from the monarchies of the past, we began to translate, *equality of opportunity* into *mediocrity* and *conformity*, to the neglect of *leadership* and *excellence*.

Here in New Mexico we represent in our diverse cultures: Anglo, Native American, Hispanic, a microcosm of the American Continent, in both its past and present: its legacy and its promise. I hope that we can continue to cherish and value and respect our diversity to grow and evolve and seek the best intellectually and culturally in terms of leadership, excellence for ourselves as well as our families in a true dignity of human *co-operation* that characterizes the great nation that we can and should become.

What *Histories And Dynasties*, the story of the novel points out about our human natures in general, and in particular, about our natures as Americans is our *human condition*: that the human race is linked together, whether we like it or not, all one family among its multiple kinds and species, for both good or ill, through the past, through the present, through evolution of individuals, families and nations in their *histories and dynasties* on this small planet of Earth.

Histories And Dynasties is a new kind of novel, a novel that focuses on ourselves, on us Americans, above all, on each individual self and person; it explores our past, our present, our American nature, character, history multiple races and cultures, whether or not we will succeed or fulfill what we set out to become. It is like no other novel that you have ever read or will read, a new kind of narrative that embraces every human being, written in a language of the 20th century, of today.

Appendix

Appendix

Regarding:
Seasons Of The Mind, Arlene Zekowski
(George Wittenborn, 1969)
and
The Multiple Modern Gods, Stanley Berne
(George Wittenborn, 1969)

An Open Letter to the Writer of:
It Must Be Said: I Took It Personally
(*Margins*/15, pp. 10, 11, 64

Dear Martha Jacob,

Because you have permitted yourself the indulgence of misinterpretation (though I must say I do admire your rage, your guts, your frankness: "The following is an attempt to throw every wrench possible into the workings of . . . Berne and Zekowski's master plan") you must permit me, regardless of your avowed prejudice, to at least set certain facts into perspective.

Margins is, along with *Cosmep*, and the *International Directory of Little Magazines*, a very important fulcrum for the Alternative Publishing Scene. But *alternative publishing* exists only because the publishers and editors of the Establishment have closed their doors tight upon your generation and the contemporary scene. And before you, they closed their doors upon their own contemporaries—ourselves and those of our generation. And even the generation before ours: Witness Anaïs Nin's litany of complaints over the fate of all her published works—"for years and years, scarcely one review despite the 'promises'

of critics, editors, publishers—and worse yet, virtually no distri-
bution!" (*The Diary of Anaïs Nin*, Vol. III, p. 259).

And what about the generation before the generation before the generation before the generation before ours? The generation of Melville, Hawthorne Whitman. Let me quote a passage of the "Preface" to the *American Samizdat and Postmodern
Anthology*, that Stanley Berne and I are preparing: it is from
Richard Chase's article, "The Fate of the Avant-Garde," included
in our *Asapma* "Preface."

> . . . the serious writer of the nineteenth century was
> painfully on his own. We are surprised to find the most
> isolated of these writers pleading for what we shall
> call an avant-garde movement. Thus Melville begs his
> contemporaries to 'confess' immediately the greatness
> of Hawthorne. . . . 'By confessing him,' in Melville's
> well-known words, you thereby confess others; you
> brace the whole brotherhood. For genius, all over the
> world, stands hand in hand, and one shock of recogni-
> tion runs the whole circle round.

Chase continues his article by describing how America refused to elevate itself or show pride in literary or intellectual or
creative excellence by enforcing an almost suicidal apartheid isolation upon its greatest writers, cutting them off from the main-
stream of American life. The Publishing Establishment in
Melville's time? Read that neglected novel of his: *Pierre*. Or if
you don't want to be reminded of the past, Richard Kostelanetz
has written a monumental study with encyclopedic documenta-
tion on the continuing alarming censorship of intellectual and
creative leadership in America, what amounts to true *literary
fascism* on the part of our present Publishing Establishment: fa-
miliarize *yourself* with the facts in his *The End of Intelligent
Writing*, excerpted in previous issues of *Margins* and reviewed
by Tom Montag in #14.

However, I do not believe that contemporary writers in
America, including writers like ourselves involved in new
forms of human creative life and spirit, should be treated *any
worse* than any other American segment group or minority,
demanding recognition and respect and yes, receiving it: Native
American Indian, Black, Chicano, Gay Liberation, Women's Liberation, etc., are all doing their part to change America into the
true Democracy *that it presently is not*. Why should the writer
suffer oblivion, neglect or disrespect in his lifetime, as he did in
Melville's generation? He or She too, is part of the "human es-

tate." And in case it slipped your mind, that is what *Alternative Publishing is* all about. To make all our *differing* voices heard, because they haven't been heard, they have been denied a hearing, some longer and more than others. You do not understand what American Democracy is all about, if you still believe in the myth of the "melting pot." Unless you prefer being WASPish (pardon). Bob Bacon, a Mohawk Indian, from *Akweasne Notes* (Vol. 6, #3, p. 3) writes the following poem:

Equality?

> Yellow, white & black man/When will you understand/I do not want equality-/Just freedom and some land./. . . . It's not that I am lazy/I work to help my own/But I'm not money crazy/So please leave me alone./Take your integration/Take your civil rights/And melt them in your melting pot/That always comes out white./I'd rather be an Indian/I'd rather be myself/Than one of many plastic puppets/Crowded on a shelf.

Would you accuse Bob Bacon's poem on *equality* of being "elitist" or "fascistic" in attitude, as you have our writing? No, you wouldn't dare show prejudice or intolerance, even if you don't understand the importance of someone's right to reject *your* values and substitute his own.

Yet, in this respect, we and Bob Bacon *are the same.* Separate but equal. And respectful of each others' rights and dignities.

No one is denying you your right to read and enjoy novels, even though the television media is more successfully projecting them than their original media of the book. I for one enjoyed *War and Peace* on the PBS-BBC television series much more than wading through Tolstoy. In fact, aside from the documentaries (which on the whole are generally worthwhile), what we are seeing on television (the soap operas, the detective and mystery series, the ethnic and racial "just folks" folksiness, etc.) are really chapters and episodes from *novels,* except that in the centuries before television and radio, they first appeared in newspapers and magazines. But I'm sure you knew that. Narrative will never again write itself in the future, spend itself so wastefully ("they [the novels] pour to waste," remarked Virginia Woolf) like it did before the advent of television. However, no one is denying you the right to read novels written in the narrative structure of "Gone with the Wind."

As for the electronic media, I too look at television good and bad. But I don't relate to the bad anymore than I should think you do, so there is no reason for you to feel, as you put it, "so hopelessly mediocre." Milton, in the *Areopagitica*, defending freedom from censorship and freedom to publish, made it quite clear that *both* good and bad books were *always* harmful and misread, and misunderstood, *only* by people of inferior taste and judgment. The same holds true for television.

But I am genuinely surprised at your falling into the old semantic trap of calling what escapes you "literary fascism." That is like calling people you don't agree with or even want to understand: "communists." I thought by now the majority of us were incapable of falling for that "canard."

As for mass man, we *all* live in a mass society, but that doesn't mean we're living in a democratic one. We are angry yes. Angry against our generation which failed us: traitors to truth, to the dialogue of diversity, of multiplicity, to civil liberties muzzled by the era of "McCarthyism." *Our* generation, spawned Watergate and Richard Nixon. And though Nixon is no longer with us, Watergate still is. If Watergate is the symbol of oligarchic corruption, wealth and power, then it runs through the fiber of all our American life, above all in the Publishing Establishment which drives out the good by means of the bad, which censors literary art and authenticity by polluting us with the meretricious and the tawdry of the non-book and the cult of the adolescent superstar Hollywood "success myth," and the tyranny of a pop culture, as *undemocratic* and *unrepresentative* of the diversity of American society as the more invisible faceless subtle tyranny of the elitist corporate power structure influencing government and legislation.

Watergate proved one thing. We are *free* only in being aware, in possessing the truth, in placing principles above loyalties to those who seek to buy our consciences with promises they won't keep, in knowing our priorities involve ethical choices. Only then can we regain our dignity and self-respect as human beings. And maybe someday be truly democratic.

But until this comes about I shall remain a libertarian. And continue to rage. And to cry out. *And to make distinctions between high art and low art.* Because in the end. All literature worth anything must be of worth to others. Most especially it must lead. And it leads by distinguishing the good from the bad, the high from the low, the true from the false, the pure from the corrupt, and contributes to a country's pride and self-image.

No, we are not yet living in a democracy, but rather in an oligarchy. Because a true democracy, Martha, is one in which the people participate and where respect for the best leadership, for excellence, is sought for and encouraged. Not just in politics but in all sectors, above all in art, in literature, because the creative artist seeks in beauty and in new forms of order, the most healthy expression of the human psyche, of the human spirit, of the human being's hunger for order, for harmony, for fulfillment, in a largely unsatisfying, chaotic, frustrating, insecure world. That is why Shelley manifestoed to us all: "Poets are the unacknowledged legislators of the world." As a traditionalist novelist even E. M. Forster emphasizes:

> He (Shelley) legislates through creating. And he creates through his . . . power to impose form. . . . And form is as important today, when the human race is trying to ride the whirlwind, as in those less agitating days of the past, when the earth seemed solid and the stars fixed. . . . *Form is not tradition. It alters from generation to generation. Artists always seek a new technique, and will continue to do so.* . . . Works of art in my opinion, are the only objects in the material universe to possess internal order, and that is why, though I don't believe that only art matters, *I do believe in Art for Art's Sake.*   (from *Two Cheers for Democracy*)

My ultimate objection to your review was that *it was not a review*, but a diatribe against, a misinterpretation of "Notes Toward an Aristocratic Literature," the *Preface* by Stanley Berne in both books. My one regret is that you made no objective or humane attempt to let the works speak for themselves. This you failed to do. And in this you failed yourself and your responsibility to *Margins* readers.

Arlene Zekowski

Index